Weather

313 - 881 - 7787

Lakes Erie, St. Clair, Huron

Allen Petz
1215 Rice Ave
Hamilton Ont
L9C 4R3
388-1893

SAILING FROM START TO FINISH

Sailing from start to finish

Yves-Louis Pinaud

Translated by James and Ingeborg Moore

THIRD EDITION

Adlard Coles Limited London

Granada Publishing Limited
First published in Great Britain 1967
by Adlard Coles Limited
Frogmore, St Albans Hertfordshire AL2 2NF and
3 Upper James Street London W1R 4BP
First published in France as Pratique de la Voile

This translation copyright © 1967 Adlard Coles Limited
Second edition 1971
Second impression 1973
Third edition 1975

ISBN 0 229 11548 9
Filmset and printed in Great Britain by BAS Printers Limited
Wallop Hampshire

ACKNOWLEDGEMENTS
Photographs
Keith Beken, Jean-Claude Chigot, Alain Gliksman, Yves-Louis Pinaud
Artist and designer
Jean-Olivier Heron assisted by Silvie Rollin

Sailing from start to finish

Contents

Chapter 1 — How a yacht sails

Chapter 2 — Helmsmanship

Chapter 3 — Racing and competition

1

How a yacht sails

For centuries the sailing ship was a vessel used for carrying cargo or fighting battles. The sharply defined functions which these two missions imposed on it are altogether alien to the sailing yacht of today. Its new purpose, together with the recent progress made in fields of science which are not exclusively nautical ones, like aerodynamics and hydrodynamics, has made it an entirely new creation and one which is virtually independent of its past and its traditions.

It is often said that naval architecture is both an art and a science. This emphasizes the fact that, besides tank tests, wind tunnel tests and theoretical calculations, intuition, sensibility and a good eye for line play a very large part.

In this book, which is written mainly for practical yachtsmen and instructors, I have tried to present the theoretical side of each problem in a diagrammatic form to make it easier to understand.

The reader must never forget, though, that this kind of presentation is deliberately much simplified, the purpose of the book being the practical side of sailing and not naval architecture.

When man first tried to use the wind to drive a boat, he obviously set up some kind of screen at right angles to the wind, and this worked as long as the wind blew towards the destination he wanted to reach.

It did not take him long after that to manage to sail towards a point that did not coincide with the wind direction by pivoting the sail round the mast and angling it to the wind. But the poor efficiency of the sails and the unfavourable hull shapes prevented him from going further than using the wind over the right (starboard) or left (port) quarter. This is called sailing **before the wind.**

It was of great use in parts of the world under the influence of directionally stable winds such as the monsoon regions, the eastern Mediterranean and others.

But before going any further we must explain a phenomenon, the importance of which has too often been underestimated in sailing instruction. The wind which moves a sailing yacht is not the same as the wind experienced by a stationary observer.

If we imagine a yacht being carried along by a current on a windless day, its crew will feel a wind which is created by the movement of the boat through the stationary mass of air, in the same way as a skier descending a slope feels the wind rushing past him.

Thus a sailing boat moving under normal conditions is subject both to the atmospheric or true wind (W_T) and the wind of its own speed (W_S), the two combining to make an artificial wind called **apparent wind** (W_A). This is the only wind to be taken into account in analysing the movements of a sailing boat. . . .

The *apparent wind* has a speed and direction notably different from those of the true wind.

When a boat pushed by a wind sails on a course which coincides with the direction of the true wind (i.e. runs dead before the wind), its apparent wind is much less than the true wind, because the wind of its own speed (W_S), diametrically opposed to the true wind (W_T), must be subtracted from the latter: $W_A = W_T - W_S$.

At the same time, the true wind and the apparent wind have obviously the same direction.

On the other hand, if a yacht goes onto a course other than dead before the wind, for example if the wind comes over the quarter (broad reaching) or on the beam (reaching), it uses an apparent wind which no longer comes from the same direction as the true wind and which can, in certain cases, be stronger even than the true wind.

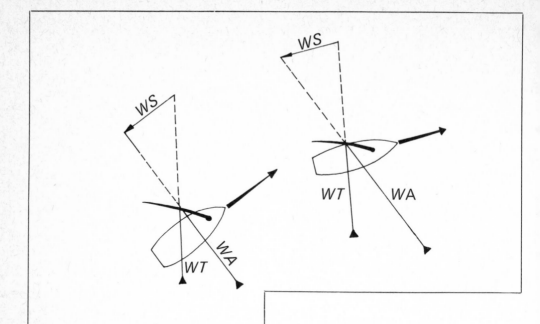

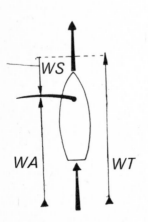

The flag at the mast top of this boat moving at high speed is a "wind vane" or "burgee". It indicates precisely the direction of the apparent wind, much better than "dog vanes" or "tell tales" tied to the rigging.

Although it is often absent from beginners' boats and, even more serious, from instructors' boats, experienced helmsmen consider it an item of gear which they would not be without.

The wind vane in the picture indicates the apparent wind as striking the boat at right angles to its course, but when one takes into consideration the boat's speed it is logical to assume that the true wind is coming over the left (port) quarter. The direction of the waves (almost identical to the boat's course) confirms this assumption.

The boat is sailing on port **tack**. Its apparent wind differs in direction from the true wind and it is probably stronger.

sailing before the wind

Set up against the wind like a screen, the sail presents one of its surfaces (the concave one) to the airflow which exerts pressure on it. The airflow is thus **suddenly interrupted** and continues in a disturbed flow forming more or less violent eddies on the other side of the sail (the convex or leeward side). The exit of the airflow is said to be **turbulent.**

Actually, wind tunnel tests have shown that if a relatively high pressure exists on the windward side, the low pressure created on the leeward side fills up spasmodically with confused eddies: the airflow does not become normal again until a point about three times the sail height downwind.

The sailing ships designed essentially for down-wind sailing were left defenceless against the fury of the elements. Since they could only flee from a storm, they were often swept on to inhospitable shores and smashed to pieces on the rocks.

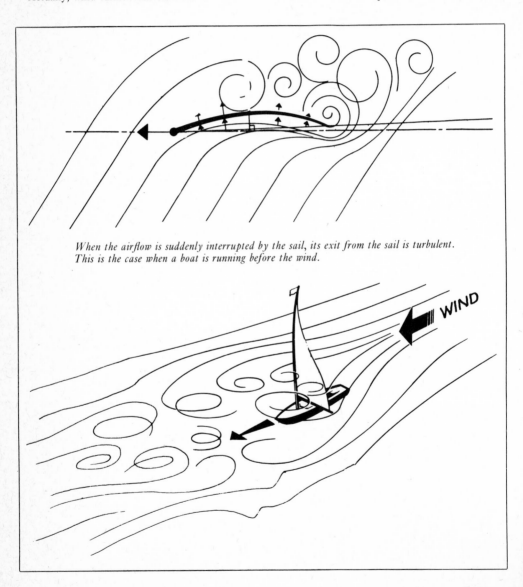

When the airflow is suddenly interrupted by the sail, its exit from the sail is turbulent. This is the case when a boat is running before the wind.

WIND

Running before the wind, even in modern sailing yachts, remains a very dangerous business, as is shown by this photograph. The boat's balance is constantly in jeopardy. Like a vehicle without brakes speeding down a steep slope the boat, carried along by the wind, lurches headlong, and it takes a very skilled crew to avoid a capsize. In racing even experienced helmsmen dread the downwind leg if it is blowing hard.

The first step towards a greater freedom for the boat in relation to the wind direction was the appearance of the first fore-and-aft rig: the lateen sail in the Arab world and the lugsail or gaff sail in western waters. From then onwards ships could sail with the wind on the beam.

The improvement of hulls, which had hardly been changed since antiquity, logically followed.

It is easy to see that if a beam wind exerts pressure on a sail set almost at right angles to its direction, while the underwater body (the immersed part of the hull) offers a strong resistance to lateral movement, the boat will have a tendency to give way under the side pressure (*make leeway*) and to lie over (*heel*).

The flag on the buoy indicates the direction of the true wind, which is evidently on the beam of the heeling boat. No. 4779 is head to wind, her sails are shaking. The third Star is on port tack.

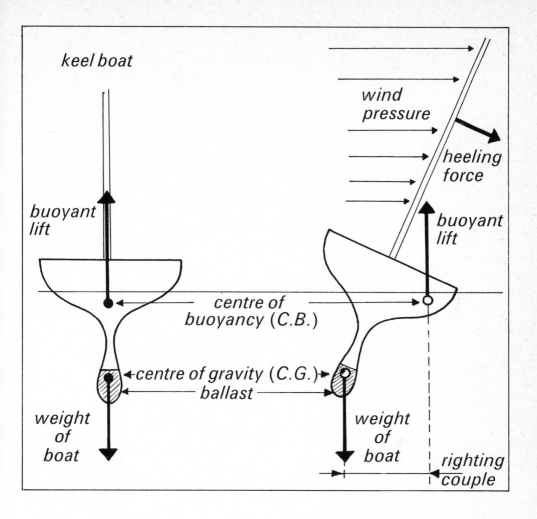

To be able to sail under these conditions, the underwater body must possess certain characteristics: it must resist leeway by presenting lateral resistance; it must resist heeling by its shape and the influence of ballast, the weight of which the hull must be able to carry; and finally it must possess reasonably fine lines so as not to have too much resistance to forward motion.

A single-hulled sailing boat behaves in fact like a float, subject to Archimedes' law. *Stability* is the first and foremost condition for safe navigation.

This depends above all on the shape of the float and the position of its centre of gravity. The larger the hull and the lower the centre of gravity, the more stable the boat.

This stability is a function of the **righting couple,** which is composed of *two equal forces* which are *opposed* to each other in direction:

1. *Downwards:* the weight of the boat, acting through the *centre of gravity* (C.G.).

2. *Upwards:* hydrostatic pressure (buoyant lift), acting through the *centre of buoyancy* (C.B.).

When the boat is on an even keel, the two centres are in the same vertical plane.

When the boat heels, the C.B. moves to the side to which the boat heels.

In this way a righting couple is established.

This increases to the same degree as the boat heels, but not indefinitely. At a certain angle of heel it ceases to exist and the boat capsizes.

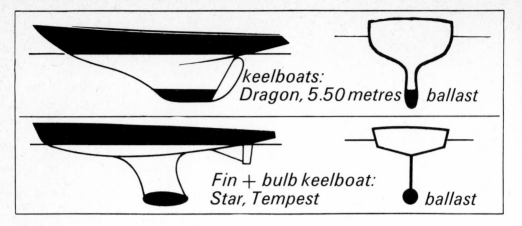

keelboats:
Dragon, 5.50 metres   ballast

Fin + bulb keelboat:
Star, Tempest   ballast

The effect of the righting couple can be increased by some kind of ballast:
either fixed ballast, at the lowest point of the plane of lateral resistance (*fin keel or bulb keel*); or movable ballast, which in dinghies is provided by the crew sitting as far outside the hull as possible. In their particular case, and contrary to keel yachts, the righting couple is at its maximum with the boat on an even keel.

A dinghy must be sailed on an even keel.

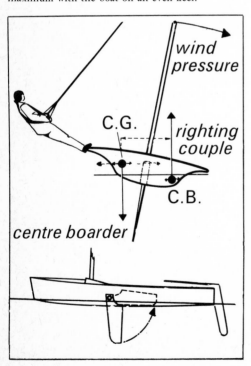

wind pressure

C.G.

righting couple

C.B.

centre boarder

If, in a dinghy, the crew do not sit out far enough, the boat capsizes.

But not too much . . . or else the boat capsizes to windward. The crew of a dinghy are responsible for the stability of the boat. Here two helmsmen seem to have forgotten this.

Provided with an efficient sail plan and plane of lateral resistance, as well as adequate stability, the fast and refined sailing yachts of today can make use of winds from practically any direction and, if necessary, sail a **port** or **starboard** course of less than 40° off the true wind. Despite this enforced concession of 40°, the reason for which we will soon see, the boat is said to be sailing into the wind. *This is close-hauled sailing.*

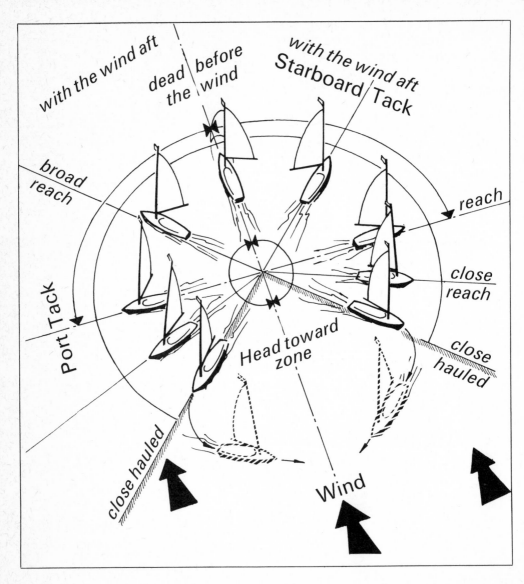

Compare the course this boat is sailing to the direction of the true wind as indicated by the flag flying from the stern of the moored committee boat or the one on the small buoy. Also note the difference in direction between these two flags and the wind vane (racing flag) at the masthead of the sailing boat which shows the apparent wind.

But what phenomenon is it which enables a sailing boat to derive its motion from an airflow which can be nearly opposite to its direction of movement? The explanation is given by this fundamental law:

the resultant force of a moving current striking a surface is at right angles to that surface, irrespective of the direction of the current

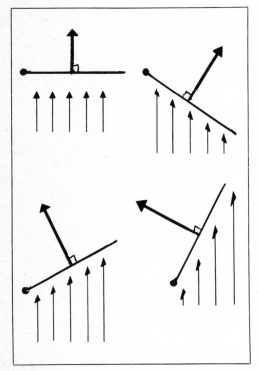

The sail, basically a triangular plane, can describe an arc of 90° either side of the hull's centre-line. Since it can be "fixed in position" at any point on this arc, mainly by means of the *sheets*, it can be set to the wind at many different angles, allowing different courses to be sailed: *before the wind*, *broad reaching*, *reaching*, *close reaching and close-hauled*. Though the principles underlying the functioning of the sails are principles of aerodynamics, it must be pointed out that most of them are altogether peculiar to sails and to sailing on different courses

and are but loosely connected with the other aspects of that science. Considering that sails use the wind from many directions from running downwind to close-hauled, it would be absurd to compare them to aeroplane wings, parachutes or even kites, all of which utilize the wind at relatively constant angles of attack.

The problem is best dealt with by first considering the aerodynamic output of a modern mainsail. Once the principles governing the mainsail are known, it will be easy to apply them, suitably adapted, to the other sails: jib, genoa and spinnaker, all of which are, in fact, concave planes, usually having three sides.

The way in which the panels of cloth which make up the sail are put together gives the sail its concave shape. Due to the fact that the trailing edge (*leech*) is not fixed it becomes "open" in the upper part of the sail and "closed" in the lower, and the sail is thus slightly helicoidal, i.e. it twists with respect to the mast.

The airflow will have the tendency to roll itself up, so to speak, from bottom to top in following this shape.

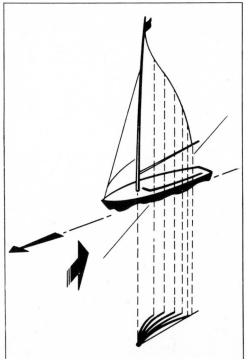

Sail profiles at different heights. They are similar in the jib.

The thrust acting on the surface is the resultant of all the forces exerted by the apparent wind.

of 10 knots are 11 times as strong as those exerted by a wind of 3 knots.

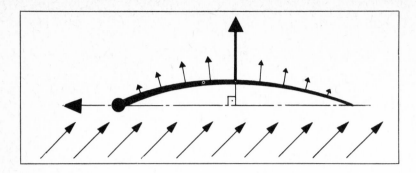

These grow proportionately to the square of the speed of the airflow. For example, speeds of 3 knots and 10 knots are not proportionate to each other as 3 to 10 but as 3^2 to 10^2, which is 9 to 100. This is to say that the pressures exerted by a wind

To simplify the interpretation of wind speeds, reference is made to the *Beaufort Scale* which, incidentally, provides some particularly eloquent examples. You can now calculate, for instance, the difference between a light breeze of 5 knots and a storm of 60 knots.

Beaufort wind scale

Beaufort Number	Description	Wind Speed in Knots	Characteristics
0	Calm	0	Sails hang limp. Sea like a mirror.
1	Light air	1–2	Leaves on trees begin to stir. Ripples are formed.
2	Light breeze	3–7	Small wavelets are formed. Branches of trees move.
3	Gentle breeze	8–12	Boats heel appreciably.
4	Moderate breeze	13–17	Small boats prepare to shorten sail. Frequent white horses.
5	Fresh breeze	18–22	Small boats reef.
6	Strong breeze	23–27	Large yachts shorten sail. Large waves begin to form.
7	Moderate gale	28–32	Trees bend. Small boats make for harbour. Sea heaps up.
8	Fresh gale	33–40	Large yachts are reefed right down. Moderately high waves of greater length.
9	Strong gale	41–47	Boats heave to. Trees may be uprooted.
10	Whole gale	48–55	
11	Storm	56–62	Sea covered with driving spray.
12	Hurricane	Above 62	

In some old almanacs one can find rather more imaginative comments, as, for instance, for Force 7: "Make for port . . . and think of those out at sea."

As a matter of interest it can be pointed out that in a force 1 wind (2 knots) the pressure is 0·018 lbs. per sq. ft. sail area, in a force 3 wind (8 knots) the pressure is 0·28 lbs. per sq. ft., in a force 5 wind (20 knots) it is 1·8 lbs. per sq. ft. and in a force 7 wind (30 knots) it is 4·0 lbs. per sq. ft.

sailing and apparent wind

In order that the sail may take up its concave shape, it is obviously necessary for it to be set at a certain angle to the airflow. Even for sails with a very slight curvature this angle must not be less than around 10 degrees. This is one of the reasons why a sailing boat has to turn away from a direction straight into the wind. We shall call this angle *alpha*.

Diagrammatically, the wind force on the sail acts at right angles to the chord of the sail curvature, and it can be assumed that its point of application (**centre of effort**) is somewhere near the centre of the area of the sail. *As we shall see, this is so no matter what the angle of incidence between the sail and the airflow.*

This is the **aerodynamic force**.

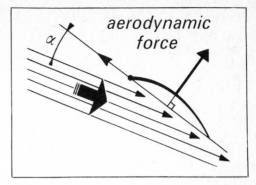

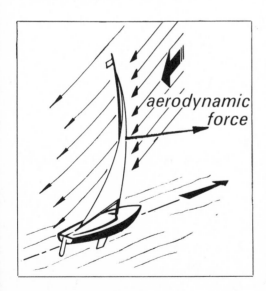

Judging from the direction of the apparent wind indicated by the wind vane, alpha *is very small, just large enough for the sails to fill.* ▶

21

Knowing that the hull of a sailing boat is so designed that it moves easily in a fore-and-aft direction whilst opposing sideways movement (*lee-way*) with a *plane of lateral resistance* (keel or centreplate) it is possible to imagine how a **boat moves forward** as soon as pressure comes onto the sails.

Even if angle *alpha*, i.e. the angle of incidence between the sail and the airflow is very acute (it must not, however, be less than 10 degrees), the boat will still make progress.

So that the boat can move *in a forward direction* it is necessary *for the aerodynamic force to be directed further forward than at right angles to the hull's centre-line*. In practice, this means that the sail is set at a certain angle to the centre-line. We shall call this angle *beta*, and it is another factor which prevents the boat from getting closer to the wind.

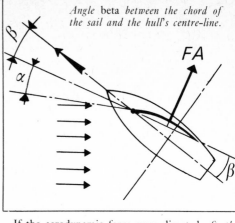

Angle beta *between the chord of the sail and the hull's centre-line.*

If the aerodynamic force were directed *aft, the boat would move astern.*

One can sometimes see racing helmsmen using this method to extricate themselves from difficult situations.

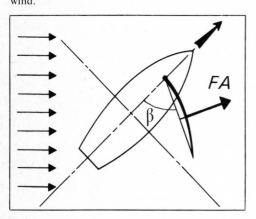

Left: Aerodynamic force directed forward: boat moves forward.

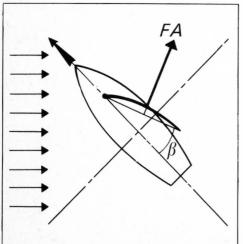

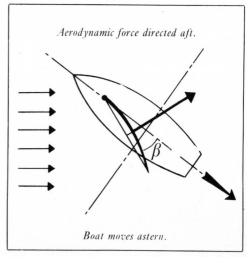

Aerodynamic force directed aft.

Boat moves astern.

sailing on the wind

Now that we know that a sailing boat can really move into the wind, the next step is to see how a sail behaves under these conditions. From the moment the sail takes up and holds its shape, and with a minimum angle of incidence with the apparent wind of around 10 degrees, the air flows smoothly and without interruption over the windward as well as the leeward side of the sail. **The flow is said to be laminar.**

(Laminar: if the flow of a fluid, in contact with a surface, follows the shape of that surface in continuous filaments.)

Wind tunnel tests have shown that the *flow remains laminar* as long as the air does not strike the sail at an angle (with the chord) *of more than 22–25 degrees.*

Beyond this angle, the flow tends to become *turbulent.*

Laminar flow gives rise to two phenomena.

One occurs on the side of the sail which is immediately struck by the apparent wind (the concave or windward side), the other on the leeward or convex side.

On the windward side the filaments of air are deflected and slowed down through contact with the sail. They then gradually return to their original direction.

On the leeward side, the airflow is not in contact with the sail. The filaments of air are accelerated because they have to cover a longer distance. They rejoin the airflow deflected by the windward side.

The difference in speed between the airflows on either side of the sail causes a strong suction to leeward of the sail.

Experiments undertaken by Eiffel show that the *suction is three to four times as strong as the pressure on the windward side. Thus the aerodynamic force is the sum of pressure to windward and suction to leeward. However its magnitude mainly relies on* **suction.**

When the flow becomes turbulent, and more particularly so when *running before the wind*, the suction decreases drastically and deprives the sail of a large part of its driving power. The aerodynamic force is thus diminished. It appears then, that the aerodynamic force is greatest when the sail **deflects** the airflow rather than **interrupts** it as it does before the wind.

This fine balance is necessary when *sailing on the wind*. A sailing boat is obviously then a prisoner of the course it has to follow, and one must seek to maintain this laminar flow whenever this is possible.

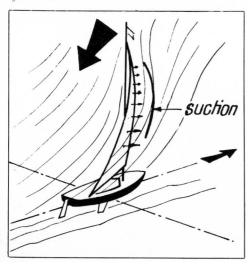

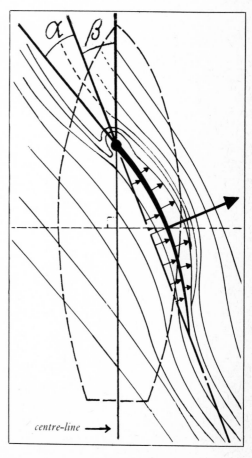

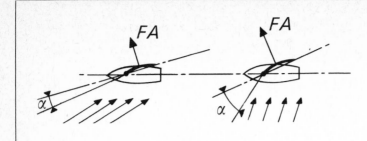

*Below right : With the sail stalled. A 5.0.5 running
downwind in a breeze exceeding force 5.*

*Below : With the sail not-stalled. These two Flying
Dutchmen are close-hauled in a force 4 wind.*

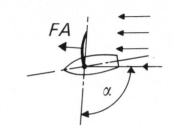

With the sail stalled, angle alpha *is very
large, or at least larger than 25° (running
and broad reaching).*

magnitude of aerodynamic force

The magnitude of the aerodynamic force is a function of three factors which are:

1. *The angle of incidence* between the sail and the airflow (we know that it should not exceed 25°, and wind tunnel tests have shown that the aerodynamic force comes into action the moment the sail fills—around 10°—and increases in strength until the angle has reached approximately 22°).

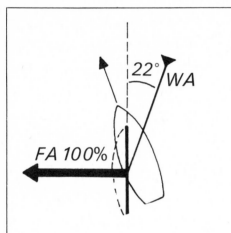

A sail is not flat but has a normal camber, i.e. 1/10; the optimum angle of incidence is reached when the sail is just full (when the luff stops lifting).

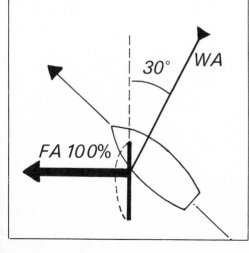

2. *The importance of sail camber.* In his experiments Dr. Manfred Curry demonstrated that with an airflow of 30 ft. per sec. (20 knots) maximum efficiency is obtained from a sail with a camber of 1/7.

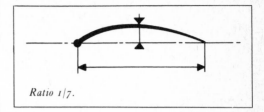

Ratio 1/7.

A ratio of 1/7 represents a relatively heavy camber, clearly greater than those of mainsails and jibs but more or less normal for modern spinnakers which are used on courses closer than dead before the wind and frequently even with the apparent wind around 45° off the course sailed.

The fullest of modern mainsails have a camber of 1/10, which is already very full. They are fine for reaching but do not perform well close-hauled. In fact it takes an angle of incidence (angle *alpha*) of more than 10° for a sail of this camber to fill properly. The problem can be overcome by using a bending mast and boom.

By being flexible, these take out much of the fullness but can restore it as soon as it is needed. (Chapters 2 and 3.)

3. *The speed of the airflow.* This last factor plays a fundamental role. We have seen that the aerodynamic force increases and decreases in proportion to the square of the wind speed. This reveals unexpected possibilities. Let us go back to our definition of the apparent wind, the resultant of two components:

the true wind (WT),
the wind caused by the movement, or speed, of the boat (Ws).

The intensity and direction of the *apparent wind* are variable, since they are subject to the influence of several factors, notably that of the true wind.

To simplify explanations, we will assume that we are dealing with a true wind which is constant in direction and strength, blowing over the surface of water which is free from currents. Two variable factors nevertheless intervene:

1. The different courses a boat can follow in relation to the true wind (points of sailing);

2. Variations in the boat's speed.

Depending on the course sailed in relation to the true wind, the speed wind (Ws) must either be **deducted** from the true wind (when running: $W_A = W_T - W_S$) or **added** to it when beating to windward.

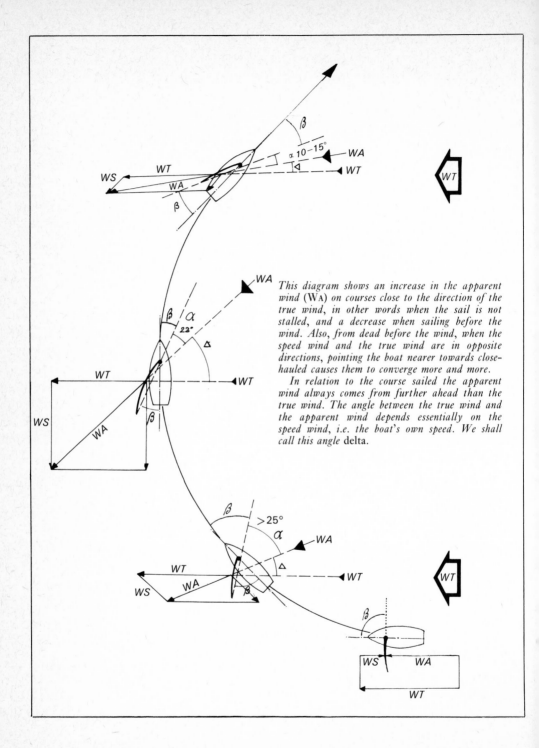

This diagram shows an increase in the apparent wind (WA) on courses close to the direction of the true wind, in other words when the sail is not stalled, and a decrease when sailing before the wind. Also, from dead before the wind, when the speed wind and the true wind are in opposite directions, pointing the boat nearer towards close-hauled causes them to converge more and more.

In relation to the course sailed the apparent wind always comes from further ahead than the true wind. The angle between the true wind and the apparent wind depends essentially on the speed wind, i.e. the boat's own speed. We shall call this angle delta.

It is when the sails are not stalled that a boat benefits from the maximum aerodynamic force. However, not all types of boats reach their maximum designed speed in the same conditions.

A boat of light construction such as a dinghy can reach higher speeds than a keelboat with exactly the same sail area and sail shape. Consequently, its apparent wind will be stronger than that of the keelboat and its scope for sailing un-stalled considerably increased.

Likewise, multihulls like catamarans and trimarans are capable of attaining speeds much in excess of those reached by conventional single hulls.

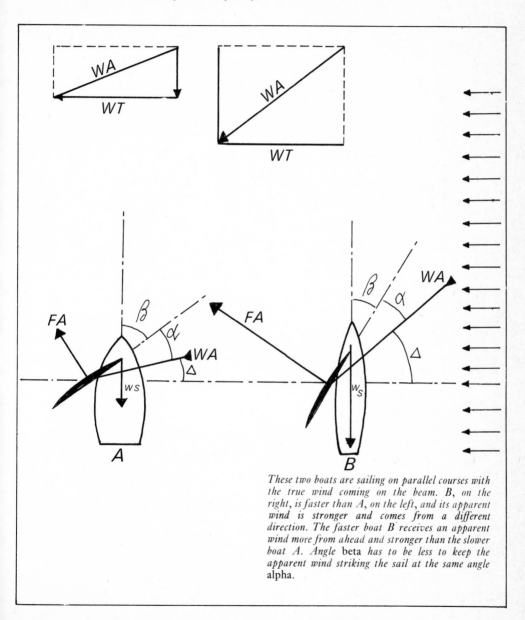

These two boats are sailing on parallel courses with the true wind coming on the beam. B, on the right, is faster than A, on the left, and its apparent wind is stronger and comes from a different direction. The faster boat B receives an apparent wind more from ahead and stronger than the slower boat A. Angle beta *has to be less to keep the apparent wind striking the sail at the same angle* alpha.

conversion of the aerodynamic force (F_A)

Transmitted to the hull by means of the mast and rigging, the aerodynamic force can be resolved into two components:

— a beneficial force which is always parallel to the hull's centre-line: the *driving force* (F_D);

— a useless lateral force at right angles to the hull's centre-line, which causes *heeling* and *leeway*: *the side force* (F_S).

Variations in the intensity of these two factors are closely linked with the *orientation of the sails* in relation to the centre-line.

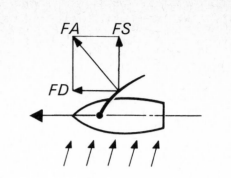

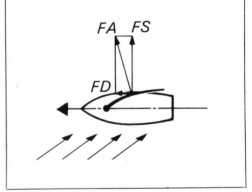

Theoretical diagram when angle beta *is less than 90°.*

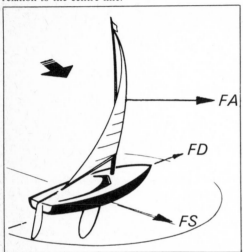

If, for example, on a course dead before the wind the sails, angled at 90° to the centre-line, provide an aerodynamic force parallel to the driving force, the side force is practically nil. But as soon as the sails are sheeted in closer to the centre-line (broad reaching, reaching, close-reaching and close-hauled) the aerodynamic force is no longer parallel to the driving force and we experience a side force whose magnitude varies from case to case. It becomes steadily stronger, when changing from downwind towards close-hauled.

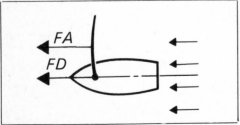

However, the submerged part of the hull and particularly the plane of lateral resistance (keel or centreplate) exert a force on the water at right angles to the hull's centre-line. The water offers a resistance which is opposed to this side force (Fs).

The centre of lateral resistance is near the geometric centre of the submerged part of the hull.

Yet the sail must not be sheeted in too far (angle *beta*) since the aerodynamic force then produces in the hull an unnecessarily large side force (Fs) and a much reduced driving force.

Despite the effect of the plane of lateral resistance the boat cannot be prevented from making a certain amount of leeway. Its true course is at an angle to the centre-line. We shall call this angle *gamma*.

It is absolutely imperative always to trim the sail with angle *beta* as large as possible for any particular course in order to gain the maximum driving force (FD). This driving force will in its turn give the boat a higher speed. We will thus obtain the greatest efficiency: **resistance to leeway increases as the boat's speed increases.** The faster a boat goes the less leeway it makes. Angle *gamma* becomes very small.

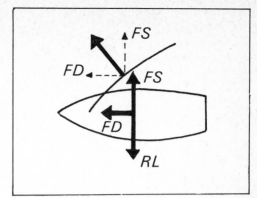

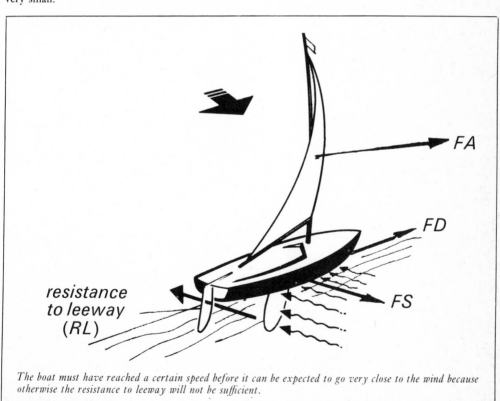

The boat must have reached a certain speed before it can be expected to go very close to the wind because otherwise the resistance to leeway will not be sufficient.

The aerodynamic force (FA) is at its maximum when the chord of the sail forms an angle of about 22° to the airflow, but we must not lose sight of the fact that it already has an appreciable magnitude from the very moment the sail fills at an angle of incidence of about 10°.

This is very important because when a boat is sailed extremely close-hauled its sails **deflect** the airflow with a very small angle *alpha*.

Practice, probably even more than experiments in wind tunnels and tanks, has proved that a boat can be made to perform better, that is to say go faster and closer to the wind, if angle *alpha* is reduced to the minimum and *beta* increased at the same time.

Experiments have yielded the following figures:

Alpha 22°	..	..	FA	100%	FD	20%
Beta 5°	..	..	Fs	50%		
Alpha 11°	..	..	FA	70%	FD	28%
Beta 12°	..	..	Fs	38%		

Note the different trim of the sails in these two boats. The one on the right is sailing with a smaller angle beta *than the one on the left. However, with both boats steering parallel courses, the one on the right uses a larger angle* alpha. *It consequently experiences a greater aerodynamic force, but since this is closer to being at right angles to the centre-line it exerts a very strong side force. Its course made good is less favourable than that of the boat on the left.*

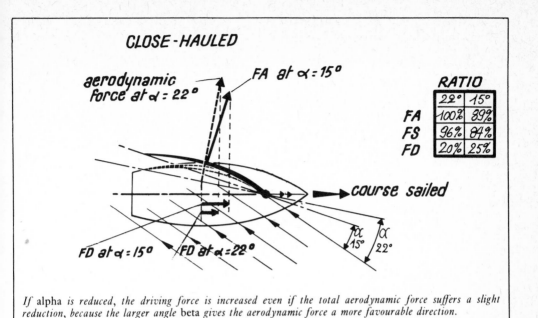

CLOSE-HAULED

aerodynamic
force at α = 22°

FA at α = 15°

course sailed

FD at α = 15°   FD at α = 22°

α 15°   α 22°

RATIO	22°	15°
FA	100%	89%
FS	96%	84%
FD	20%	25%

If alpha *is reduced, the driving force is increased even if the total aerodynamic force suffers a slight reduction, because the larger angle* beta *gives the aerodynamic force a more favourable direction.*

Note the magnitude of angle beta *on this boat sailing close-hauled in a wind of force 1–2: the boom indicates the angle at which the sail is trimmed in relation to the centre-line (mast-tiller).*

β

To reach a point which lies in the eye of the wind a boat must sail close-hauled on port and starboard tack alternately. And even though a fast boat, as we have seen, has to cover a longer distance on either side of the axis of the true wind to reach this point than a slower boat (because angle *delta* is larger) it is more than certain that it will take less time to do so. This succession of turns with the wind coming alternately from the left and the right (*port tack and starboard tack*) is called **beating**.

Due to frequent changes in the direction of the true wind one tack is always becoming more favourable than the other. The observant helmsman will not fail to take advantage of this and thus cover the shortest possible distance.

If, when sailing close-hauled on port tack, he notices that in order to get his sails to fill he has to alter course and point further away from his aim

(*bear away*), he will conclude from this that the wind has *veered* several degrees to the right, i.e. it is **heading** him. He will go about at once onto starboard tack to take advantage of the fact that the wind has **freed** on that tack and allows him to *point closer* to the point he wants to reach.

If one studies angles *alpha*, *beta*, *gamma* and particularly *delta* one understands why a sailing boat is limited in how close it can go to the axis of the true wind. Exactly how close depends on the combined characteristics of the hull and the sails.

A slow boat will hardly be able to better the angles *alpha* and *beta*, and even if *delta* is not very large, *gamma* on the other hand will be considerable (due to the low speed). The boat will thus give the impression of being very close-winded, but in fact, because of the leeway it makes, its course will be far removed from the axis of the true wind.

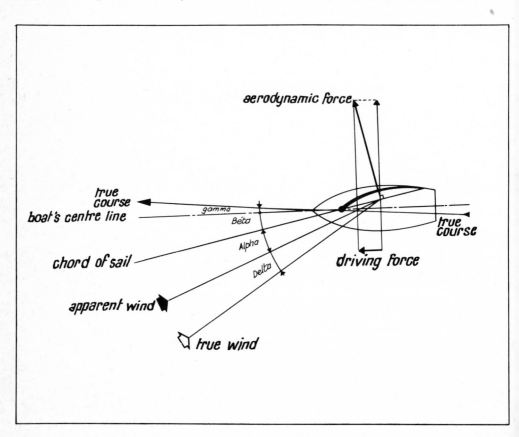

Beating. These Stars racing are going for a mark of the course which lies ahead and dead to windward and have chosen opposite tacks, close-hauled.

resistance to forward motion

Even the best designed hull gives rise to resistance to forward motion which diminishes the driving force.

There are five kinds of resistance:

1. *Resistance caused by heeling*

When a boat heels its hull shape becomes asymmetrical and this adds to resistance to forward motion. With keelboats heeling is inevitable and part of their very conception. Their hull is designed with this in mind. Besides, the increase in waterline length which can be brought about by heeling compensates to some extent the additional resistance caused by the asymmetry of the hull, so that at a small angle of heel the resistance is not very considerable.

For example, the figures for a Dragon (according to Baader) are:

Angle of heel 5°, increase in resistance 1%;
Angle of heel 15°, increase in resistance 4%;
Angle of heel 30°, increase in resistance 25%.

A dinghy, on the other hand, is not designed to sail heeled, and the asymmetry of its hull is much more pronounced even at small angles of heel. This means that particularly in strong winds the boat suffers a powerful resistance to forward motion and is subject to violent helm pressure. In light winds, on the other hand, the boat must be intentionally heeled very slightly in order to reduce the wetted surface, resistance from which is strongest at very low speeds (amounting to 80—90% of the total resistance). The resulting hull asymmetry also gives the boat a slight weather helm which improves the "feeling" of the boat.

2. *Resistance caused by leeway*

Leeway causes the boat to move obliquely through the water, and this provokes the formation of a mass of eddies, the so-called induced drag. Many experiments have shown that this induced drag increases considerably with the angle of leeway. Approximate figures for keelboats suggest an increase of 14% of the total resistance to forward motion for an angle of leeway of 2°, of 56% for an angle of 6°, and of 106% for an angle of 10°.

Tank tests on models have shown that the resistance to forward motion is increased by 50% if a boat sails at an angle of heel of 25° and with an angle of leeway of 5°.

3. *Dynamic resistance (wave-making resistance)*

The volume of the hull which is immersed during motion displaces an equal amount of water, consequently this motion is accompanied by the formation of waves.

Every boat moving through the water creates a bow wave and, except at very low speeds, a stern wave. The distance between their crests (wave length) cannot normally exceed the waterline length of the boat. It has also been found that the speed of a wave is a function of its length. It therefore follows that a boat cannot normally move faster than the wave system attached to its waterline length (photo on the left). This is what is called the critical speed of a boat. Light boats, however, can escape this rule. What happens is that the passage of the flat parts of the hull over the flow of water generate lift which changes the immersed volume of the hull.

This is what is called *planing*. The boat detaches itself from its stern wave while the bow rides up until the "bow wave" is clearly amidships and, in addition, much less pronounced. When planing, the boat meets with a much reduced resistance to forward motion and is capable of reaching spectacular speeds. But the rules of the apparent wind still apply, with two additions: firstly, it is possible when planing to sail un-stalled when *off* the wind, right up to a broad reach. In fact, as the boat's speed increases so the apparent wind draws ahead so that the sails can be sheeted in and set at a favourable angle of incidence (ill. below). Because of this, planing is not usually possible on courses close to the wind. Before the wind, when the boat's "speed wind" diminishes the true wind instead of augmenting it, planing will not occur except in very strong winds and even then the speeds reached will be lower than those attained on a reach. In any event, the technique of planing is of fundamental importance in racing when it can enable some competitors to make spectacular gains.

4. *Impact resistance* (ill. below)

This is due to the hull hitting a moving body of water, i.e. the waves. Weight plays an important rôle here, which is why a keelboat which is heavier and has more inertia is rather better off than a dinghy. A longer waterline allows it to negotiate a series of short waves at a time, but since the weight of a boat governs the speed with which it accelerates, a heavy keelboat takes longer to recover than a light dinghy once it has been stopped.

5. *Skin friction*

The viscosity of the water is responsible for a thin film of water adhering to the entire surface of the immersed hull. Its thickness and regularity depend on the state of the hull surface. It is therefore important to check very frequently that all underwater surfaces are smooth.

This boat sailing at high speed has just encountered a wave. The wind on this particular occasion was in excess of force 7, which means a pressure of more than 4 lbs. per sq. ft. sail area.

directional balance of a sailing boat

Balancing a boat means balancing the *centre of effort* [(C.E.) the centre of pressure of the aerodynamic force] and the centre of lateral resistance (C.L.R.) against each other.

The position of the C.E. in relation to the C.L.R. changes with the course sailed (i.e. the angle between the sail and the centre-line), the boat's speed and the angle of heel, and also is affected by the camber (curvature) of the sail. If the C.E. is very slightly *aft* of the C.L.R. the boat has a tendency to come up into the wind by turning round its C.L.R.

The boat is then said to carry **weather helm**. If, on the other hand, the C.E. is appreciably *forward* of the C.L.R. the boat has a tendency to fall away from the wind.

It is then said to carry **lee helm**.

It is the position of the mast along the centre-line that is largely responsible for the balance of a boat.

If the mast is too far aft, the boat will carry weather helm and vice versa. The designer usually specifies that the mast be put in a position where it will give the boat a very slight weather helm if the sails are correctly trimmed on a close-hauled course (which is the one on which a boat must be tuned). By virtue of their entirely different hull shapes a dinghy designed for sailing upright can only be allowed an angle of heel of a few degrees, while a keelboat will be much more tolerant.

If a dinghy is rigged with mainsail and jib (sloop rig) where the overall C.E. is the combination of the individual C.E.'s of the two sails, it is possible to steer the boat without the help of a rudder.

With a una-rigged boat (Finn) which only possesses a mainsail this is not possible. In either case the aim is to dispose the C.E. in such a way that the rudder needs to be employed only to guide and control turns. In fact, one must remember that every movement on the rudder slows the boat down.

The crew then, as soon as they have the boat well under control, must seek to establish perfect balance between the C.E. and the C.L.R., because it is in this condition that the boat is likely to reach its optimum speed.

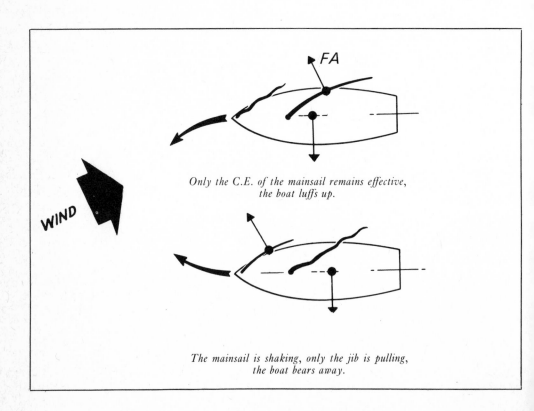

Only the C.E. of the mainsail remains effective, the boat luffs up.

The mainsail is shaking, only the jib is pulling, the boat bears away.

Note how delicately this helmsman handles his FINN (una rig) on the wind : the boat is certainly very well balanced. It is also interesting to see that angle beta *(angle between sail and centre-line) is quite considerable although the wind does not exceed force 2 to 3.*

details of a racing dinghy's equipment

1 Wind vane (or burgee) balanced by counter-weight.
2 Head of mainsail: point of attachment of halyard.
3 Main halyard locking device.
4 Mast fitting for spinnaker sheave.
5 Mast fitting for shrouds, forestay and trapeze wires.
6 Outer end of cross trees (spreaders).
7 Pivoting joint of cross trees.
8 Outer end of spinnaker boom with hook.
9 Hand grip and adjustment on trapeze wire.
10 Spinnaker boom fitting to take topping lift (upper wire) and downhaul (lower wire).
11 Stemhead fitting to take forestay and jib tack shackle.
12 End of trapeze wire with two rings: upper one for sailing close-hauled, lower one for reaching.
13 Bottle screws for adjusting tension of shrouds.
14 Fairlead for shock cord that keeps trapeze wire under tension.
16 Boom fitting with gooseneck.
17 Double purchase to adjust tack of mainsail.
18 "Window" enabling helmsman to see to leeward.
19 Slot in deck with longitudinal and transverse

20 wedges to hold mast.
    Kicking strap.
21 Jam cleat for jib sheet.
22 Track and adjustable slides for jib sheets.
23 Sheet winch.
24 Sliding traveller on main sheet horse; adjustable by purchase on either side.
25 Mainsheet purchase.
26 Pivoting joint of tiller extension.
27 Trumpet cleat for adjusting rudder blade depth.
28 Toe straps
29 Block for spinnaker guy.
30 Metal rudder stock.
31 Bailer flap.
32 Boom.
33 Clew outhaul and black band.
34 Lead for spinnaker sheet.
35 Pocket for full-length batten.
36 Seam.
38 Lifting rudder.
39 Top of centreplate.
40 Winch base mounted on centreplate case.
41 Chain plate to which shroud is attached.
42 Wire guard to prevent spinnaker from slipping under the hull if the halyard breaks.
43 Spinnaker guy.
44 Pivoting, retractable centreplate.

THE OPTIMIST

This new edition has been printed largely to cover a modern development, I would almost say a necessity of the present and future times.

Since 1968 the Optimist, which had been slowly spreading through Europe anyway, has gained impetus to carry it to the forefront of the European and international scene; it has been helped in this both by its energetic committee and by support from official and semi-official sources.

The Optimist explosion, which surprised nobody in the small boat world, has started a transformation which, to my mind, is more of an instructional revolution than a technical one, and represents an accelerated expansion without parallel in the history of yachting. Because the Optimist is an extremely stable little boat, designed for single-handed sailing from the earliest age (say 6–7 years to 12–14 depending on the size of the child), it enables children to discover for themselves the pleasures of sailing and, above all, racing.

● *The basic principles* of sailing an Optimist are the same as those of sailing other dinghies. It would therefore be superfluous to discuss trim, sheets, handling and tactics when these are all dealt with in detail later in this book. Nevertheless young Optimist helmsmen and, perhaps more important, those parents and instructors who teach them, should take note of three specific techniques which are important when racing Optimists and which represent differences from accepted practice in other dinghies. These variations stem from the concept of the boat itself, hull, rigging and sail which are all individual.

● *To Windward.* If the Optimist heels to an alarming angle when closehauled in a stiff breeze, do not try to reduce it by luffing to 'feather' the sail as you would in any other dinghy. You should renounce the modern method and revert to the old fashioned technique of maintaining heading and easing the sheet. Angle *alpha* is reduced by increasing angle *beta*, because angle of the apparent wind to the boat remains unchanged. You may not work higher to windward but you keep the boat going, for an Optimist which is pinched too high quickly slows to a halt and even picks up stern-way due to its hull shape and lightness. We should add that, as a general rule, and even in calm conditions, the Optimist should never be sailed too close to the wind, due to its being vulnerable to resistance to forward motion (p. 34). You should always have a fairly large angle *beta*, even in light winds (angle between the sail and the centre-line of the boat; chapter 1 and page 39).

● *Wind aft*, and particularly on a dead run, (trim, p. 48), the Optimist is fastest when heeled to windward (p. 49). This reduces wetted area.

When gybing, as described on pp. 70–77 and accompanying fold-out, the young helmsman should remember that the boom will be obstructed if the dagger board is not lowered out of the way (it will have been raised for sailing off the wind as noted on p. 60).

The individual rigging of the Optimist requires special advice as regards fitting out, but this does not absolve you from reading the following pages.

mast

After fitting a small wind vane or burgee on top, the heel of the mast should be poked through the hole in the thwart and then lodged in the mast step. This is movable fore and aft, thus permitting adjustment of mast rake. It is easy to alter mast rake on the Optimist (pp. 44 and 45) as it has no rigging; it is simply a question of adjusting the position of the heel. As a rule, the mast should be upright, but take care that the boom is horizontal when there is no tension on the sheet. Should the aft end (clew) be lower than the boom jaws (tack) it is a good idea to move the mast heel aft so as to realign the rig. Avoid the situation where the boom rests on the transom when the sail is sheeted hard down. This would have the effect of stretching the leech of the sail and thus reducing efficiency (sails, chapter III, pp. 188–203).

On the other hand, if the boom is too high aft, the mast heel should be moved forward to rectify the situation and, indeed, to make the boat look right. In any event, it is the cut of the sail and, more particularly, the length of the leech, which decides proper adjustment. There are rare exceptions to this rule which could be quoted, but it seems unwise to draw hasty conclusions as to good or bad performance of one Optimist as compared with another; it is more profitable to look for reasons for speed differences in shape of sail or hull (pp. 123 and 124).

the sprit

This represents an extremely important factor in sail trim. There are two different methods of setting it up. One has hooks and the other a two-part pulley. The second of these obviously allows great control over general sail trim for racing (p. 46).

light weather

Minimum tension on the pulley so as to ensure plenty of flow in the sail (aerodynamics, p. 25— total sail thrust). Equally, do not pull too hard on the sheet as this would immediately provoke creases from head to clew, which are particularly harmful to sail efficiency. We might also repeat that luff and foot should have a minimum tension.

medium weather

Windspeed 10–15 knots is about force 3 in the Beaufort scale. All the factors above should be more firmly tensioned, which will give rise to a crease parallel to the sprit, but which will disappear when the sail is sheeted home; if not the sprit tackle should be eased.

heavy weather

Tension should be harsh along all edges of the sail; luff, foot and sprit should be hauled out as much as possible.

kicking strap

Its action is intimately linked with sail trim for different wind conditions. This is described in detail on pp. 47 and 48.

final advice

When running in a strong wind, the Optimist tends to bury its bow, so the helmsman should position himself against the transom and never allow his sheet to run out too far (see pp. 51 and 52). Constructional details and advice on training are dealt with later, on page 123 et seq.

2

Boat handling

Books of instruction on sailing are very much the fashion: there must be some twenty of them on the market at the moment. I doubt if similar efforts have been made in support of other sports. One might ask oneself, however, to what extent the authors of these books overestimate the difficulties of learning and underestimate those of perfection.

Practical dinghy sailing is essentially a very mobile sport like ski-ing or horse riding. While it is necessary to acquire a knowledge of the technical and theoretical aspects, this does not by any means do away with the need for experience, and all the books in the world cannot replace this. One cannot hope to make progress in the art of sailing without going through a two-fold apprenticeship: theory and practice.

It is possible for the newcomer to familiarize himself with a sailing dinghy, under the guidance of an instructor or experienced friend, in a few hours and go on to more advanced instruction. But whilst it is certainly desirable to get down to practicalities as soon as possible, it is no less essential to do so with extreme care. Sailing is and will always be a dangerous sport, even more so for the lone sailor than for those taking part in a race.

Before going into this lively subject, I would like to make some recommendations:

● *Estimate the force of the wind correctly*
Beginners are very much given to underestimating the strength of the wind, particularly when it is off shore and the sun is shining. In such conditions one can see inexperienced sailors set out to sea whilst knowledgeable helmsmen think twice before they rig their boats. Do not play the rôle of "trail-blazer" but take your lead from those who are more experienced.

● *Wear a life jacket*
This is a piece of gear which should be as familiar to dinghy sailors as hunting caps to riders and shin pads to footballers. You might have to be in the water for a long time after having tired yourself out trying to right your capsized boat.

Now some practical details:

● *Never go sailing without shoes*
Bare feet are out of place on a boat. It is better to persuade yourself to wear shoes before breaking a toe on a self-bailer as I once did while tacking. Shoes with anti-slip soles and with unobtrusive lacings that do not get caught everywhere are undoubtedly the best solution. Foam rubber boots of the kind worn by skin divers are very useful but not very robust and also rather expensive.

● *Always be well clad*
Even in fine weather, when it is hot on land, one always feels cold on the water, and feeling cold seriously slows down reflexes. Put on oilskin top and trousers or a one-piece suit. No-one can endure for long exposure to cold water in strong winds. Exposure suits (wet-suits) are a real asset if one has to be out on the water for several hours, especially if it is not the middle of summer. These suits are particularly valuable in preventing the body undercooling if you capsize and have to spend some time in the water.

If you have delicate hands wear gloves rather than get sore hands for fun. It is possible to harden the skin on your hands by soaking them in a 50% solution of formalin or brine for 10–20 minutes a day for a fortnight.

rigging the boat

the wind vane (burgee)

It always amazes experienced helmsmen to see how many beginners think they can do without a wind vane.

The purpose of this piece of gear is more than to give an air of elegance to the boat: it indicates the direction of the wind at any moment. It is important to the boat's performance on all points of sailing, and from the point of view of safety it is an absolute necessity. It is only the wind vane which ensures a safe gybe in strong winds when a capsize would otherwise be inevitable. Paul Elvström, four times Olympic champion, never sails without one.

The first operation then is to fix a wind vane to the masthead, on the forward side of the mast.

advice

Now cast a glance at the ends of the spreaders. If they are the slightest bit rough, they must be covered with adhesive tape. The constant chafing of the sail against the spreader ends off the wind will soon damage it and eventually wear a hole.

stepping the mast

On the simplest of boats the mast step consists of a simple socket designed to hold the foot of the mast. Sometimes the step can be adjusted by means of different devices, in which case it is best to try the mid-way position first.

With the boat on the ground or on its trailer place the foot of the mast into the step. Pull the mast upright and hold it in a vertical position while someone else makes the shrouds fast to the chain plates and the forestay to the stemhead fitting, *leaving them fairly slack.*

But the setting up of the mast is by no means finished yet. It will now be necessary to adjust the angle the mast takes up in relation to the vertical: this is what is called the *rake*.

adjusting the rake

The most accurate way in which to do this is to use the main halyard as a plumb line by attaching a weight of some sort to its end. At the same time one

puts the forestay under tension: the mast gets pulled forward, but *its movement is checked by the length of the shrouds.*

If the plumb line hangs absolutely parallel to the mast when the hull is perfectly horizontal, *the rake is nil.*

If the plumb line hangs forward of the mast, the mast clearly has a *forward rake*, whereas if it hangs aft of the mast, the mast is *raked aft*. As a general rule, the mast ought to be inclined aft. This makes allowance for the fact that the tension of the kicking strap on the boom will tend to pull the mast forward by bending it. The desired rake will be obtained by shortening the shrouds, if necessary, where they are attached to the chain plates.

Adjustment by eye is not sufficiently accurate. An approved method is to measure the distance between the end of the plumb line and a point on the after side of the mast, usually the black band which marks the lower limit to which the sail can be set, or the gooseneck fitting.

Since the height of masts varies appreciably from

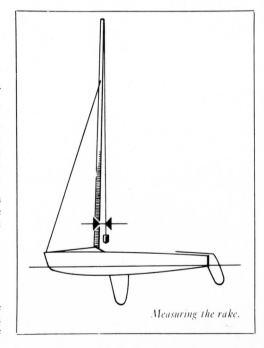

Measuring the rake.

one type of boat to another, the rake is not expressed as an absolute measurement in millimetres but in *thousandths*, that is to say in millimetres per metre.

For example, a rake of 40 thousandths for a luff of 6 metres corresponds to a distance of 40 × 6 = 240 mm. between the plumb line and the mast.

In boats where the mast is flexible and has a tendency to bend forward to any degree, a rake of between 20 and 70 thousandths is generally adopted. To start with, it is best to try a rake of 40 thousandths.

Once the length of the shrouds has been determined and they have been fixed to the chain plates, it is advisable not to tighten the forestay and thus the rigging is slack when the sails are not set. In fact, exaggerated tension on the standing rigging while the boat is not normally used could impose too much strain on the mast under the influence of temperature changes: quite often the temperature drops appreciably during the night and the steel wires of the rigging contract. If the rigging was already taut during the day, the pressure on the mast can then become so great that the mast takes on a permanent bend. This is quite a common occurrence. A good idea is to tie all the shrouds together with a piece of shockcord which takes up the slack in them, so that the mast does not sway about on the mooring thus causing all points of the rigging to suffer sudden jerks and stresses.

You have now completed the initial preparation.

For national or international classes the associations give more or less precise instructions on the subject of mast rake. In the 420 the distance between the masthead sheave and the outside edge of the transom is measured. On average it should be 6.10 m. (20 ft). In the 5.0.5. two measurements are taken from the same point, namely the outside edge of the transom: one to the after edge of the foot of the mast (3.16 m. = 10 ft 4 in.), the other to the after edge of the mast at deck level (3.11 m. = 10 ft 1½ in.). In the 470 instructions are less precise. It is merely suggested to adopt a rake aft of 5 degrees.

In a new boat there is the additional consideration of having to allow for a very noticeable stretching of the shrouds during the first few hours out, as a result of which the rake will decrease.

Finally, it will be found useful in strong winds to increase the rake to make both the jib leech and mainsail leech set better.

Without any doubt it is only while sailing it that you can hope to find that fine adjustment which will produce the best performance from the boat, but we shall come back to that later. You must be able to master the steering of the boat well before dealing with such a delicate matter. (p. 82 et seq.)

From now on the mast can be set up and taken down, without altering the length of the shrouds, by undoing them at the chainplates.

The boat is now put *head to wind* before the sails are hoisted.

the jib

First of all the tack is made fast. The foot of the jib, or at least the forward third or half of it, when hoisted, must come down to deck level for optimum aerodynamic efficiency.

The jib is now hoisted.

Tensioning the halyard is a delicate operation which calls for a certain feel. If one pulls hard on the halyard this transfers itself automatically to the luff of the jib and the result is that the mast is pulled forward. But if the shrouds have been adjusted in length beforehand, the mast finds its correct position at once. A halyard made of steel wire is recommended, or at least partly of wire. With synthetic rope which possesses a certain elasticity it is impossible to tension the halyard accurately. How much luff tension is applied to the jib has to be carefully judged according to the wind strength. While the crew hoists the sail, the helmsman pulls out on the forestay, the amount of pull depending on the strength of wind, and this determines how hard the jib is hoisted home.

The general rule is **strong** tension in **strong winds**, so that in a seaway the whole of the rig is rigid and does not become stretched; **light** tension in **light winds** will give the rig a certain flexibility.

This operation completed, it will be noticed that the forestay is slack: it performs no other function than that of a safeguard to prevent the mast falling over if one of the jib fittings or the fore halyard breaks.

The hanks are now superfluous, always assuming that the jib has a stainless steel luff wire. Anything but stainless steel wire is too elastic and does not allow an accurate adjustment of mast and sails.

The sheet, with the jib hauled in taut, ought to be in line with the bisector of the angle between foot and leech. If the sheet lead can be moved, it is set up in the desired position; if it is permanently fixed, the tack of the jib must be raised or lowered. Lowering it as far as possible has the same effect as moving the lead aft, and vice versa. But this method is far from perfect. What must be avoided is for the air to escape by the foot of the jib. Instead, it must be led past the leeward side of the mainsail to cause the required suction there (see p. 23).

the mainsail

The battens in the mainsail should be 2 to 5 mm. (1/16–3/16 in.) shorter than the corresponding pockets except if the pockets have elastics fitted against which the battens are pushed in.

If the sail possesses a full-length batten like the 420 or the 5.0.5. then this must be under stress between the luff and the leech. As a general rule the batten should be lightly tensioned in light winds and tied in hard in strong winds.

The bolt rope at the foot of the mainsail is now fed into the boom groove and made fast at the tack. Most boats have a special fitting with a pin or hook, or else a shackle. Frequently these kinds of fixture do not allow the sail to set perfectly at the tack, and small creases cannot be avoided. They do, however, allow the gooseneck to be slid up and down without interfering with the track fixture.

The mainsail is now made fast *temporarily* at the clew. The kicking strap is eased right off, as is the mainsheet.

After having fixed the head of the mainsail securely to the halyard the mainsail is hoisted, the luff rope being fed carefully into the mast track.

If the boom is adjustable in height at the mast it should be fixed in the highest position, except in a very strong breeze. The sail is hoisted as far as it will go, unless a black band indicates the maximum position. The boom is then gradually pulled down to obtain a light tension on the luff. Then the boom is made fast with whatever means is provided for this purpose. The screws with which the track, in which the gooseneck slides, is fitted to the mast should be checked frequently, they take a considerable strain.

If the gooseneck is in a fixed position on the mast as it is on the Firefly, it is obvious that the tension on the luff can only be adjusted by the halyard. In all cases it is important that the fullness of the sail be well distributed. This can only be achieved by painstaking adjustment. As the tension of the luff is increased, so the fullness of the sail is partially taken up and at the same time moved nearer the mast, thus giving rise to large creases which can only be got rid of by giving the mast a bend forward in the middle. In *light winds* one seeks to obtain *maximum fullness* in the sail, at the same time avoiding the formation of small horizontal creases alongside the mast which indicate that the tension on the luff is too light. In *strong winds* it is necessary at the same time to *keep the sail low and put the luff under maximum tension*, without going outside the limits permitted by the class rules. This is when the large vertical creases we spoke of before will make their appearance, but they will normally disappear as soon as the sail is sheeted home.

Slack mainsail and jib luffs make a sorry sight, not to mention the loss of efficiency.

Only now do we proceed to adjust the tension along the foot by means of the outhaul. The adjustment is the same as that for the luff: *strong tension* in *strong winds, maximum amount of slack in light winds* to give the sail its maximum fullness. It will not always be possible to avoid small creases going upwards from the after part of the foot.

Whilst making the adjustment along the foot it is a good idea to have a look at the whole of the sail to check how the fullness is distributed over its area.

It is always advisable to try and get rid of the vertical creases but at the same time only apply the minimum of tension to the foot of the sail. In fairly strong winds one can proceed in the same way as for the luff and tension it until a horizontal crease appears. This will disappear as soon as the sail fills and the boom bends slightly. The clew is then securely fastened by means of a lashing long enough to allow several turns round the boom and through the cringle as well. This precaution will prevent the after part of the boom groove from opening out or the sail tearing at that point when it is sheeted in hard.

the kicking strap

This plays a two-fold rôle as safety device and means of adjustment. It is vitally important.
a) **Safety**
It holds the boom down and stops it from lifting. Its influence is of particular value during a gybe in strong winds because it keeps the leech taut and prevents a "Chinese gybe".
b) **Adjustment**
By applying tension to the kicking strap the mainsail can be flattened to a greater or lesser degree. It has a direct influence on the boom by pulling it down and forward at the same time.

Consequently, and depending on the amount of tension applied, it simultaneously causes:
— the boom to bend slightly downwards in the middle.
— the leech of the mainsail to become taut.
— the masthead to move aft and the upper part of the mast, from the hounds upwards, to bend.
— the boom to press on the mast making it bend forward in its lower part.

The kicking strap is of particular importance on boats that do not possess an adjustable mainsheet horse (Firefly, Cadet, etc.) when it comes to sailing anywhere between close-hauled and reaching.

With the mainsail kept very flat by the kicking strap the sheet can be used to control the angle between the sail and the centre-line and *the angle of incidence between the apparent wind and the sail* (chapter I, angle alpha).

However, for the same wind force the kicking strap must be tensioned differently according to the point of sailing. It is particularly desirable in moderate winds to release the tension somewhat on a reach and a run in order to give the mainsail back some of its fullness.
— *Light winds :* tension negligible on all points of sailing.
— *Moderate breeze :* moderate tension close-hauled, less tension reaching.
— *Strong breeze :* strong tension on practically all points of sailing.

On certain dinghies the mast is not held in place at deck level. In that case the action of the kicking-strap in pulling the boom forward cannot be checked, and there is a risk of the mast being distorted too much and some times even breaking.

This accident usually occurs on a reach in very strong winds. This is how it comes about:

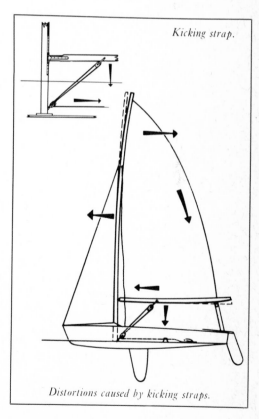

Kicking strap.

Distortions caused by kicking straps.

47

The jib has been hoisted home hard, thus making the whole of the rigging rigid. If the kicking strap is now pulled down hard, the mast in bending releases the tension on the rigging (in fact, as the mast bends the hounds are lowered by an inch or two). Close on the wind the boom is set at a very small angle to the centre-line and its pressure is directed much more forward than sideways. Also, the mast is held in place at three points on deck: the jib tack, the chainplate of the weather shroud and the mainsheet.

But as the boat bears away onto a reach or a run the mainsheet is paid off and no longer puts up any resistance to the wind pressure which now pushes the whole of the rigging forward. The jib luff slackens and the mast is held solely by the two shrouds. Through the pull of the kicking strap the boom, for its part, exercises a very strong sideways pressure on the mast. The mast, swaying back and forth and from port to starboard under the influence of every wave and puff is put under considerable stress.

In practice the mast can be relieved in two ways:

1) by re-tensioning the jib after having set the kicking strap, in order to tauten the rigging;

2) by slightly releasing the kicking strap when bearing away, which tensions the rigging to some extent. This is the most logical solution.

final advice

Before rushing off to do battle with the seas it is a good idea to safeguard yourself against unpleasant surprises by checking whether all the gear works as it should: the sheets, the centreplate in its case, the rudder.

While you are not too sure of yourself in executing manoeuvres, always use the rudder in the fully down position.

the trim of the boat

Newcomers to dinghy sailing soon realize the importance of the lateral trim of the boat, particularly when an extra strong puff makes their boat heel over. They react instinctively by **sitting out**. On the other hand if, as the puff dies down, the boat returns to an even keel and under the effect of the counterweight starts to heel to windward, the crew does not always notice it immediately. In this abnormal position the boat takes on a ridiculous trim which is particularly harmful to speed.

A dinghy is generally designed to be sailed as upright as possible, with only a slight heel of up to 10°. In very light airs this heel can be progressively increased to make the boat more sensitive on the helm and to allow the sails to set better, and at the same time reduce the wetted surface of the hull (**skin friction**—chapter 1).

If the helmsman sits to windward, at right angles to the centre-line, he has his **aftermost** hand on the tiller while his **forward** hand holds the sheet.

This is an absolute rule. For instance, if the boat is on the port tack, the helmsman, if he is sitting to windward, holds the sheet in his left hand and the tiller in his right. If he changes over to sit to leeward his handholds are immediately reversed.

The stronger the wind, no matter what the point of sailing, the more upright the boat must be sailed. *This is called lateral trim.*

In light airs the boat is deliberately heeled slightly.

Optimists heeling.

The wind has dropped slightly and the crew in each of the two boats, with remarkable co-ordination, has come in from the trapeze to keep his 5.0.5 sailing at the correct angle of heel.

The *longitudinal trim* of the boat is less obvious to beginners but nevertheless important. They often weigh the stern of the boat down too much and forget that the transom must under no circumstances drag in the water because this gives rise to considerable turbulence. Not only does the boat's speed suffer but, and this is far more serious, the boat goes "soft" on the helm and loses all feel. This is as disastrous as heeling to windward.

● *When sailing close-hauled* the crew should move forward until the transom is just clear of the water and produces no turbulence.

If the wind is strong the crew can move further aft as the boat gathers speed, making sure all the time, though, that no undue turbulence appears at the transom. As a result of the crew moving aft in strong winds the bow of the boat is lifted fractionally out of the water and the boat becomes more sensitive on the helm.

● *Off the wind* in a fairly strong breeze, in order to help the boat to plane, the crew should move aft without, however, immersing the transom. If the wind drops temporarily, the helmsman or the crew (or both of them) must immediately move forward to stop the boat from squatting by the stern.

It follows that the crew must be constantly on the move, not only athwartships to keep the boat upright but also fore-and-aft, getting their weight back amidships as a puff dies down, for instance.

This 5.0.5 sailing in a wind of force 3 to 4 owes its speed mainly to its perfect lateral trim.

Several factors are responsible for the boat yawing (going off course).

First of all there is the fact that in a fresh breeze the modern dinghy is generally faster than the swell and when running before the wind tends to dig its nose in every time it catches up with a wave. At that moment the resistance to forward motion is very marked (impact resistance). The boat is slowed down and at the same time the wind pressure increases, but the nature of this increase is not beneficial (W_s diminishes, while W_A increases). Being a particularly lively and sensitive piece of equipment, the boat seeks to escape from this embrace by "writhing" in the water and either bearing away or luffing up very suddenly. Efforts to correct the boat's movement on the tiller often make things worse.

The fact that the centre or centres of effort are now very far out from the centre-line helps to intensify the rolling movements of the boat. The crew will have to remain rather far aft in order to lift the bow clear of the water and be careful to keep the boat sailing perfectly upright.

If the rolling persists the area of mainsail presented to the wind will have to be reduced by hauling in on the mainsheet but at the same time keeping the boat dead before the wind (the wind vane comes in useful here). Usually it is not too difficult to prevent the boat from shooting up into the wind, but sailing by the lee is a problem and once an involuntary gybe has occurred capsizing is inevitable.

It is important to check the position of the centreplate and make sure that it is not all the way up. It should be 1/4 to 1/3 down. Finally try to get the waves, wherever possible, square on the transom. Whenever the boat decelerates the waves have a violent effect on it and make it luff or bear away very abruptly.

While it is easy on a sloop to get a good lateral trim (by winging out the jib or spinnaker opposite the mainsail), this is not so on a una-rigged boat where the asymmetry of the sail area is very marked.

Here the skill of the helmsman counts for even more. Una helmsmen will benefit from memorizing the preceding remarks thoroughly, especially what has been said about reducing the sail area presented to the wind (boom angled at 50° to 60° to the centre-line only).

A una-rigged boat is always heavier forward than a sloop and tends to dig its nose in more readily. But rolling, with the boom out at right angles to the centre-line, is also caused by the twisted shape of the sail. Its upper part is at an angle of more than 90° to the centre-line, while the lower after part sets at less than 90°. The different pressures are directed towards opposite sides of the centre-line, and it follows that the boat is constantly pushed from one side to the other.

If the helmsman has his boat well under control, and if the class rules do not forbid it, as is the case with the Finn, it is often a help to lift the rudder slightly to get a "better feel" of the boat. Even in strong winds the lateral trim of the boat can be better controlled if the rudder is slightly lifted.

The centreplate is always down on a beat. As the boat bears away it is raised progressively: half down on a reach, a quarter down on a run.

. . . they have not read the preceding page!

trimming the sheets

Before embarking on this subject it will be necessary to refer back to chapter 1 to familiarise ourselves thoroughly with the way a boat sails. The sailing boat is a moving object amid an air mass which is itself in motion. It is not simply the *true wind* that matters but the combination of the true wind and the wind created by the boat's movement. This is the *apparent wind*, and it is indicated by the wind vane at the masthead.

There are two basic modes in which a boat sails under the influence of this apparent wind:

● *On the wind*, when the wind produced by the boat itself augments the true wind. To the observer on board the apparent wind is then stronger than the true wind. This is the case when sailing *close-hauled, full and by, on a close reach, a reach* and sometimes, for boats like ice yachts and land yachts, *on a broad reach*. There is no doubt that the faster a boat can go (by virtue of its design, its water-lines and sailplan) the wider is its scope for sailing on the wind.

● *Before the wind*, when the boat, by its movement, reduces more or less appreciably the pressure of the true wind on the sails. This is the case when *running, broad reaching* and, with very slow boats, even *reaching*.

It can be concluded that a boat attains its maximum speed when sailing in an "unstalled" condition.

It has been found in wind tunnel tests—as indeed in practice—that the boat performs best *if the sails are trimmed to an angle of around 22° to the apparent wind*.

It is immediately obvious then that optimum performance can only be achieved by careful trimming of the various sails in relation to the apparent wind.

For the purpose of determining the angle, since sails can vary so greatly in fullness, it is customary to take the chord of the curvature at the height of the C.E.

In theory, if set at an angle of 22° the sails are 100% efficient. It is therefore essential, with the boat sailing close-hauled and making practically no leeway due to its speed, to maintain this angle all the time. This is not the easiest thing to do, since the true wind is never constant in speed and direction. Every time it changes, the apparent wind changes, too.

Whenever this happens it is essential to both alter course and re-trim the sails as quickly as possible.

The wind vane now plays an important rôle, not only in strong winds when the helmsman has to take very quick action, but also in light airs when the reactions of the boat are much slower.

We know that when a boat goes very fast, the leeway made is practically nil. In other words, the slower a boat is the more leeway it makes. On the other hand, the closer a boat is pushed up into the wind, the slower it will go. It is therefore when sailing close-hauled, and particularly when beating, that leeway is most marked, and must be reduced as much as possible (chapter 1).

Close-hauled, when beating, the angle of incidence is very small and the luff of the sail close to lifting.

Lifting: A sail is said to be lifting if it shakes, lightly, along the luff, or, quite strongly, over its entire width from luff to leech.

In a *strong wind*, if the sails are sheeted in too hard, the boat will heel at an exaggerated angle. The crew reacts by easing out the sheets. The sail lifts and the boat comes back to an even keel, but it has lost all its speed and sometimes even stops completely.

No-one is expected to sail with a protractor: with sails of medium camber the optimum angle for efficiency is the one at which the luff is just short of lifting.

Sailing correctly demands intuition and feeling in simultaneously handling the tiller (luffing up or bearing away) and trimming the sail or sails (luffing up reduces the angle between the sail and the apparent wind). The skill of great champions lies in the fact that they can foresee wind changes and anticipate the manoeuvres necessary. In this way their sails are always correctly trimmed and their boats, even in strong winds, always sail nearly upright without being subjected to constant heeling and subsequent righting.

How can this technique be acquired?

close-hauled

First of all, the object must be to impart as much speed as possible to the boat while staying close

The Farrant brothers, 1965 world champions in the 5.0.5 class.

to the wind (angles *alpha* and *beta*); to try and keep the boat sailing as upright as possible (lateral trim) by the crew sitting out. You will notice that this is by no means easy, since the wind is never constant, neither in strength nor in direction. The rule is to *luff up* a little in the puffs by pushing the tiller down slightly (angle *alpha* becomes smaller). If the boat heels over in spite of this, pay the sheet off a bit to get the sails back to the correct angle to the apparent wind. The latter will actually be further on the beam since one of its components (the true wind) has increased in force.

As the boat comes back on an even keel, stop luffing, bear away slightly and sheet in.

It is only possible to proceed in this way with the mainsail if the boat has a horse or a track on which the position of the mainsheet block can be adjusted, thus allowing the sail to be trimmed to a good angle of attack. The stronger the breeze, the further down to leeward the traveller should be to reduce angle *alpha* to the minimum but to increase, at the same time, angle *beta* and get the aerodynamic force to be directed as far forward as possible.

If the true wind (W_T) increases in strength: This is the case when a sudden puff strikes the sail. The speed of the boat and therefore the speed wind (W_s) do not respond immediately to this increase. Only one component, the true wind (W_T) is changed, and this causes the apparent wind to come from further aft. The apparent wind seems to **free**.

The true wind shifts from W_{T1} to W_{T2}: the apparent wind shifts from W_{A1} to W_{A2}; it changes in direction and strength. The wind is said to be **freeing**.

It means that it strikes the sail from further abeam, and if no adjustment is made to the course sailed or the angle of the sail to compensate for this new incidence, the boat will respond by heeling violently (the angle of incidence of the sail is too great).

If the true wind (W_T) comes from further aft, the apparent wind (W_A) will obviously free, too. The same procedure must be followed.

If the speed of the boat drops (boat stopped by a wave): Only one of the components, the speed wind (W_s) changes, the other component, the true wind (W_T) remains constant. The apparent wind (W_A) changes in direction (it frees) and strength (it is weaker than before). The boat's speed wind W_{S1} shifts to W_{S2}. Consequently, the apparent wind goes from W_{A1} to W_{A2} and the angle of incidence is greater.

A gentle luff would be indicated to avoid the boat heeling in this puff.

Instead of hanging out like an acrobat this helmsman would do better to luff up and ease the sheet a bit.

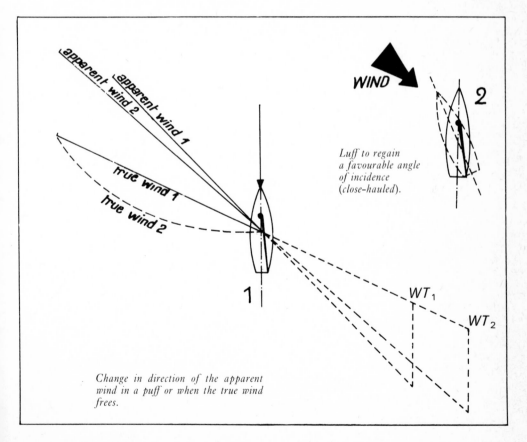

WIND

Luff to regain a favourable angle of incidence (close-hauled).

apparent wind 2

apparent wind 1

true wind 1

true wind 2

1

2

WT₁

WT₂

Change in direction of the apparent wind in a puff or when the true wind frees.

The wind seems to be **freeing**.

This may give the impression that it is possible to go closer to the true wind, but the slowing down of the boat causes it to make considerable leeway, and luffing up in this case would be a *grave mistake*. On the contrary, the boat must be made to gain speed as quickly as possible by easing the sheets slightly and making sure that it is not stopped again by another wave.

great mistake, because the true wind when it weakens does not change in direction, and going about, even if done in the most perfect manner, will do nothing to improve matters, rather the opposite.

It is obvious that a fine adjustment of the angle of incidence of the sail can only be achieved if the boat has a horse or track on which the mainsheet block can be "played" at the same time as the mainsheet is hauled in or eased off.

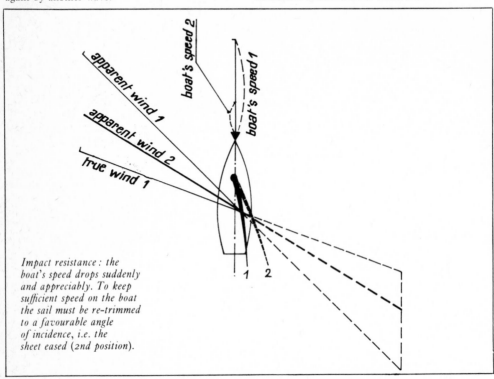

Impact resistance: the boat's speed drops suddenly and appreciably. To keep sufficient speed on the boat the sail must be re-trimmed to a favourable angle of incidence, i.e. the sheet eased (2nd position).

Every time the wind drops slightly, especially between puffs, the sheets must be eased to give the sail a bit more fullness. Also, and more important still, the traveller must be reset more or less amidships so that the sail sets at a favourable angle of incidence. What actually happens is that the speed of the true wind drops suddenly while the speed of the boat remains constant. The apparent wind moves further ahead, and in order to keep up the boat's speed it is necessary to bear away a little (the power developed by the sail depends on its fullness, and whilst there are moments when the sail must be flattened by bending the mast, there are others, like this one, when the sail must be given its maximum fullness).

In these conditions beginners often think the wind "is heading" and hasten to go about. This is a

in strong winds

In strong winds, on boats which do not possess a mainsheet horse (Heron, Mirror, etc.) strong tension on the kicking strap will flatten the mainsail, and it is by means of the sheet alone that the angle of incidence of the sail can be regulated. It is not possible with this simplified arrangement to go extremely close to the wind.

It is possible in this way to get the better of the puffs, but as soon as the wind drops the tension on the kicking strap keeps the sail too flat. It would really be necessary continuously to adjust its tension.

in light winds

In light winds, while always keeping as close to the wind as possible, it is above all necessary to sail the boat in such a way that does not make too much leeway.

If you feel the boat slow down without the wind having weakened or the luff of the sail shaking, the sheets must immediately be eased a bit: the angle of incidence is clearly greater than it should ideally be and angle *beta* is too small.

The wind vane is invaluable here, providing it is sensitive.

As soon as the boat gathers speed again, luff gradually and sheet the sails in slightly.

As I pointed out in the paragraph on **lateral trim**, it helps to make the boat heel slightly and so give it more feel on the helm and reduce the wetted surface. It follows that the position of the crew is of great importance. There is nothing more difficult than sailing close-hauled in light airs. It calls for utmost attention on the part of the helmsman, who has to be on the look-out for the slightest puff.

While this does not require anything in the way of physical effort, it certainly calls for a high degree of sensitivity. Sailing in light airs is a special art.

If the wind is light but there is a swell, the boat must be prevented from slamming into every wave. By increasing the angle of heel and easing the sheets somewhat it is possible to reach a fair speed and the boat can then be gradually coaxed closer to the wind.

Resistance to leeway (R_L) grows as the boat's speed increases, thus

angle gamma is reduced

(chapter 1)

The helmsman of this 420, close-hauled knows how to sail his boat at maximum speed.

reaching

In sailing full and by, on a close reach or on a reach the first requirement is gradually to raise the centreplate, and this at the same time brings it further aft. The boat will then be more responsive to the helm since the C.L.R. has moved aft.

In boats with a *dagger plate*, e.g. the Europa Moth, the plate can only be moved fractionally aft, since the centreplate case is only little wider than the plate itself.

While this system has the advantage that the small centreplate case does not interfere much with the space in the cockpit and only a very small amount of water is dragged along inside the case, it is inconvenient in many ways. We need only remark on its tiring and awkward operation and the danger involved in running aground, when serious damage is not uncommon.

In the puffs, **ease the mainsheet and pull the helm up,** keeping the boat sailing quite upright. Then trim the jib. As soon as the boat starts to plane,

A very common fault with beginners when they bear away. Note the rudder angled across the transom and the boat trying to luff because the mainsheet is still sheeted in while the jib is eased.

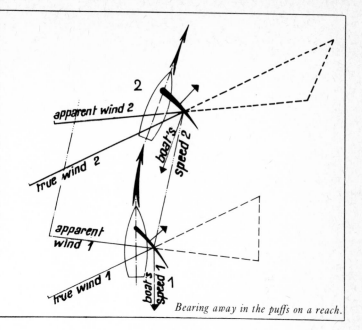

Bear away in the puffs and at the same time ease the sheets to direct the aerodynamic force further ahead and thus diminish leeway. It is a serious mistake simply to keep the boat sailing upright by sitting out further without bearing away and thereby keeping angle beta *constant. It not only gives rise to a turbulent airflow but to an unfavourable direction of the aerodynamic force, as a result of which the boat makes very considerable leeway. By bearing away, the boat benefits longer from the puff because it momentarily continues with it in the same direction.*

Bearing away in the puffs on a reach.

sheet the sails in gradually at the same time hauling your wind to get back on the normal course. As the puff subsides, continue to luff and sheet in a bit more. When reaching, the boat is not pinned to a course as close to the wind as possible, so the important thing is to strive always for maximum speed by directing the aerodynamic force well ahead.

On this point the boat is still sailing unstalled and benefits from optimum sail efficiency. It is important to preserve the air flow over the sail. Any change in speed or direction of the true wind entails a sudden and notable change in the apparent wind. A turbulent flow caused by angle *alpha* being too great (stalling) must be prevented by easing the sheets (at the same time benefiting from a larger angle *beta*). By bearing away momentarily the boat follows a course rather more before the wind and benefits longer from the effects of the puff, while the undesirable leeway is considerably reduced (FA directed very much ahead).

Let us state then, that in order to restore a laminar flow over the sail we must quickly reduce the angle of incidence of the airflow until the airflow is deflected as little as possible; at around 10°, the aerodynamic force will, of course, be greatly diminished.

What is important throughout is that the boat should be kept upright and planing as long as possible.

In light winds the commonest mistake made by beginners is to sheet the sails in too far on all points of sailing. Besides this, they do not pay sufficient attention to changes in wind speed and direction. Consequently, since the apparent wind changes all the time, they are unable to trim their sails so that they perform efficiently and start thinking that their own boat is inferior. Very often after a race in light winds one can hear newcomers say: "My boat won't go . . . ."

So far we have been talking about sailing "on the wind". By contrast, if the boat sails "before the wind" (running or broad reaching) its speed depends chiefly on the resistance to forward motion (position of crew and total weight of boat).

In light winds, one must above all avoid "dragging the stern"; in fresh winds, digging the bow in.

CLOSE-HAULED : *luff in the puffs ;*
REACHING : *bear away in the puffs and ease the sheets.*

On all points of sailing keep the boat as upright as possible.

Use the rudder gently and as nearly as possible in sympathy with the action of the sails.

sitting-out

Modern dinghies, light and over-canvassed as they are, possess a very low inherent stability, and it is the influence of their crews alone which not only keeps them from capsizing but enables them to put up such a remarkable performance, particularly if they can be prevented from heeling to more than 10°.

Because dinghies are so light it is at the same time essential and very effective for their crews to sit or hang out. In addition, the ample beam of dinghies also contributes to this effectiveness. On keelboats the influence of these efforts is less noticable, but even there the crew have to get out. The further the crew of a dinghy can get out, feet secured by toestraps, the greater the resistance to heeling. This position is extremely tiring and after a very short time produces violent muscular pains in the abdomen and thighs of anyone not used to this kind of exercise.

Before launching yourself on a course of athletic training destined to strengthen the muscles so that they can tolerate these prolonged contractions, it might be advisable to adjust the toestraps until the sitting-out position is almost . . . comfortable.

It is better to sit out moderately far for a long time than to throw oneself out full-length to impress the audience and stay there for but a few seconds. It follows that the toestraps must be fitted rather low and, above all, adapted to the physique of every particular crew. Obviously short-legged persons can comfortably use toestraps higher up than those with long legs.

It is therefore recommended that the toestraps should be fitted with some means by which they can be adjusted in height if this is not already provided. A comfortable position and maximum efficiency when sitting-out make sailing the boat immeasurably easier. One cannot point this out too often.

By adopting good habits right from the start you ensure quicker success in racing later on. But it is too soon to deal with what is required in the way of

These toe straps are too high and do not allow helmsman and crew to take up a very "comfortable" sitting-out position.

Helmsman and crew of this 420 are in a very efficient sitting-out position. Nevertheless, the attitude of the crew is not very orthodox but certainly extremely tiring on his thigh and abdominal muscles. The attitude of the helmsman is classical. The boat seems a bit too far down by the bow. ▶

sitting-out in racing. It calls for intensive physical training and this is described in chapter 3 (**preparation for racing**).

As far as the system of suspending the crew completely outboard on a wire (the trapeze) is concerned, this can only be employed if the helmsman is highly skilled in handling his boat. Without this mastery, helmsman and crew involve themselves in "contretemps" with which they will not fail to amuse the spectators but which are just as likely to spoil their taste for sailing after they have capsized several times.

Yvonne Duvelleroy, several times French champion, demonstrates an excellent sitting-out position. Note the angle between sail and centre-line and the long toestrap which can be adjusted on the cockpit floor.

Classical position of Finn helmsman in a fresh breeze.

Star crews adopt rather strange attitudes to keep the boat upright.

tacking

In tacking, the boat uses its momentum to carry it through the sector of the turn in which the sails do not impart drive to it. This manoeuvre is easy enough in a heavy boat with plenty of speed, but it can present difficulties for a dinghy with rather low inertia, particularly if the wind is strong and if the boat is being stopped by waves (chapter 1). Under these circumstances beginners often fail to go about: this is called missing stays. It will repay us, therefore, to look at some points of theory. . . .

Keeping up the boat's speed is of the utmost importance, particularly in the first phase of the manoeuvre when the boat is brought "head to wind".

In order to maintain a powerful **driving force** the sails must be kept pulling for as long as possible so that the maximum use can be made of the *aerodynamic force*. It is fatal to **ease** the sheets before the boat has come up very nearly head to wind.

If we refer back to what was said concerning the directional balance of a boat we find that as long as aerodynamic force is derived from the mainsail the boat turns of its own accord round its centre of lateral resistance, and all that is needed is to control the movement with the rudder gradually to bring the boat *head to wind* (chapter 1).

In any case, in tacking the tiller must not be moved abruptly nor, what is more, must the sheets be let fly too soon. In strong winds the boat will otherwise refuse to go about.

We can now proceed to complete the manoeuvre, which will greatly contribute to our mastery of the boat: as soon as the boat reaches head to wind with the sails shaking, bring it gradually round to the other tack by hauling in on the mainsheet, without touching the tiller. Remember to have the centreplate completely lowered or else the boat will drift sideways. This exercise is excellent practice for tacking and should be repeated again and again.

In light winds and calm waters the boat will go about by itself if it is deliberately heeled a bit more. The tiller need only be used to control the manoeuvre, to "round off" the turn and to preserve the boat's speed. The moment the boat points into the eye of the wind, ease the sheets. Let the boat come onto the other tack and do not haul in the sheets until you are sure that you have gone well past the axis of the wind. All the same, the boat will have slowed down and should not be brought back to a close-hauled course until it has picked up speed.

Constant practice of this manoeuvre will soon make perfect. The important thing to remember is not to sheet the sails in too soon and not to be in a hurry to get the boat pointing high again on the other tack. Both are serious mistakes which inevitably give rise to pronounced leeway.

In the photograph on the opposite page you can see that the jib is fluttering while the mainsail is still pulling, helping the boat round.

The photographs on this page show, left, the boat pointing head to wind. The crew changes sides with his back to the mast. The boat's lateral trim is perfect. Right : the turn is continued on the other (**starboard**) tack.

In strong winds and a lively sea you should, above all, take care not to tack at a moment when it looks as though you will hit a particularly big wave. The boat will immediately be stopped. If the waves are from the same direction as the wind, they will probably strike the hull at an angle of around 40°. The turn must be started at the crest of one wave and the boat got through stays (past the eye of the wind) while it is in the trough, so that the next wave pushes the bow round.

The more closely the direction of the waves coincides with that of the wind, the more precisely the manoeuvre must be timed, for if a wave reaches the boat before it has got through stays there is a great risk that it will be knocked back and stopped.

In such conditions it is of the utmost importance to keep speed on the boat as long as possible, which means chosing a moment to tack when the sea is least disturbed and, above all, not easing the sheets too soon.

The sails must be kept sheeted in as long as possible and the movement of the boat accurately controlled until it comes head to wind. This is the moment for some energetic action on the helm to get the boat onto the other tack as fast as possible. The sails are sheeted in only gradually as the crew moves over to weather. The lateral trim plays an important part here. If the sheets are hauled in too soon, the boat will heel over violently and out of control, and since the boat has lost most of its speed by now, a strong puff could easily capsize it.

The helmsman, if the boat has a mainsheet horse amidships (Finn, Moth, FD, 420, 470, 5.0.5.), changes sides facing forward. He exchanges helm and sheet behind his back at the moment he passes the boat's centre-line. If the mainsheet is hauled in from aft (as on the Firefly) the helmsman makes the half-turn facing aft. It is easier this way to change over sheet and helm, but the helmsman momentarily loses control over the course he steers and this can be extremely dangerous.

The crew always changes sides with his back to the mast so that he can safely duck under the kicking strap.

A half-hitch takes the strain of holding the sheet off the fingers.

Opposite page, top: the helmsman starts the turn by pushing the helm down, but keeping the sail sheeted in. Above: the boat goes through stays. Below: the turn is completed, the sail is pulling on the other tack. The helmsman retrieves his tiller extension.

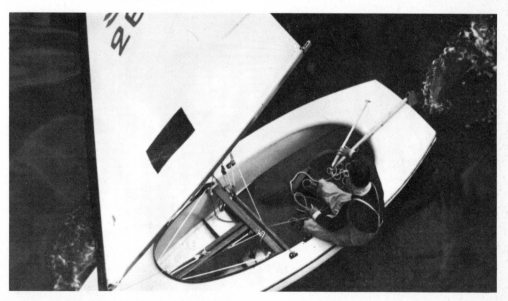

gybing

Definition: changing tacks by bearing away (a boat is said to be "bearing away" when it turns away from the wind). In other words, it is the opposite to tacking, which begins by luffing up, i.e. turning the bow into the wind. In gybing it is the stern, or the transom, which is turned into the wind (figures 1 and 2). It is immediately obvious that the sail does not work in the same way and that the speed of the boat is affected in different ways in either case.

In tacking, the sail approaches the centre-line gradually and goes over onto the other tack "gently". The boat experiences a gradual deceleration and then a gradual acceleration.

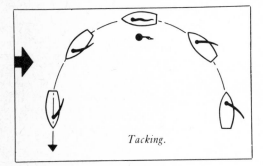

Tacking.

In gybing, the change from one tack to the other is abrupt. The boat loses very little speed if any, and the whole manoeuvre is performed at great speed, depending on the wind, of course.

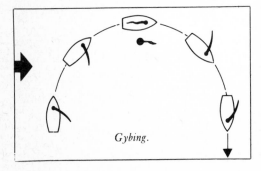

Gybing.

The sail is swung completely round and sets on the other tack, taking the boom with it in a sweeping movement, often hitting the helmsman on the way.

In tacking the going across of the sail from one tack to the other happens practically by itself, (the helmsman can assist it by hauling in on the mainsheet).

In gybing it is necessary to take deliberate action and, in strong winds, even go so far as to induce the sail to come across by bearing away to an exaggerated degree.

The helmsman hauls hard in on the mainsheet and at the same time bears away further.

The boat's lateral trim is therefore very much in danger of being upset, particularly at the moment when, after having passed the centre-line, the sail presents its entire surface to the wind on the other tack.

How will this gybe end?

manoeuvre?

It is possible by gybing to follow a direct course when tacking would mean sailing a loop, slowing the boat down and altogether taking much longer. Herein lies its whole *raison d'etre*.

All this contributes to making gybing a very tricky manoeuvre and it is fair to say that it is responsible for most of the capsizes that occur in fresh winds.

But why then undertake such a delicate

It follows then that gybing is a manoeuvre aimed at saving time. But of course it is of benefit only if a boat has to *change tacks before the wind*.

The difficulties and dangers of gybing depend mainly on the strength of the wind and the state of the sea. They can be considerably reduced by a perfect technique.

Above all, any abrupt changes of course must be avoided, like going suddenly from a reach on one

weaker because the boat follows a course that coincides with the direction of the wind ($W_A = W_T - W_S$), chapter 1.

Consequently, it is at the moment when the wind

Gybing round a mark.

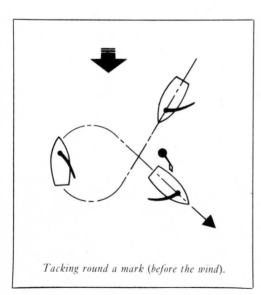

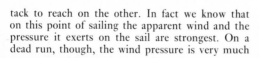

Tacking round a mark (before the wind).

The lateral trim of this Finn running in a strong wind is perfect. The helmsman can now undertake a gybe.

tack to reach on the other. In fact we know that on this point of sailing the apparent wind and the pressure it exerts on the sail are strongest. On a dead run, though, the wind pressure is very much

is from dead aft that the sail can be made to go across with the least violence.

Nevertheless, the manoeuvre can only be performed with safety if the boat is in perfect lateral and longitudinal trim.

You must at any price avoid going through the last phase of a gybe just as the boat is running up the ascending slope of a wave, because as soon as the bow comes in contact with such a mass of water, however fleetingly, the boat will slow down and, immediately, the wind pressure on the sail will increase ($> \mathrm{Ws} \rightarrow < \mathrm{Wa}$).

With the boat perfectly upright and dead before the wind, the gybe begins like this:

On a sloop, with the jib sheets completely freed, helmsman and crew move towards the centre-line of the boat, always keeping well aft. The centre-plate is 3/4 up or even further, so that it offers the least possible side resistance whilst still giving directional control. This enables the boat to "side-slip" rather than heel and then luff up (too much centreplate causes it to "trip over itself").

The helmsman hauls the mainsheet in as hard as possible to bring the lower part of the luff into the wind. (The boom must be at 45° to the centre-line.) At the same time he puts the helm up lightly to bear away and get the boat to sail by the lee. In this way he makes *the wind get behind the lower, after part of the mainsail.*

As soon as this has happened, the rest of the sail will almost instantaneously follow, and the helms-

Gybing in strong winds should not be attempted until the technique of running before the wind has been properly mastered.

This simplifies matters considerably and there is much less danger of capsizing. However, it is the last phase of the manoeuvre, when the sail comes across and sets on the other side, which is the most dangerous. Whichever way it is handled, the transfer of pressure from one side to the other is violent, and the success of the exercise depends entirely on the skill of helmsman and crew.

Even in a force 6 wind short lulls are bound to occur, and the ideal is to gybe precisely then.

In any event, do not adopt an attitude of "we'll show them!" and gybe right in the middle of a squall, but always time it so that the apparent wind is weakest, that is to say *when the boat is at its maximum speed in relation to the wind.* This will hardly be in a squall but when the boat has reached a steady speed, neither during an acceleration nor during a deceleration (impact resistance!).

man then has to reverse the helm and put the boat back before the wind. The crew's part consists in making sure that the boom goes across at the correct moment. The mainsheet is gradually paid off; it plays the rôle of a shock absorber. During the entire manoeuvre the boat must remain as upright as possible, and the helmsman and crew ensure the lateral trim by shifting their weight in perfect synchronization with the transfer of the wind pressure from one side to the other. The slightest lack of concentration will **immediately** cause violent rolling to which the waves will contribute. The kicking strap plays an essential part here, because it has to keep the boom down as low as possible.

A particularly well executed gybe in a force 6 wind.

On a *una-rigged boat* the boom is very low and Heaven help the helmsman who gets in its way: stopped in its swing it cannot get across to the other side quickly enough and the boat starts to heel. (To avoid unpleasant consequences the centreplate should be almost completely raised.) The end of the boom digs into the water and prevents the sail from easing right off. The result is a *broach-to*, followed by a capsize. The helmsman can avoid this by letting the tiller go and allowing it to go down to leeward. The boat will then come up into the wind and right itself.

This gybe in a strong breeze will certainly end in a capsize. Too much plate is down and makes the boat "trip over itself". The boom is held fast by the water. The helmsman should have let go of the tiller to allow the boat to come up into the wind and right itself.

A boat going very fast behaves in the same way as a car without brakes. Decisions must be taken in split seconds and agility and self-confidence are of the greatest importance.

Gybing single-handed, in particular, requires a high degree of skill, and the one-man boat (e.g. Finn or Moth) is a training boat *par excellence*.

The skilled single-handed helmsman is without doubt a past master in handling a boat and can adapt himself to any task he is asked to perform on a larger boat.

For anyone training for racing, single-handed sailing is essential if he wants to make rapid progress.

The one-man boat also has the enormous advantage of forcing the helmsman to take full responsibility for what he does: a fundamental necessity in yachting.

The last phase of this gybe looks like coming off well. The boat is sideslipping and the helmsman, bent low, is ready to use his weight as a counterbalance on the other tack.

Excellent starting position for a gybe. The boat is perfectly upright and the helmsman, ready to shift over to windward to preserve the lateral trim.

In very strong winds, and despite all efforts, the una-rigged boat does not want to gybe and can only be made to do so in the way just described.

The worst being over, it only remains to reverse the helm and by gradually bearing away resume the proper course for the next mark.

Gybing, as the most tricky manoeuvre in sailing and particularly in racing, is feared as much by experienced helmsmen and even champions as it is by the innocent beginner.

It is in the way they perform a gybe that helmsman and crew prove their real skill.

A successful gybe in strong winds, although it does not call for outstanding muscular effort, requires top physical fitness. Fatigue and cold slow down one's reflexes quite considerably.

after a capsize

Although a capsize is often the logical result of a beginner's mistake, it does not follow that experienced helmsmen are immune to this mishap. On the contrary, after having passed through the first stage of initiation, helmsman and crew are tempted by their newly acquired self-confidence to take risks.

Risks like gybing in a strong breeze, carrying a spinnaker when people with common-sense are content with winging out the jib, etc. There is no shortage of reasons for a capsize!

Since this is so, the ability to right a capsize quickly and efficiently without wasting one's energies or mishandling the gear is as essentially a part of expert dinghy sailing as all the other skills.

preventative measures

In rough conditions, when the chances of a capsize are numerous, it is advisable to keep order on board. All ropes' ends and sheets tucked away and, if possible, made fast; spinnaker pole correctly stowed and held in place with shock cord; spinnaker stowed in its bag—so that the capsize does not have to be followed by an impromptu treasure hunt! The rudder, too, especially if it is a metal one, and the centreplate if it is not permanently made fast, should be similarly secured with a lashing.

On boats which do not possess a means of tensioning the halyards by levers, the halyards must not be made fast with complicated knots, because the sails must be capable of being got down in a hurry.

Losing your head won't help you sort things out quickly.

what to do

A capsize is not always so sudden that the crew have no opportunity of intervening. When all seems lost, the best policy is to let go of the helm and the sheets and hope for the boat to come up into the wind. It may do this by itself and right itself. If the trick does not come off, the most important thing is not to make matters worse by letting the boat turn turtle, keel up and mast down (often in the mud or sand!).

the boat will right itself fairly suddenly and the helmsman must quickly get back into the cockpit to balance the boat, sails flapping, while the crew hoists himself back on board over the transom. All that remains to be done is clear up the mess and set off on a reach with the bailers open to get rid of any water shipped.

Under no circumstances must you hang on to any part of the boat's interior or climb onto the gunwale by stepping on the mast or centreplate case, or haul yourself up by the sheets. If neither of

This crew is committing the serious mistake of not wanting to get wet. Instead he puts his weight on parts of the boat's interior in climbing out over the gunwale.

In a two-man boat one of the crew has to sacrifice himself and jump into the water at once to hang on to the bow and keep the boat pointing into the wind. Meanwhile the other climbs over the side keeping his weight well aft, and stands on the centreplate. As soon as the sail has raised itself from the water,

the crew has managed to stay on the boat, they have to swim round it and pull down with both arms on the centreplate, which must, of course, be lowered if the capsize has occurred on a reach.

If the boat has turned completely over, one of the

The worst is over, they have prevented this Flying Dutchman from turning turtle. I would be slightly worried about the centreplate, though.

crew gets up onto the hull and levers on the centre-plate until the mast is horizontal (if the water is shallow it is advisable to make sure beforehand that the masthead is not buried in the mud), after which he can stand on the centreplate and proceed in the way just described.

Getting the boat to come up is not everything, one must also stop the movement at the right moment.

A capsized boat lies across the wind and drifts before the wind hull first, its mast and sails pointing into the wind. If you set about righting it without any further preparations, you will be under the lee of the boat and as soon as the mast comes up, the wind will strike the sail and the boat will come down again on your head. The only way to proceed in a strong wind is to right the boat against the wind. For this it must be turned round until the mast and sail point down wind. As the boat comes up it does so against the pressure of the wind which

slows down its movement, and you can use your weight to balance the wind pressure on the sails. Metal masts which are common on dinghies have a disadvantage as far as safety is concerned: they should be fitted with some foam material to prevent them filling up with water. Without this precaution the weight of the mast will quickly turn a capsize into a complete 180° inversion. Once the mast is full, the weight of this column of water may completely defeat your attempts to right the boat. At best it will take a superhuman effort. The mast then comes up rapidly and its momentum will inevitably pull it over to the other side. If you have a hollow mast and have by chance managed to right the boat after all, give the mast time to empty itself before climbing back on board.

With a bit of practice these manoeuvres become relatively easy. You can put some fine summer's day to good use by practicing your capsize drill.

What agility! But the crew is still underneath the boat.

Phew! That's righted that one. And to think that we have to carry on now and maybe go through the whole business all over again.

tuning the boat

A day on which a light breeze is blowing and the water is relatively calm and without current is the ideal for setting out on a series of tests to try to obtain *perfect tuning* of the boat.

The centreplate is completely lowered, the sheets hardened in and the boat is sailed close-hauled with a slight heel of about 5°.

With the mainsail and jib normally sheeted in, the jib must not backwind the mainsail (cause it to lift). If this happens, sheet the mainsail in a bit further, i.e. bring the boom nearer the centre-line. If at this moment the boat tries to come up into the wind and is heavy on the helm when you try to get it back on course, it carries **weather helm**. It cannot, under these conditions, develop its maximum speed since the rudder is no longer in line with the centre-line and sets up a strong resistance to forward motion.

The next step is to ease the jib sheet a little and let the boom out a bit further. The boat should now re-gather speed and yet will point very little further off the wind. But if it still carries weather helm, the centreplate, if it is a pivoting one, should be raised a little. If it is a dagger plate the same purpose will be served by inclining it aft. With the boat still at a very slight angle of heel the tiller is now let go. If the boat shoots up into the wind it is obvious that despite everything that has been done the overall *centre of effort is AFT of the centre of lateral resistance.*

The first thing to do now is to check on the *rake of the mast*. The way to measure this has been explained at the beginning of this chapter under **rigging the boat**.

But it is almost certain that this will put itself right before long. After the boat has been in use for some time the shrouds will have stretched and this reduces the rake.

Several things can be done to obtain a perfect balance between the C.E. and the C.L.R.:

1. The tack fitting for the jib can be **moved forward** provided that the class rules permit it.

2. The foot of the mast can be **moved forward**, as long as the same rake of 15 to 30 thousandths is preserved.

3. The C.L.R. can be **moved aft** by moving the centreplate aft. This is a tricky operation and one has to make quite sure in advance that the plate will still fit into the centreplate case.

If the boat behaves in the opposite way, that is if

it bears away when the helm is released after the centreplate has been lowered or moved forward and the mainsail sheeted in as close to the centre-line as possible, the boat carries **lee helm**. The procedure to follow is then the opposite.

The boat should be tested in this way on both tacks. If the helmsman notices very quickly that his boat does not behave in the same way on both tacks (i.e. if it carries weather helm on the starboard tack and lee helm on the port tack) he can be fairly certain of finding the cause of this by comparing the length of opposite shrouds and cross trees, the amount of lateral play the mast has at deck level and, if he finds nothing wrong with any of these, the lateral flexibility of the mast itself or the flatness of the rudder or centreboard. In fact, with wooden masts the two halves, traditionally made by glueing together two pieces of wood with the grain running in opposite directions, cannot be expected to react in exactly the same way.

The spruce used for masts can be "coarse fibred" or "large grained" and possess very little elasticity, or "close fibred" or "fine grained", in which case it is noticably more rigid and at the same time more elastic. So if the mast maker has joined a fine-grained piece of wood to a coarse-grained one, the difference in the lateral flexibility of the two parts will be most noticeable. Remember that under the influence of the kicking strap on the boom on one hand and the tension of the mainsheet on the other, the mast is simultaneously pulled forward and to windward. On one tack then, the mast will bend more than on the other, and that will be on the "coarse-grained" side.

It is possible partly to remedy this discrepancy by fitting what is called a *diamond* as explained later on in the section on **masts**. If this is not sufficient, the only other solution, simple if not cheap, is to have another mast. To avoid surprises of this kind anyone buying a boat is advised to examine the texture and behaviour of his mast at the time the boat is delivered. Needless to say, the same goes for the boom. But more and more modern dinghies are fitted with metal spars which are of equal flexibility along their whole length. To get back to the faults that can be put right without much fuss (difference in length of shrouds and cross trees), it can be said that a shroud which is too short or a cross tree which is too long make the mast bend more to windward. All these imperfections taken together cause the mainsail to be too flat on one tack and too full on the other.

Most boats are either balanced in a fresh breeze but carry lee helm in light airs, or they are balanced in light airs and carry too much weather helm in strong winds.

The aim should be to tune a boat in such a way that it is almost perfectly balanced close-hauled in a light breeze and heeling very slightly; as soon as the heel increases the boat should show a tendency to come up into the wind. One can then be sure that it is capable of being tuned to maximum speed.

In stronger winds a good balance can be obtained by increasing the angle between the mainsail and the centre-line and having some of the centreplate up, while the mainsheet should be hauled in hard to flatten the sail as much as possible.

When all these adjustments have been made, the helmsman should give some time to watching closely the behaviour of the jib luff in order to determine where the jib sheet leads should go. If the jib is well trimmed, the luff should lift over its entire height as soon as the boat is luffed up very slightly when close-hauled. If, however, the luff lifts in its upper part first, the sheet leads are too far aft. Vice versa, if the luff lifts in its lower part first the leads are too far forward.

On a sloop which does not possess adjustable sheet leads the same effect is obtained by shifting the position of the tack. In the first case it is too low, in the second too high.

In any case, the jib must not shake along the leech. If it does, even with the sheet hard in, the sheet leads are too far aft or the tack too low. This is easily cured.

Once the jib has been attended to, and the boat still does not handle satisfactorily, I should think it advisable to carry out a small examination which, although it might seem superfluous, may reveal the chief cause of all your troubles: measure the distance between the transom and the centre-line of the centreplate and compare your findings with the official building plans. Mistakes can always occur during the building of the boat, and the centreplate case might be an inch or so out. Since the relative positions of C.E. and C.L.R. are critical for the boat's performance, any interference with them has noticeable effects.

Finally, the whole trouble may be that the rudder is slightly warped to one side or that there is too much play in its bearings.

After all is said and done, the best way of tuning a boat is still to sail it against another boat of the same class which is known for its speed and its ability to point high. But don't think you can blindly copy everything on the other man's boat

and hope to make yours go just as well. In fact, it is almost certain that his sails and mast are slightly different and that the total weight of the crew as well as the weight ratio between helmsman and crew are not the same.

Question the best performers in your class, those that beat you regularly, on the way they sail their boats in certain weathers and on different points. 'Did you tighten up on your rigging today?', 'Did you set the mainsheet traveller right out to leeward?', 'Was your centre-plate right down?' etc. etc. Don't be shy, and try not to blame the wind for all your disappointments. Take along a tape measure and measure anything which is likely to be of importance: position of centre-plate axis, of foot of mast, of mast at deck level, all from the outer edge of the transom, and then the length of the cross trees, and why not the shape of the rudder and the centreplate? If you are certain that there is no reason why your boat should be slower or point less high yet, despite all, you get nowhere: have your sails looked over by an expert, if possible. Alternatively, compare them with those of the boats that perform better than your boat by hoisting the sails ashore with the boats side by side, closely watching the behaviour of the mainsail and jib leeches as the sheets are played.

One of the first steps in tuning is to make the sails set well

the mast

The mast plays an essential rôle in the behaviour of the boat, all the more so since most adjustments made in tuning the boat have some effect upon it.

Holding up the sails is not its sole purpose; by deliberately bending it out of its original shape the maximum drive can be derived from the sails in any wind: in light airs the maximum fullness is wanted in the mainsail (chapter 1), and in these conditions the mast is so adjusted that it gives the sail this fullness when the boat is close-hauled. In strong winds, on the other hand, the mainsail must be as flat as possible and the leech very open to help the air flow smoothly off the sail. In either case it is the mast which is adjusted to give the desired effect. In strong winds the necessary curvature in the mast can be produced by hauling down hard on the kicking strap.

The large majority of sailing boats, dinghies as well as keelboats, have cross trees, or spreaders, fitted to their masts. In many cases, particularly on dinghies, the mast is held at deck level by movable wedges. Both cross trees and wedges influence the bend of the mast between the hounds and the foot of the mast, either by accentuating it or diminishing it. Their effect is not separate, though, but joint.

The tension of the shrouds is, first of all, caused by the tension put on the jib luff when the jib is hoisted. An additional cause, once the sails fill, is the resistance to heeling. Let us look more closely at this phenomenon.

When the airflow (apparent wind) acts on either side of the sail (pressure on the windward side, suction on the leeward side) it is the windward shroud that has to take the main strain, but only to the extent to which it has to RESIST THE RIGHTING FORCE, i.e. the ballast in keelboats or the crew sitting out in centreplate boats.

One can easily imagine a boat without fixed or movable ballast being flattened by the wind. In that case practically no strain would come on the windward shroud.

Also, in boats with a trapeze, the strain on the windward shroud *is only proportional to the weight of the helmsman sitting out*, since the crew on the trapeze, for his part, eases the strain on the shroud by his weight.

cross trees

Let us start by analysing the function of the cross trees.

First of all, it must be said that they must be

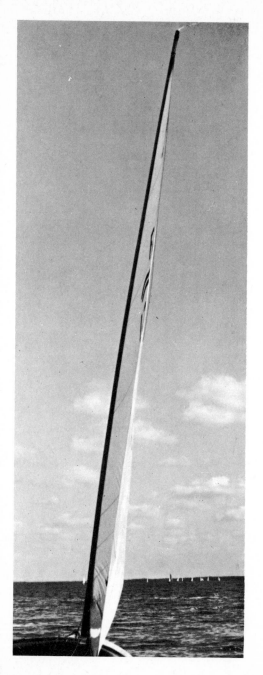

hinged on the mast in such a way that the push they exercise is in the right direction and can be very accurately controlled.

There are two kinds of cross trees or spreaders:

— Long cross trees which push the shrouds out so that they form an angle between the mast fitting and the chain plates;

— Short cross trees which lead the shrouds in a straight line from the mast fitting to the chain plates.

first kind

The tauter the luff of the jib, the greater the pressure of the shrouds on the cross trees. They push the mast forward, unless they are limited in their movement by forward and aft stops.

This forward movement of the mast will continue until the shrouds are stretched in a straight line from the chain plates to where they are attached to the mast. But the windward shroud also takes the strain of resistance to heeling. So its push on the cross tree and through it on the mast is bound to be greater than that of the leeward shroud.

To these different strains put on the mast are added the effect of the kicking strap (p. 47) and the pull of the mainsail and jib sheets. Thus the cross trees are initially contributing to bending the mast, but from the moment the shrouds are straight or the movement of the cross trees is deliberately stopped, they stop the mast from bending further.

second kind

The principles are the same, except that instead of being first pushed forward the mast is immediately stopped by the short cross trees.

What can we conclude from this? To start with, if we have a very rigid mast we can make it bend by a strong pull on the jib luff in combination with long cross trees. On the other hand, if we have an excessively flexible mast, short cross trees will prevent it from bending too much.

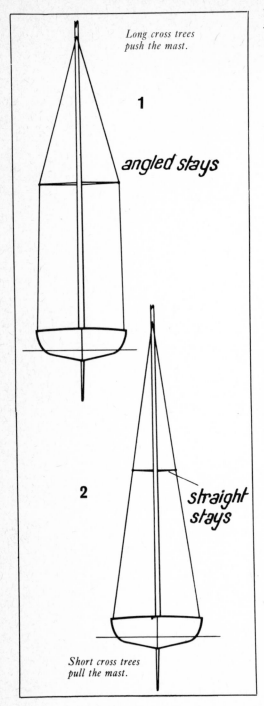

Long cross trees
push the mast.

1

angled stays

2

straight stays

Short cross trees
pull the mast.

This 5.0.5 has long cross trees. Note how the leeward shroud is slack.

Also, the angle through which the cross trees are allowed to pivot should be greater for a stiff mast than for a very supple mast.

On the other hand, the weight ratio between helmsman and crewman must be considered.

If the crew is relatively light in relation to the helmsman, the helmsman, when sitting out, will offer resistance to heeling and thereby impose a much greater strain on the windward shroud than if we had the opposite case of a light helmsman and a heavy crew. This points out the necessity of altering the length of the cross trees when changing one's crew, but always with a view to the stiffness or flexibility of the mast.

For it must never be forgotten that whatever the weight of the crew on the trapeze, the oblique pull downwards pulls the mast to windward and causes it to bend sideways, twisting the sail and opening the leech.

This phenomenon slows the reactions of the boat down, and while this is desirable in a fresh wind it has adverse effects in a moderate or unsteady breeze. As soon as the crew gets out on the trapeze the boat goes dead and becomes difficult to helm.

It is a good idea to give careful consideration to the correct length of the cross trees and not to put too much trust in standard lengths as delivered in standard boats. They are generally too long, but then that is a good thing since they can always be shortened.

For a full mainsail the cross trees must be longer than for a flat mainsail. In the former case excellent results are achieved in light winds with a flat sea, because, through the forced bending of the mast, the fullness of the sail becomes well distributed without the tension of the leech having to be adjusted. The sheet and the kicking strap can now be used quite independently.

In light airs it is also worth letting the mast have completely free play at deck level. It is not until vigorous action is taken on the sheets, i.e. in strong winds, that it becomes necessary to control the movement of the mast at deck level to avoid excessive bending forward.

This brings us to the adjustment of the mast where it passes through the deck while its heel, as we know, rests lower, either on the keel or the extension of the centre-plate case. It is done with a number of wedges.

This mast broke on a spinnaker run when, owing to the bending of the mast, the gate which holds the mast at deck level broke. It was blowing very hard, several wrecks bear witness to that.

It is equally necessary to control the degree to which the mast can bend backwards. While it is desirable to increase this bend in strong winds to flatten the sail and make the boat go better to windward, in light winds the sail must be given all of its fullness. For this the windward spreader must exert more side pressure.

It follows that the cross trees can only work efficiently if the mast passes through a gate at deck level. The pressure of the windward spreader can then be directed as necessary.

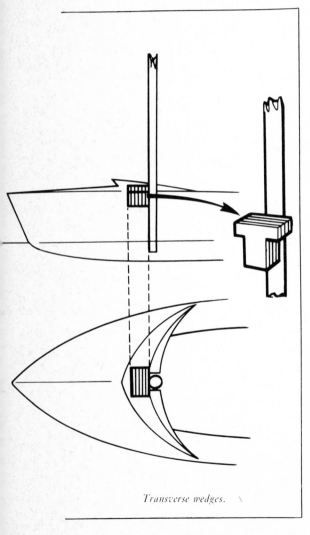

Transverse wedges.

mast wedges

As soon as the wind freshens, necessitating the use of the kicking strap and rather energetic action on the sheet, the mast must be blocked laterally and controlled in its forward movement by a system of lateral wedges in the deck gate.

This can be done in two ways:

1. by a number of small wooden shapes 5 to 10 mm. thick which are inserted forward of the mast (see diagram); and

2. by a remote-control system as used in the 5.0.5. and FD (see diagram p. 90).

This method of adjustment, especially by the second system, produces spectacular results. For example, in a force 3 wind, close-hauled, with the mast blocked forward and the mainsail normally sheeted in, the sail is full and the boat carries slight weather helm. By removing one or several of the wedges or releasing the tension on the control system, the mast is allowed to bend. The sail flattens, the leech opens, the boat becomes easier on the helm and, although it does not point so high, will go appreciably faster.

Here are some hints on how you will get a better performance out of your boat.

In light winds, on a calm sea, with a normally full sail and a fairly rigid mast, the shrouds should be fairly taut, the mast left unchecked by wedges forward and, if possible, allowed some lateral play.

If the sea is choppy the jib luff should be slackened off a bit so as to give the whole of the rig more flexibility.

In moderate winds the jib luff must be tauter. As soon as the crew starts to get out on the trapeze, the mast must be blocked forward to counteract the detrimental effect of the trapeze on the mast (which I mentioned before).

If the boat then carries weather helm you must not, under any circumstances, try to remedy this by experimenting with the centre-plate. Before unblocking the mast again, try to balance the boat by setting the mainsheet traveller to leeward. Not too much, though. If the boat still continues to yaw in the puffs instead of gathering speed, gradually unblock the mast as much as necessary. If the water is calm, the mast must be blocked more than if there is a sea running or the water is choppy. In the latter case, apart from releasing the mast at deck level, it is a good idea to slacken the whole of the rigging a bit. For this purpose high-performance boats like the 5.0.5. and FD have a sheave or similar arrangement for controlling the jib or genoa halyard and the shrouds underway.

As the wind freshens, the mast wedges are removed altogether, the kicking strap is hardened in. If, despite this, the boat heels right over in the puffs, the rigging must be slackened. The mast will then be pushed to windward and the sail will start to lift slightly.

On the other hand, the pull of the jib-sheet must be given some attention. The sheet fairlead, which is set right forward in light airs, is moved progressively further aft as the wind freshens, in order to open the leech.

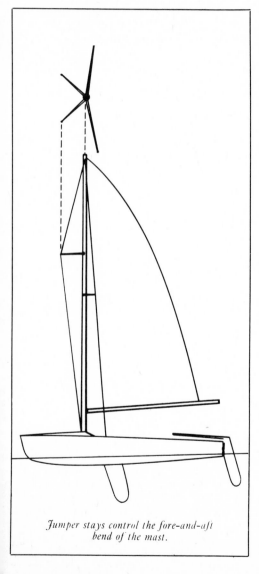

Jumper stays control the fore-and-aft bend of the mast.

Finally, increasing the mast rake by slackening the jib halyard makes beating easier in strong winds.

To sum up, it can be said that a well-tuned boat relies essentially on its mast. It is a question of playing with the tension of the rigging, the limits to which the mast will bend and sometimes with its rake aft.

To do this, you really have to know your mast and its reactions. Therefore, if you have a clever crew who can helm the boat while on the trapeze, take the opportunity to inspect your mast sometime in a force 2 to 3. Standing on the foredeck, study it from all angles. You can be certain that in this way you are going to learn a great deal about the performance of your boat and its sails.

The forward movement of the mast in light airs can be limited by transverse wedges inserted in front of it. When the mainsheet is hardened in, the pressure of the boom on the mast is checked and the sail keeps its fullness. But it is then necessary for the top of the mast, above the hounds, to be rigid, otherwise the pull of the mainsheet will be transmitted via the leech of the mainsail and will pull the top of the mast aft. Held in place by the jib luff and unable to yield to the pull, the mast will only bend from the hounds upward. This will cause the sail to flatten excessively in its upper part and reduce its efficiency.

This situation can be remedied by two stays of fine steel wire fitted before the mast, between a point level with the masthead sheave and a point about mid-way between the deck and the hounds. This is called a *jumper stay*. It is advisable to make it adjustable, since obviously the jumper stay must be taut in light winds and slack in fresh winds when the mast needs its full flexibility. The lower point of attachment is usually a tensioning device of the Highfield lever type.

On masts which are too flexible jumper stays give excellent results, but they are also a source of trouble if a spinnaker is used, since this has a habit of getting entangled in them.

If, despite long cross trees, the mast bends sideways when the boat is close-hauled, with its middle section curving into the wind, the mast is obviously very flexible indeed. This is easy to cure by fitting a pair of stays alongside the mast to make a *diamond*.

This means fitting a rigid short spreader on either side of the mast and leading across each a thin steel wire stretched from the hounds to a point on the mast at deck level.

Ideally, the mast and sail should be a perfect match. It is possible to alter a mainsail in such a way as to make it fit a mast perfectly, but I shall deal with that later.

In strong winds, when it is desirable that the mast should bend aft, the transverse wedges in front of the mast are removed. However, if the gate is very large it will be necessary to prevent the mast being pushed sideways by the boom by holding it in place by longitudinal wedges. The mast is then sure to be guided into a fore-and-aft bend. One cannot be too careful, though, and in order to prevent the mast bending excessively the wrong way with a following wind it is recommended that its movement is blocked by a transverse wedge aft of the mast.

System by which the limits of mast bend can be instantly adjusted.

On large boats possessing lower shrouds and runners the possibilities of controlling the mast are even more varied.

In light winds the lower shrouds must be slackened off so that the cross trees alone are effective and cause the mast to bend slightly. In strong winds they must be firmly tautened, as indeed must the whole of the rigging, to give the mast rigid support. The mast is pulled to windward, causing the mainsail to flatten and the slot between the jib and the mainsail to widen at the same time. The wind-flow past the leeward side of the mainsail is thus accelerated and the suction improved (chapter I).

Perfectly taut runners enable firm tension to be put on the jib luff, which must in no circumstances be allowed to sag when the boat is close-hauled. If there is a **preventer backstay**, a wire running from the masthead to the stern of the boat, this is also put under firm tension so as to bend the mast in its upper part and help to flatten the mainsail. With very strong jumper stays it is possible to do without runners and use only a preventer backstay. Many 5·5 metres are thus equipped, enabling their

The mast of this Star is stayed by lower shrouds, runners and jumper stays.

crews to carry out manoeuvres with great speed.

When a sail is hit by a strong gust it must be able to "spill" the air. The sail normally sets in a helicoidal (twisted) shape (chapter 1), that is to say it is "open" in its upper part and "closed" in its lower part, and as the wind increases the whole sail must be progressively "opened", i.e. flattened.

By bending the mast to a greater or lesser degree it is possible to use one single, full-cut mainsail for anything from light airs to very strong winds.

The same does not, unfortunately, apply to the jib, since it cannot be adjusted in this way. The jib luff can never be made to curve forward; the only alteration that can be made to the luff is to make it concave (sag) by releasing tension on it, and this is always detrimental.

special considerations

The classical una-rigs (Finn, Moth, OK) would appear easy to tune because they have an unstayed mast, but since this very fact prevents the mast from having any play at deck level, all the necessary adjustments have to be made by modifying the rake of the mast by moving its foot forward or aft (see chapter 3, fittings).

Close-hauled in a fresh breeze the mast is bent aft to flatten the sail. By hauling in hard on the sheet the boom can be brought right down to the deck, the mainsheet traveller being set as far to leeward as possible.

In bending aft, the mast should produce a flattening of the sail in its upper third and at the same time help to "open" the leech. If this result cannot be obtained one should not hesitate to plane down the mast, along its leading edge, in those places where it does not seem to be flexible enough (see illustrations on pages 84, 85). A mast which is flexible in its upper third is ideal, but the sail must have been cut to match it exactly.

Planing the mast down is a delicate operation which must be undertaken with great care.

Two tools are essential: a small, very sharp plane set to take off very thin shavings, and a drill 1 mm. in diameter.

The latter is used to "sound" the thickness of the wood. The mast being hollow, it would be disastrous to plane off too much.

Thanks to a flexible mast this Finn seems quite happy in a very strong wind.

To start with, drill several holes with a hand drill, about 5 in. apart and in offset rows on either side of the forward centre-line of the mast. The holes must not pierce the wood completely, and this obviously demands a lot of skill.

In the upper third of the mast the wood can be planed down to a thickness of 5 mm. If this does not give the desired flexibility, 4 mm. still gives enough strength for the mast not to break. Halfway up the mast at least 6 mm. are needed, and in the lower third 8 to 10 mm.

It is a good idea to proceed in instalments and to try out the sail in between, since the effect of your efforts can only be appreciated by careful observation of mast and sail working together. When the job is finished and you are satisfied with the result do not forget to plug the drill holes and revarnish the mast.

If the yard making the mast is prepared to go to the trouble it is possible to get, right from the start, a mast precisely to specification, but this calls for a sharp eye and a lot of time.

Finn masts, for example, fall into three categories: stiff, medium and flexible.

The following test can be applied to ascertain their flexibility:

The mast is put across two trestles, one at the masthead and the other where the mast goes through the deck.

In this position the mast will bend under its own weight. The bend must not exceed 13 cm. (5¼ in.) in a mast classified as "flexible", or be less than 8 cm. (3¼ in.) in a mast classified as "stiff".

The mast is then loaded with a weight of 20 kg. (44 lbs.) suspended equidistant from the two trestles. For a flexible mast the maximum bend must not exceed 20 cm. (7¾ in.), for a stiff one 12 cm. (4¾ in.). A medium mast should have a camber of around 15 cm. (6 in.).

However, as was pointed out earlier on, the camber must not be regular because the mast must follow the round of the luff of the sail closely.

As far as the lateral flexibility of the mast is concerned, it is always the same no matter if the mast is classified as stiff, medium or flexible. Tested in the same way with the same weight, the camber sideways must not exceed 12 cm. (4¾ in.) nor be less than 6 cm. (2½ in.).

The upper part of the mast, about 5 ft. down from the masthead, should be more flexible than the rest.

If the mast is too supple, wooden battens can be glued to it and planed down as much as is necessary.

It is definitely preferable, though, to cut a sail to fit a particular mast than to try and force the mast to match the sail, unless you want to be faced with a broken mast you cannot repair.

The mast rake on una-rigged boats is generally more marked than on sloops and ranges between 50 and 90 thousandths, with the exception of the

The mast in this case seems too flexible to adapt itself perfectly to the sail in a fresh breeze.

Moth, whose mainsail has a very long leech which makes it impossible for the mast to be raked aft.

The choice of mast for a una-rigged boat as far as flexibility is concerned depends on the weight of the helmsman. A helmsman weighing 11 stone will use a much more bendy mast than one weighing 14 stone. But in any case, for serious competition in the Finn class the helmsman's weight should be above 11 stone (154 lb.) and he should have strong muscles.

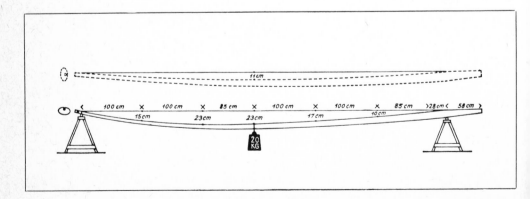

the trapeze

The trapeze is the most recent and most valuable aid for the better use of live ballast since the beginnings of yachting. It plays a rôle of vital importance in dinghies, whose stability is a function of the righting couple that can be applied. Efforts have constantly been made to improve this righting couple, first with sacks of sand during the times of the sandbaggers, and more recently with sliding seats as in sailing canoes (they are coming back again on single-handers) and certain dinghies like the Hornet. Compared with other methods, the trapeze is simpler and cheaper. Contrary to common belief it does not call for acrobatics and is much less tiring and wearing on the muscles than the classic sitting-out position using toestraps. It looks like being generally adopted for all dinghies from 12 ft. upwards.

The trapeze consists of two parts:

1. A steel wire attached to the mast at the hounds, the other end terminating in a ring of some kind. Port and starboard wires are kept under tension by a piece of shock cord via fairleads on the hull.

2. Some kind of harness; anything from a wide belt lined with foam rubber to a special "couche" incorporating adjustable braces and legs. They are attached to the trapeze wire by a metal plate on which a downward facing hook is welded or bolted.

how to use it

The crew must get out on the trapeze as soon as the boat can no longer be kept on an even keel by the usual sitting-out method using toestraps. For the purposes of terminology and irrespective of tack or course sailed (on or off the wind) we will consider the crew as he would be in the normal sitting-out position, i.e. at right angles to the centre-line, so that one part of his body can be said to be **forward** (towards the bow) and the other part **aft** (towards the stern).

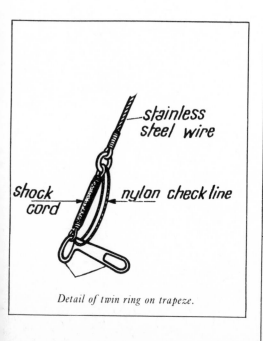

Detail of twin ring on trapeze.

getting out

With the jib sheeted in and the sheet passing round
the winch, or failing this, a cleat on the windward
side, the crew gets hold of the trapeze ring with his
forward hand and slips it into the hook on his
harness. His **aftermost** hand keeps the jib sheet
taut by pressing it against the gunwale.

With his **aftermost** foot still under the toestrap
and that leg kept straight or lightly flexed, the crew
now draws his **forward** leg right up so that the heel
touches his seat and places the middle of his sole
firmly against the chain plate or the bottlescrew of
the weather shroud. After having checked once
again that the trapeze ring is firmly attached to the
harness hook, the crew grabs the grip handle on
the trapeze wire with his **forward** hand and pushes
himself outboard *with his forward leg alone*.

In fact, the forward leg performs this operation
alone because the trapeze wire, being attached to
the mast at a point forward of its attachment to the
harness, will try to pull the crew towards the bow.
He must hold his position aft of the shrouds by
pushing against this pull with his forward leg.

Whilst launching himself outboard, the crew
slides his aftermost hand along the jib sheet. He
then places his aftermost foot against the gunwale
to maintain good balance, and as soon as he is in
this position lets go of the grip handle and with his
forward hand takes over the jib sheet.

He must avoid at all cost supporting himself on
his forward arm by hanging on to the grip handle.
In fact, all the weight must be taken on the harness.
By using his arm, he would very quickly get tired.

getting in

The crew once again seizes the grip handle with his
forward hand, takes his aftermost foot off the gunwale and puts the heel on the side deck. By progressively bending his forward leg, he gets back to
a sitting position, with the forward leg completely
bent and the foot resting on the side deck.

Except when told to do so by the helmsman the
crew must never relax tension on the jib sheet. In
this way, he can get out again very quickly without
jolting the boat violently.

going about

If getting in from the trapeze is immediately
followed by a tacking manoeuvre, the crew bends
the *aftermost* leg and with his forward leg finds a
foothold in the cockpit. He then proceeds with the
change-over from one side to the other in the usual
way, by making a half-turn with his back to the

*Getting out on the trapeze. Note how the crew has his
forward leg bent in the classical position.*

mast so that he can duck under the kicking strap.

On a reach, the procedure is the same, with the
only difference that the crew has greater difficulty
in getting out quickly because both he and the
helmsman are sitting further aft. The end of the
trapeze wire must have two rings attached to it to
allow for the two different positions.

advice

If spreaders are used as part of the rigging, one
must make quite sure that the trapeze wire does
not get wrapped round the shroud. If this happens,

as it sometimes does, the shroud gets pulled off the spreader as soon as the crew puts his weight on the trapeze wire. Needless to say, this can have very unpleasant repercussions if it is blowing hard. To avoid it happening, the two wires can be joined, at the height of the spreaders, by a short piece of shock cord fixed in its middle to the forward side of the mast.

the fact that the harness will stretch once it is attached to the wire.

The harness must always be fitted with an open hook so that the crew can detach himself quickly in the event of a capsize to windward.

To prevent the ring slipping out of the hook when the crew pulls himself up by the grip handle, it is advisable to join the ring to the grip handle by a short length of shock cord which pulls the ring up.

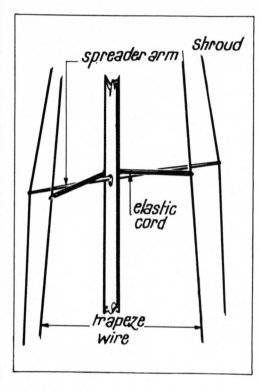

The trapeze is correctly adjusted for length and the crew's position is perfect. Note the shock cord just above the cross trees.

length of trapeze wire

The crew must be suspended from the wire in such a way that he is as near as possible at right angles to the mast. The angle may be less than 90° by 3° to 8°, particularly off the wind, but it should never be more, because with the boat sailing upright the shoulders of the crew would be too near the water and he would have extreme difficulty in getting back into the boat, especially if the boat heeled to windward.

The length of the trapeze wire and its ring must be calculated with great care, taking into account

advice to helmsman

The use of the trapeze is less tiring for the crew than hanging out by toestraps, but it can become strenuous if, in a fresh breeze, it means getting in and out all the time. It is therefore the helmsman's job to spare the energies of his crew by not luffing up too hard, thus making the boat heel to windward.

having to play the jib. It goes without saying that the helmsman must not give his crew too many "wettings".

Close-hauled, the helmsman must helm the boat with great precision and, above all, never let go of his sheet.

On a reach, he must trim the mainsheet very quickly, in particular sheet it in immediately a puff dies down.

Which of the two has made the mistake? Did the helmsman luff up too hard? Did he let go of his mainsheet? Or maybe the crew waited too long before getting in when the wind dropped?

the crew must not get in from the trapeze unless the wind drops

In fluky winds the helmsman must go as far as to sit to leeward to allow his crew to stay out. He must economize on the crew's strength, especially since off the wind he has to get in and out much more often and with great rapidity, apart from continually

The foremost requirement for getting the best out of the trapeze is that the boat is correctly helmed.

A top helmsman can sail and even race quite safely with a real greenhorn on the trapeze, just as a mountain guide can take "a sack of coal" up Mont Blanc.

But, on the other hand, the best crew will not tolerate a fool at the helm who lets him drop into the water every five minutes.

How to do it and how not to do it.
Above: Fogh/Peterson, world champions.

the spinnaker

The spinnaker is a very special kind of headsail since it is cut extremely full. Because of this it must be used with a rather large angle *alpha*.

Whilst modern spinnakers can be used close reaching, that is unstalled and with laminar flow, their use cannot be extended to courses very close to the wind (where angle *alpha* is very small). This means they are set only if the course which the boat is following is at a rather large angle to the wind, that is at best on a reach and more particularly before the wind.

A spinnaker can be of considerable size, depending on the type of boat, and if it is well set it is capable of increasing the boat's speed quite appreciably. However, in order to "pay", its area must be at least equal to that of the mainsail and jib together, otherwise it will take something not far short of a hurricane to justify its use. In anything less it will just be a distraction for the crew on the downwind leg, which is tricky enough as it is (Cadet, Merlin, Hornet).

Held up only at three points: the head, tack and clew, the spinnaker is certainly the most beautiful sail a boat can set, if not the most efficient. Unless it is correctly trimmed, it collapses and immediately loses all its shape and power. Yet the spinnaker must be considered like a conventional sail (main sail or jib) because it also has a luff (leading edge), a foot and a leech (trailing edge). One cannot really speak of spinnaker "sheets" then (a sheet being the rope by which a sail is trimmed to the wind) but only of "one sheet", namely the one passing to leeward of the mainsail. The windward rope which controls the leading edge of the spinnaker is the *guy* and the point at which it is attached becomes the *tack*.

It is a sound idea to experiment first with the spinnaker on dry land on a day when the wind is not too strong.

Place the boat stern to wind. With the sheet and guy attached to their respective corners the spinnaker is laid on the deck, luff and leech well separated. The "sheets" are passed through their leads, outside the rigging (shrouds and stays).

In this way the spinnaker, once it is hoisted, can swing freely from port to starboard forward of the jib and forestay. On some dinghies the leads are fitted on the transom, on others they are on the after part of the side decks between 1 and 4 ft. forward of the transom (5.0.5, Flying Dutchman). While it is useful to have the guy lead nearer the mast, the sheet lead is wanted as far aft as possible, so one has to settle for a compromise.

To prevent the spinnaker sheets slipping through the leads when the spinnaker is hoisted, it is advisable to make their ends fast to something in the cockpit (horse or toestraps) by a simple knot.

The spinnaker is then hoisted.

As it goes up the head is watched carefully to make sure that it goes up to the sheave without getting caught up in anything.

One end of the spinnaker boom is put through one of the cringles which now becomes the tack. The topping lift and downhaul are attached to their fitting in the middle of the boom, and finally the other end of the boom is clipped onto the fitting provided for this purpose on the forward side of the mast.

The spinnaker sheet and guy are now hauled in until the spinnaker fills and is drawing properly. To find the correct positions for the sheet and guy, the guy is hauled in first until the luff begins to shake, then the sheet is hauled in or paid out until the leech is just at the point of lifting. The important thing is to give the luff a favourable angle of attack. Since the boat is on dry land one is unlikely to get the optimum trim of sheet and guy; as soon as the boat is out sailing it is under the influence of an apparent wind which is altogether different from the wind experienced by a stationary boat. We then proceed to adjust the topping lift and downhaul.

The topping lift : this consists of a stainless steel wire of the right length to hold the spinnaker boom at an angle of around 80° upwards to the mast. The wire has a shock cord running parallel to it which holds the boom just a little higher if the wind is too light for the spinnaker to lift the boom.

Downhaul : this is a rope of variable and adjustable length by which the spinnaker boom can be held down when the wind is fresh and the spinnaker tends to pull the boom up.

Handing the spinnaker : the sheet and guy are paid out simultaneously until the spinnaker collapses. The boom is unshipped from the mast, the topping lift and downhaul detached from the boom and finally one detaches the tack. The tack is brought in close to the mast by hauling on the guy, then the whole of the foot is gathered in as far as the clew. Of course the sheet must have been let go in advance. The halyard is cast off and as the spinnaker is gradually lowered it is stowed in its proper place (bags under the fore-deck).

It will be necessary to repeat this exercise until it can be performed without mistake.

The first time the spinnaker is hoisted afloat it is best to choose a day when the wind is not too strong, or even better when it is very light.

Before getting under way, the spinnaker should be got ready very carefully: stowed in its bag, headboard on top, clew and tack well separated, sheet and guy shackled to their respective corners and passed through their leads.

When you are ready the boat must be steered dead before the wind. Then the different steps designed to get the spinnaker pulling as fast as possible are performed in the following order:

1. The mainsheet is paid right off so that the mainsail is pulling well. It must be remembered that during the whole manoeuvre, until the spinnaker fills, the mainsail is the sole driving force, since the jib has to be neglected.

2. Now starts the manoeuvre proper: the movements of the crew are apt to upset the stability of the boat and it is a good idea for the helmsman to stand upright astride the tiller so that he can shift his weight immediately the trim of the boat is

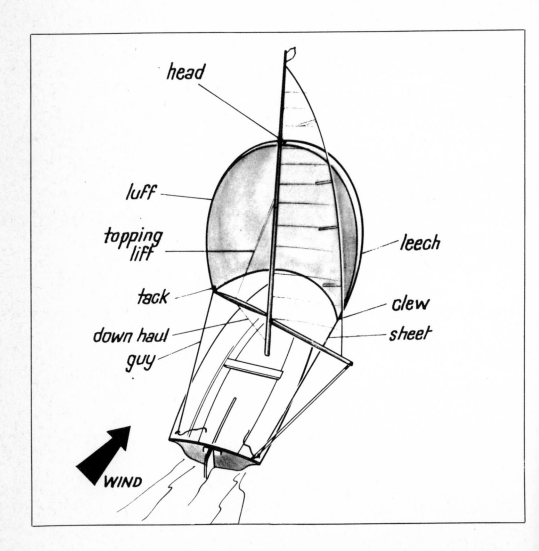

Last phase of hoisting the spinnaker. Topping lift and downhaul are fixed, the crew attaches the end of the spinnaker boom to the mast. The helmsman controls the tiller with his legs and holds the sheet and guy.

upset. Since the crew has moved forward of his usual position, the helmsman must move right aft to keep the boat level on its waterline and, above all, stop it digging its nose in (longitudinal trim).

3. The crew passes the weather jib sheet behind his head so that once the spinnaker is hoisted it is outside the standing and running rigging. He then shackles the halyard onto the headboard.

4. The helmsman hoists the spinnaker while the crew guides it as it goes up, to make sure it does not catch in the cross trees or the mast fittings. Then the helmsman trims the sheet and guy so that the spinnaker sets evenly on either side of the forestay.

5. The crew gets hold of the spinnaker boom while the helmsman keeps the boat sailing dead before the wind. To luff up or bear away would be very dangerous during this operation.

6. The crew attaches one end of the spinnaker boom to the tack, then the topping lift and down-haul to the boom and finally, pushing the boom outward as the helmsman pays out the guy, the boom end goes onto its fitting on the mast.

7. The helmsman now hauls in the guy and then the sheet until the spinnaker sets correctly, while the crew adjusts the height of the boom by means of the downhaul.

8. The crew adjusts the centreplate (about $\frac{1}{4}$

down) and tidies up the loose ends (jib sheets and spinnaker halyard).

9. The helmsman now passes the crew the spinnaker sheet and guy, which should be cleated if the wind is strong. During the whole manoeuvre the helmsman must keep the boat sailing before the wind as he stands astride the tiller controlling it with his legs.

The two can now take up a more comfortable position, but not so comfortable that they cannot shift their weight quickly to keep the boat level.

If it is blowing hard the centreplate should now be lowered to at least ⅓.

It pays to study the reactions of the spinnaker closely and do what has previously been practiced on dry land, that is, have the boom back as near at right angles as possible and also pay out the sheet as far as possible without making the spinnaker lift.

In light winds the helmsman sits to leeward, on the side of the mainsail, and the crew to windward to keep a close watch on the spinnaker luff. By continuously but gently playing the sheet he keeps the luff at a favourable angle of incidence, just the same as this is done with any other sail. The guy should be left alone as much as possible. If the

wind freshens both helmsman and crew move further inboard to damp down the rolling movements of the boat which could lead to a capsize.

Here again the wind vane is essential. This small gadget stops one making serious mistakes when sailing off the wind and particularly before the wind.

In fact it frequently occurs for some reason or other (effect of waves, altering course to avoid another boat or an obstruction) that one luffs up or bears away very slightly. Under spinnaker such deviations from the course can result in a very near capsize. For example if, when running dead before the wind in a fresh breeze, you are forced to bear away you will be running by the lee and risk an involuntary gybe. It is therefore advisable to consult the wind vane immediately after every change of course to make sure you are on the right one.

Most of the adjustments made to the spinnaker must be made through the sheet (to leeward). Yet the strain on the guy is always much greater than that on the sheet and, especially in strong winds, the guy must be made fast in some way, either by a jamb cleat or by taking a turn round an ordinary cleat, to stop it being carried away in a squall. If this happens, the tack gets blown forward until

the boom hits the forestay. The centre of effort of
the spinnaker has now moved far to leeward, the
mast gets pulled over and a capsize is quite likely.
This cannot happen if the guy is made fast and the
spinnaker is handled like an ordinary sail.

If the puffs are very strong at times, the sheet is
eased as much as seems necessary to spill the air
from the leech to the spinnaker. You can go as far
as to let the spinnaker lift and in extreme cases
even let the sheet fly altogether. With the spinnaker flying like a piece of washing the boat comes
back on an even keel. If in this case you eased the
guy off you would not spill the wind from the
spinnaker but only give rise to the unpleasant
sequence of events just described. If we consider
that on the jib and the mainsail the tack is permanently fixed we can see why on a spinnaker the
tack must not be constantly shifted back and forth.
It is obviously useful to be able to alter the angle
of attack of the spinnaker luff by changing the
position of the tack, but this is for occasional use
only.

On light dinghies the spinnaker sheet and guy
are usually of rope. Under strain from the tack the
guy stretches noticably, causing the angle of attack
to change and the boom to swing forward. It is
therefore important to choose a rope that has a
low stretch.

lowering the spinnaker

It pays to prepare this manoeuvre well in advance so that there is time to put things right if they have got in a muddle.

1. The boat is again sailed before the wind. The helmsman stands up and holds the tiller between his legs. The crew hands him the spinnaker sheet and guy.

2. The crew unships the spinnaker boom from the mast, unhitches the topping lift and downhaul and finally disconnects the spinnaker tack.

3. The helmsman lets the sheet fly and with his free hand takes the spinnaker boom from the crew and stows it inside the boat. Meanwhile the crew gets hold of the guy and gathers the foot of the spinnaker in to windward.

4. The crew ducks under the weather jib sheet and, while the helmsman seizes the spinnaker, casts off the halyard and lowers the spinnaker. He stows it in its proper place, tack and clew well separated.

5. He now unclips the halyard, makes it safely fast and puts the spinnaker headboard well in sight on top of the sail.

While he does this, the helmsman lowers the centreplate and, if possible, trims the jib sheet so that the jib is drawing.

6. The crew takes up his usual place and takes over the jib sheet.

gybing

First of all the boat is brought dead before the wind, and the helmsman takes up the same position as for hoisting the spinnaker.

1. The mainsail is gybed first. This can be done by the helmsman. If it is made the crew's job he must first hand the helmsman the spinnaker sheet and guy. The jib, too is sheeted down to leeward so that it does not get in the way during the manoeuvre.

2. The crew unhitches the spinnaker boom from the mast and passes the end across forward of the mast. The helmsman lets the spinnaker go to windward by easing the sheet and guy which now interchange names (sheet becomes guy, guy becomes sheet).

3. The crew clips the free end of the boom onto the new tack and unhitches the other end of the boom from what was the tack, and finally fixes the boom back on the mast.

4. While the crew puts the boat in order the helmsman trims the spinnaker and then passes the crew the sheet and guy. This done, they can resume their new course.

Under spinnaker the centreplate is operated by the helmsman who also takes responsibility for maintaining the boat's stability (lateral trim), since the crew usually stays to windward.

First stage of gybe. The crew, both hands on the kicking strap, is about to pull the mainsail over to the other side. The helmsman continues to bear away while keeping the boat perfectly upright.

The sequence of the manoeuvres here described is the same whatever the class of dinghy, but it might be as well to mention a slight variation adopted by top 5.0.5. and FD crews. They usually leave the spinnaker boom made fast before and after hoisting the spinnaker. During the first part of the gybe the crew handles the spinnaker sheet and guy, then he hands them over to the helmsman.

After a few outings the different spinnaker manoeuvres will start to become automatic and the time will come to try the spinnaker on a reach.

As the wind goes round on the beam the angle of attack of the luff must be adjusted by gradually easing the guy. But as soon as the spinnaker is correctly trimmed the guy must be safely belayed again to avoid the mishap we have talked about earlier.

Since the direction of the aerodynamic force is now more from the side, the force causing leeway is proportionately greater. To resist it, the centreplate must be lowered to a considerable depth, more so than on a reach under mainsail and jib alone. The crew must sit well out to keep the boat sailing absolutely upright.

The resultant force of the combined aerodynamic forces of spinnaker, mainsail and jib is enormous and calls for very precise manoeuvring of the boat.

During the first few experiments it is advisable for the crew to ignore the jib in order to be able to pay more attention to the combined working of the mainsail and spinnaker.

The latter, permanently fixed on the windward side (guy belayed round cleat) is trimmed by the sheet alone. The spinnaker boom is also held rigid by the downhaul which is kept very taut and transmits strong tension to the topping lift.

In the puffs, the mainsheet and spinnaker sheet are both eased off while the helmsman bears away, and the stronger the puff the more one has to bear off. The boat will then accelerate considerably. To keep up the speed as the puff dies down the helmsman gradually luffs up to preserve a laminar flow over the sail. He first hauls in on the mainsheet to start the boat luffing, then the crew follows with the spinnaker sheet.

When the helmsman and crew have worked out a slick routine they may bring the jib back into play. It is trimmed to a mid-way position and belayed on the windward cleat by the helmsman.

Racing dinghies generally use a very simple system. The downhaul consists of a steel wire with a hook for the boom at one end and a plastic ball at the other which locks into a fitting on the deck or the mast as the boom is rigged. The length of this cable is such that it does not allow the spinnaker boom to rise higher than is desirable for optimum performance in fresh wind (65° to 70°). Any unused length of cable is pulled inside the hull by shock-cord.

As the wind decreases in strength the boom is adjusted by the topping lift only. The topping lift runs through a small sheave under the cross trees and from there is led back down the mast to deck level where it is either taken up by a double-ended or continuous tackle which allows adjustment from either side of the boat, or it is simply belayed on a small cleat on the mast. The former method has the advantage that the crew can adjust the height of the spinnaker boom without moving from his place.

Spinnaker chute. This was first used in the International 14 ft. Dinghy. Since 1966 it has been increasingly used in the FD and since 1968 in the 5.0.5. It consists of a retrieving line, frequently a continuation of the spinnaker halyard, attached to the centre of the spinnaker. It passes down a plastic hose-pipe at the extreme forward end of the boat, before the forestay. This retrieving line makes spinnaker handling very much easier, especially in fresh winds.

combined use of spinnaker and trapeze

When the spinnaker is set in a fresh breeze on a reach, the use of the trapeze becomes necessary to hold the boat upright.

It is very important that the boat should sail on a level keel because at the slightest angle of heel it will start to luff up. The final result is usually a capsize.

The spinnaker must only be trimmed by the sheet; the guy, as well as the downhaul of the boom, must be securely belayed.

The crew has unshipped the spinnaker boom from the mast and is about to attach that end to the new tack. He then takes the other end of the boom out of the old tack and fixes it to the mast. Note the helmsman holding the spinnaker sheet and guy.

Gybing under spinnaker: top: the crew has just unshipped the spinnaker boom from the mast and is about to attach it to the new spinnaker tack. Left: operation seen from forward. Bottom: the crew attaches the boom to the tack.

Despite these precautions the spinnaker boom often moves forward in strong puffs. This is detrimental to the efficiency of the spinnaker.

To avoid this happening the guy should be led right down to the windward *chain plate*. In this way its pull is more vertical and acts in part as an extra downhaul, leaving the crew free to get out on the trapeze.

To this end a fairlead is fitted to the underneath of the gunwale and the guy led inside it. It is essential to good performance that the crew has only the spinnaker sheet to attend to.

It is up to the helmsman to trim the jib. The jib sheets are led through cleats.

On keelboats the spinnaker is usually hoisted and lowered to leeward of the mainsail, which means that some time can be saved in these manoeuvres and, what is more important, they can be left till the last minute.

But, apart from the detailed tasks allotted to each member of the crew, the procedure on keelboats is generally the same.

The spinnaker guy passes via a fairlead under the gunwale. This, together with a steel wire topping lift ensures good control of the boom. The crew is positioned aft to keep the boat in perfect longitudinal trim.

sailing in currents and tidal waters

Whether you are sailing on the sea or on a river you always have to use the current to the best advantage if it is favourable and try to avoid its harmful effects if it is unfavourable.

Currents in rivers present few problems concerning their direction and strength, but when it comes to tidal currents the sailor must be able to judge their direction and speed precisely. Changes in their direction and strength are closely linked with the movement of the tides, but they are not necessarily completely synchronized with these. In fact, there can be a difference of several hours between the turn of the tide and the effect making itself felt near the shore in the water level near the shore (low tide or high tide). The stream of the rising tide is called the *flood* and that of the falling tide the *ebb*.

We know that about 6 hours elapse between dead low water and high water, and the same amount of time between high water and the next low water.

Between the end of the ebb and the beginning of the flood, equally between the end of the flood and the beginning of the ebb, there is a slack period which very much effects the speed and direction of the tidal flow, but as has been said before, its direction on the one hand and the slack period on the other are not necessarily synchronized to the times of high and low water.

It is true that the tide runs in or out, with variable intensity, for a fixed period of time, but this can overlap by several hours the subsequent ebb or flood. Thus the flood over a given area of sea may continue to come in in the same direction several hours after high water, which means for quite some time after the tide level has started to drop. The ebb in turn will not make itself felt until two or three hours before low water and continue long after the tide has begun to rise again.

Coming back to the intensity of tidal currents, it is obvious that they are weaker at the beginning and at the end of their movement in one direction or other, and that their maximum intensity is generally experienced mid-way through each phase.

Tidal currents are sometimes very strong. The extent to which the tide makes itself felt in any given locality depends on the expanse of water and the configuration of the coast.

When the flood penetrates a large, enclosed bay it is very strong in and around the entrance. The ebb will be equally strong. Anyone wishing to enter or leave the bay will have to time this according to the flood or ebb respectively unless he wants to be faced with a long wait and, above all, expose himself to considerable danger.

Pilot guides and charts of currents are drawn up by the Hydrographic Office, and it is wise to refer to them to avoid trouble. On the other hand, if you sail regularly in the same area of water, a little observation will very quickly allow the problems of navigation to be resolved.

But the situation is more tricky, without exactly being dramatic, when navigating coastwise on tideless seas, or seas where the tide is very weak, such as the Mediterranean or the Baltic. Currents there do not follow set time-tables. They may run for several days in one direction and then disappear altogether to come back some time later either from the same or the opposite direction.

These capricious currents are connected with the dominant winds and their thermal influence on the water. For example, if a strong mistral has blown for several days it sets into motion the mass of water, and although its speed will be rather low compared with tidal currents it is, nevertheless, enough to raise and lower the water level.

How do we know that there is a current? It is very simple: you just pick a landmark and steer towards it. You will soon notice if the boat is carried to one side or the other.

In general, currents are always stronger in deep water and weaker near the coast as the water becomes shallower. When having to sail against a current it is wise to steer near the shore where its effects are less noticeable or even negligible.

On the other hand, when the current is favourable you have to get out as much as possible into deep water and pick the patches where the current is strongest, even if it is not the most direct course. You will get to the mark quicker this way despite covering a longer distance.

Nevertheless, there are situations in which it is not possible to navigate other than against the current, for example if the coast is rocky or unfamiliar.

In a following wind dinghies have an advantage over keelboats in being able to raise the centreplate

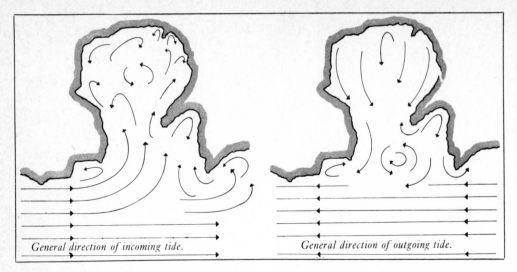

General direction of incoming tide.

General direction of outgoing tide.

The detrimental effects of the current are the same for these two yachts: they get carried to leeward. Their apparent wind is less strong than it would be if there were no current.

Quite apart from this, in going to windward the yachts suffer considerable leeway which can only be overcome by increased speed (chapter 1).

A sails freer and therefore goes faster. Theoretically, she should experience the effects of the current only.

B goes closer to the wind and is therefore slower. Because of this she makes considerable leeway, which must be added to the drift caused by the current. Her course made good and speed over the ground are very much inferior compared with A.

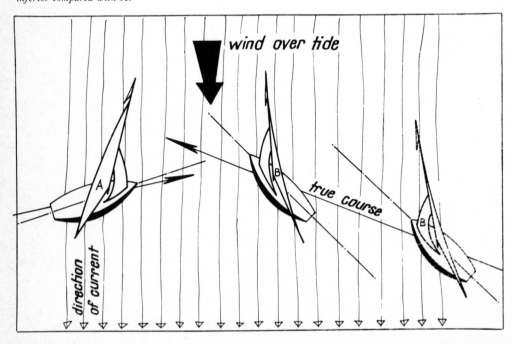

wind over tide

true course

direction of current

thus offering a smaller area of resistance to the current.

The centreplate can also be raised on a broad reach and a reach, as long as the boat does not "sideslip".

Above all the helmsman must avoid putting the boat beam on to the current, and he must concentrate all his attention on this.

If you are sailing close-hauled and on one tack the current is exactly opposite to your course, you must, of course, avoid letting the current get under the weather bow if only for a few seconds. You should rather try and offer the leeward side of the boat to the current (lee-bow the current) by luffing up whenever this is possible without slowing the boat down and in this way benefit from being pushed up into the wind by the current. There is certainly a knack in this and it cannot be done without a great deal of practice.

As for the other tack, the wind will be with the current (wind over tide), and this is particularly unfavourable. The aim must now be not to sail as close as possible but as fast as possible. A slow boat will be very handicapped under these conditions. In short, the solution, the salvation, lies in speed.

On the other hand, if the current is against the wind (wind against tide) you can make good use of it by stemming it and clawing up into the wind. This will give you the impression of laying an extraordinarily good course to windward, but do not get carried away by this and try above all to keep a good speed on the boat (resistance to leeway).

This may seem quite simple on the face of it, but it really requires a lot of intuition, because it is very difficult to estimate the true direction of the current in relation to the course of a boat sailing close-hauled. It is only by long practice or an intimate knowledge of a certain stretch of water that you can hope to become proficient in dealing with this difficult situation.

Near the shore you will frequently meet with a current in the opposite direction and this can make things easier (eddy).

In an on-shore wind it is comparatively easy to sail near the coast, but if the wind is off-shore you are likely to run into blanketed zones and even complete calms. The alternatives are obvious enough. If the wind is sufficiently strong for the boat to make up against the currents easily it is advisable to stand off from the land to find a steady, regular wind.

On the other hand, if the wind is light it pays to choose a course on which you can profit from a counter current or the absence of a current altogether.

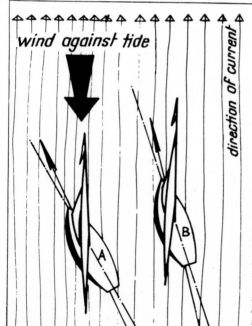

The current pushes the two yachts to windward. The apparent wind is stronger than it would be in the absence of the current.

Not only do the yachts make a better speed, but by lee-bowing the current they can sail a true course very much closer to the wind.

A is sailing at a normal angle of incidence to the apparent wind which gives her a sufficiently high speed to resist leeway.

B is pointing too close and suffers considerable leeway. She looks like making a better course, but actually her true course (or course made good) is very much the same as A's, while her speed is definitely less.

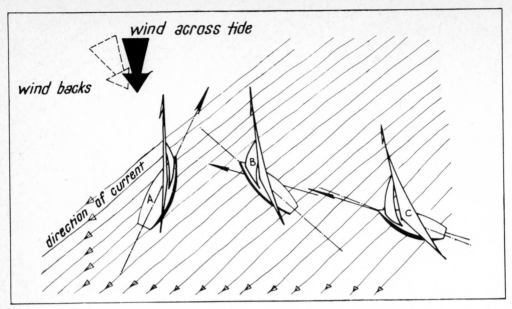

A, on port tack, profits from a freeing wind and can lee-bow the current. B and C find themselves faced with the situation illustrated as "wind over tide". B is pointing too high. C sails freer to benefit from less leeway.

Wind against tide causes this Dragon to carry a great deal of weather helm. Note how the helmsman has to pull the helm up hard.

inshore sailing

Coastwise navigation even with its dangers from shoals and possible stranding has always been, nevertheless the most normal type of sailing. The yachtsman with a small boat has no choice but sail close to the coast.

Somehow paradoxically, it seems that the week-end sailor or the "potterer" thinks he is safer near the coast. This is certainly partly true, because when a gale is forecast he can decide not to go to sea or quickly regain his home port.

However, we are not concerned with this aspect but rather with trying to understand and come to terms with the wind when we are sailing near the coast.

In fact, there is scarcely any problem when the wind blows on-shore, except that of getting away from the beach or getting out of harbour. On the other hand, if the wind blows off-shore at the time you want to come in, you are faced with having to make countless tacks. The normal, overall wind direction is always modified by the configuration of the coast. These variations in wind direction and also in force are closely linked to two factors:

— the degree to which the coastline is irregular
— the angle at which the normal wind strikes the coast at any given point.

Let us start with the simplest case.

A relatively low coastline, straight, with the wind blowing at right angles from the land. The wind is practically undisturbed until quite near the coast, but from about 100 yards out the flow returns to its normal direction. A sailing boat coming in from the sea and wishing to attain a point on the

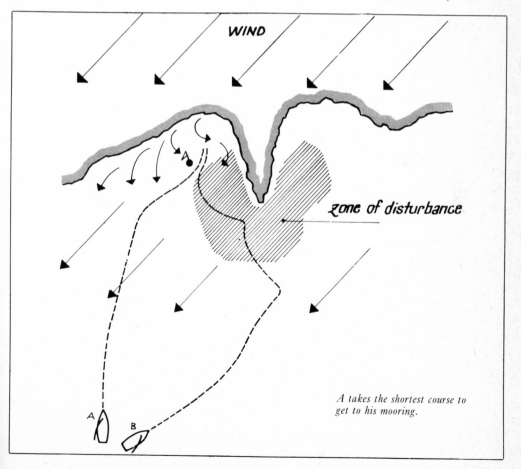

WIND

zone of disturbance

A takes the shortest course to get to his mooring.

A

B

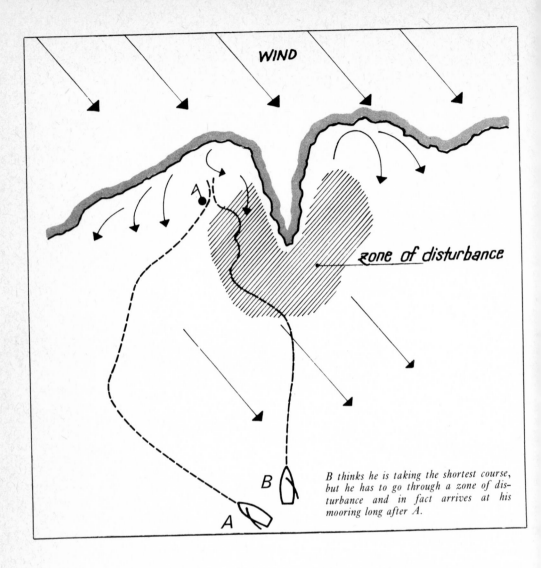

WIND

zone of disturbance

B thinks he is taking the shortest course, but he has to go through a zone of disturbance and in fact arrives at his mooring long after A.

coast exactly in the eye of the wind can beat in on port and starboard tack alternately without noticing any difference in tacks unless there is a current, in which case the helmsman will choose the tack on which the current helps him to edge up into the wind.

But if the direction of the wind is not at right angles to the coast its flow will undergo variations in direction and tend to be deflected parallel to the general line of the coast. The closer you get to the coast the more these variations are felt. Near a very irregular coastline an off-shore wind becomes very unstable. A piece of land jutting out into the water will deflect the airflow on either side and sometimes within a considerable radius all round it. The wind will vary greatly in direction and speed. A yacht coming in to pick up her mooring inshore will have to avoid passing through this zone of disturbance where the wind is turbulent and can vary in strength in a ratio of 1 to 4 as well as changing in direction by up to 60° or 120°.

A follows a course outside the zone of disturbance and will arrive at her mooring first. B thinks she has chosen the shorter course, but she must pass

through the zone of disturbance where she must tack many times, thus losing precious time compared with A.

A general rule, when the wind is off-shore, is to choose the tack which takes you most directly to the shore and at the same time to avoid any zones of disturbed wind.

This demands a keen eye and experience. It is a good idea to reconnoitre those stretches of the coast which are considered tricky and to familiarise yourself with the difficulties to be encountered.

When sailing in an irregular and light breeze in very warm and thundery weather you must look for the least little puff to help the boat along. There is always some wind under the big clouds and you have to tack to pick them out. If the wind drops altogether there is a good chance that it will come up again from the opposite direction.

When a thunderstorm is approaching the wind dies down to come up very strongly a moment later, blowing generally towards the storm. There is no absolute rule on this, but the best way to avoid trouble in a case like this is not to jump to rash conclusions.

3

Racing and competition

A race, sometimes called a regatta, is a match between two or more boats on a course defined by *marks* (buoys).

Racing is a tough competition and has led to considerable progress being made in naval architecture: in the shape and construction of hulls and sails; in the rigging and all the cunning apparatus known as fittings which contributes to the performance of a boat.

Racing often demands an athletic performance, particularly on dinghies, but it is one of those rare sports in which you can be in the top rank for many years, thanks to the diversity of boat classes.

Someone who is Olympic champion in a light dinghy class at the age of 21 can still be a top class international helmsman in a class less exacting physically at the age of fifty.

Yacht racing was adopted as an Olympic competition from the 4th Olympics of modern times. The choice of classes has evolved, passing resolutely from the imposing and majestic keelboats to the lighter classes which are widely spread throughout the world.

There are now three types of dinghies, the Finn for single-handed sailing and the Flying Dutchman and 470 for crews of two. There are two keel boats, the Soling and the Tempest, and one catamaran, the Tornado. The Soling, a three-man boat and the

Tempest, which has a crew of two, were introduced in the 1972 Olympic Games. The 470 and Tornado will be included for the first time in the 1976 Olympics in Canada.

In many countries the national authority chooses several other one-design classes in addition to these five Olympic classes, in which national championships are held. These classes have been selected by their design as well as their nationwide popularity.

Amongst the single-handers the Finn is often used in Senior and Junior Championships, while for cadets and ladies the authority might choose boats like the Moth, Firefly, Enterprise or Cadet. Two-man championships are competed for in some countries in the 5.0.5 class, classified as International Series A, which has replaced the Flying Dutchman, and is much more widespread in France for example.

For juniors, cadets and ladies a very good boat is the 420 with spinnaker and trapeze; but there are many others such as Hornet, Albacore, Fireball, Osprey, Snipe, and so on.

Whilst leaving yacht clubs an entirely free choice of classes they wish to race, the French national authority for example reserves the right to choose the classes in which the French National Championships are decided, giving the winner the title of National Champion.

Racing in dinghies, and more particularly single-handed, needs real athletic prowess and sometimes a very special physique. This imposes a stringent process of elimination on helmsmen and crews aiming at national competition. It goes without saying that in international and Olympic competition one meets genuine athletes.

Interest in racing is fostered by the complexity of the many factors involved. Before you can win a race, you must know about aero- and hydro-dynamics, and how to apply them at any given moment to impart greatest speed regardless of point of sailing or wind strength. You must be quick in movement, know how to choose the right sails for the prevailing wind and then trim them to best advantage. Finally, above all, select the quickest route between the start and finish, so as to take less time than your opponents.

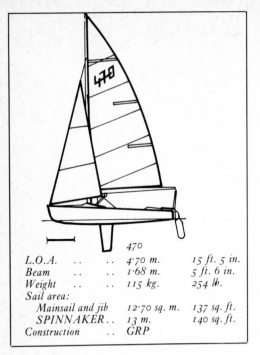

470

L.O.A.	.. ..	4·70 m.	15 ft. 5 in.
Beam	.. ..	1·68 m.	5 ft. 6 in.
Weight	.. ..	115 kg.	254 lb.
Sail area:			
Mainsail and jib		12·70 sq. m.	137 sq. ft.
SPINNAKER	..	13 m.	140 sq. ft.
Construction	..	GRP	

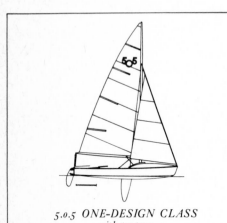

5.0.5 *ONE-DESIGN CLASS*
with trapeze

L.O.A.	.. ..	5·05 m.	16 ft. 7 in.
L.W.L.	. ..	4·65 m.	15 ft. 3 in.
Beam O.A.	..	1·94 m.	6 ft. 2 in.
Beam W.L.	..	1·22 m.	4 ft. 0 in.
Weight	.. ..	128 kg.	282 lb.
Sail area:			
Mainsail and jib	..	16·3 sq. m.	175 sq. ft.
SPINNAKER	..	20 sq. m.	215 sq. ft.
Construction	..	Moulded ply or fibreglass	

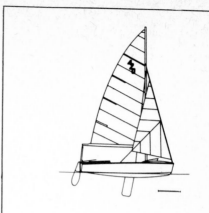

420—ONE-DESIGN CLASS
with trapeze

L.O.A.	.. ..	4·20 m.	13 ft. 9 in.
L.W.D.	.. ..	4·00 m.	13 ft. 1 in.
Beam	.. ..	1·63 m.	5 ft. 4 in.
Weight	.. ..	90 kg.	198 lb.
Sail area :			
Mainsail and jib ..		10·25 sq. m.	110 sq. ft.
SPINNAKER ..		10 sq. m.	107 sq. ft.
Construction	..	Fibreglass only	

FLYING DUTCHMAN
with trapeze

L.O.A.	.. ..	6·05 m.	19 ft. 10 in.
L.W.L.	.. ..	5·60 m.	18 ft. 0 in.
Beam	.. ..	1·70 m.	5 ft. 7 in.
Weight	.. ..	158 kg.	350 lb.
Sail area :			
Mainsail and jib ..		16 sq. m.	172 sq. ft.
SPINNAKER ..		16 sq. m.	172 sq. ft.
Construction	..	Moulded ply or fibreglass	

TORNADO

L.O.A.	..	..	6·09 m.	20 ft.
Beam	..	..	3·04 m.	10 ft.
Weight	..	..	135 kg.	298 lb.
Sail area	..	..	21·83 sq. m.	235 sq. ft.
Construction		..	GRP or cold moulded	

OK DINGHY

L.O.A.	..	..	4·00 m.	13 ft. 1 in.
Beam	..	..	1·42 m.	4 ft. 8 in.
Weight	..	..	85 kg.	187 lb.
Sail area	..	..	8·30 sq. m.	89 sq. ft.
Construction		..	Plywood and GRP	
			(permitted for amateurs)	

FINN—ONE-DESIGN CLASS
UNA-RIGGED

L.O.A.	..	4·50 m.	14 ft. 9 in.
Beam	..	1·50 m.	4 ft. 11½ in.
Weight	..	1·45 kg.	319 lb.
Sail area	..	10 sq. m.	107 sq. ft.
Construction	..	Moulded ply, strip planked or fibreglass	

EUROPA MOTH—ONE-DESIGN CLASS
UNA-RIGGED

L.O.A.	..	3·35 m.	11 ft. 0 in.
Beam	..	1·44 m.	4 ft. 8 in.
Weight	..	60 kg.	132 lb.
Sail area	..	7 sq. m.	75 sq. ft.
Construction	..	Moulded ply or fibreglass	

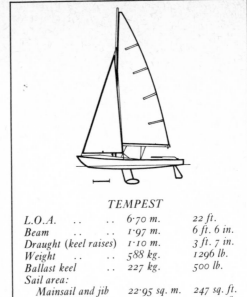

TEMPEST

L.O.A.	.. ..	6·70 m.	22 ft.
Beam	..	1·97 m.	6 ft. 6 in.
Draught (keel raises)		1·10 m.	3 ft. 7 in.
Weight	..	588 kg.	1296 lb.
Ballast keel	..	227 kg.	500 lb.
Sail area:			
Mainsail and jib		22·95 sq. m.	247 sq. ft.
SPINNAKER	..	20·90 sq. m.	225 sq. ft.
Construction	..	only GRP	

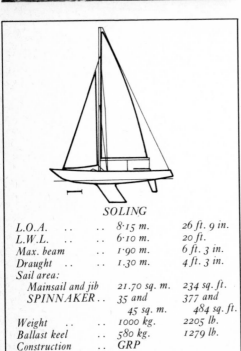

SOLING

L.O.A.	.. ..	8·15 m.	26 ft. 9 in.
L.W.L.	.. ..	6·10 m.	20 ft.
Max. beam	..	1·90 m.	6 ft. 3 in.
Draught	..	1·30 m.	4 ft. 3 in.
Sail area:			
Mainsail and jib		21·70 sq. m.	234 sq. ft.
SPINNAKER	..	35 and	377 and
		45 sq. m.	484 sq. ft.
Weight	.. ..	1000 kg.	2205 lb.
Ballast keel	..	580 kg.	1279 lb.
Construction	..	GRP	

Optimist

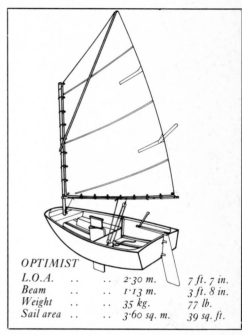

OPTIMIST

L.O.A.	..	..	2·30 m.	7 ft. 7 in.
Beam	..	..	1·13 m.	3 ft. 8 in.
Weight	..	..	35 kg.	77 lb.
Sail area	..	..	3·60 sq. m.	39 sq. ft.

Construction of the Optimist is free, that is to say that anyone interested in this small training boat may build it. In fact, amateur construction is the basis of the rapid development of the class. It used to be built only of wood but, since 1972, it has been possible to buy GRP hulls and fit them out at home. Experience seems to show that the fastest boats are those with a steady sheer and maximum length keel.

As far as building to tolerances is concerned, best results seem to come from minimum overall beam combined with maximum beam forward and aft; this optimises hydrodynamic qualities. Professional builders specialising in the Optimist are, of course, well aware of these permitted tolerances, as are producers of GRP hulls.

Class rules require that the mast shall be in one piece, that is to say it must not be laminated; the wood usually selected therefore is normally fine

grain (stiff mast). However, all types of wood traditionally associated with masts may be used, always remembering not to treat an Optimist spar merely as a kind of broomstick. Knots should be avoided and the wood should be cut along the grain, which should be fine and close. It goes without saying that this also holds good for the boom and sprit.

In 1972 the Optimist Association allowed the use of metal spars. Seen in the light of the never-ending equipment race, it might seem that this decision is not altogether in the best interests of class progress. But on a closer examination it can be seen that, because most insurance policies do not cover accidental breakages, it is perhaps wise to pay more for metal spars (which are stronger than wooden ones) at the outset. The increased cost is often less than the extra premium required to cover breakages.

fittings

In order to avoid on the one hand any equipment race and, on the other, experiment and gadgetry which can be both costly and sometimes unsafe, all Optimist fittings are clearly specified so that no loopholes exist.

In spite of the fact that yards producing the boat in series do not supply them as standard, I strongly recommend a snubbing winch for the main sheet. This reduces considerably for girls and boys the effort needed to hold the sheet in a stiff breeze.

sitting out

Pages 62–65 are devoted to this technique and you should make sure of reading them if you want to get the best out of your Optimist in brisk weather. However, it is as well to recall here that these "gymnastics" require the use of a tiller extension (often missing from training boats), which is a "must" for proper training, particularly for racing.

physical condition

From the moment the young tyro shows a desire to go on after he has learned to sail, so that he may continue to competitive standards, and the parents have resigned themselves to the cost of all this, it is important that they make him have a check-up by the family doctor. To drive home the need for this kind of examination, I draw the attention of fathers, mothers and particularly teachers, to Physical Fitness in Racing (pp. 228–239). As far as young bodies in the midst of development are concerned, it is evident that the most important parts are the abdomen and spine—which are known, in fact, to be susceptible to trouble throughout life. There should be no need, therefore, to insist on a medical examination in the first place, and on

regular physical education exercises over and above those normally undergone at school in the second place.

It is only in competition that you notice the finer points which lead to ultimate improvement. Racing is therefore important for progress. If at one time racing was somewhat looked down upon among sailing people, that's all changed now, because it represents the yardstick by which sailing is measured these days. Besides, it is absorbing, marvellous, ever changing as the fickle wind makes sure that nothing is ever the same so that your plans are constantly being set at nought. The requirement to get on as well as possible in spite of the opposition is known as *racing tactics*. This is what it's all about.

On the other hand, there are also some ploys which can be used to stop an opponent passing, and these are equally part of tactics. They should never lead to a collision, and are therefore limited by the racing rules.

The latter have been standardised for several years now. Under the control of the International Yacht Racing Union (IYRU), the racing rules are complex and fairly difficult to interpret in all their detail.

But the rules of the road as such, are fairly simple and not too numerous; they can be summarised into basic rules which it is essential to know before embarking on your first race or, indeed, on to any stretch of water where there are other boats in any numbers.

These basic rules may be compared with the Highway Code which learner drivers have to absorb while under instruction. A collision between two sailing boats may not be fatal in itself, due to the relatively slow speeds involved, but it can start a chain of events which may lead to death later. See the International Rules for Preventing Collision at Sea as well as the Rules of the IYRU. Before examining the latter, we must learn some of the definitions as set forth in the IYRU.

close-hauled

A yacht is *close-hauled* when sailing by the wind as close as she can lie with advantage in working to windward.

luffing

Altering course towards the wind until head to wind.

tacking

A yacht is *tacking* from the moment she is beyond head to wind until she has *borne away*, if beating to windward, to a *close-hauled* course; if not beating to windward, to the course on which her mainsail has filled.

bearing away

Altering course away from the wind until a yacht begins to *gybe*.

gybing

A yacht begins to *gybe* at the moment when, with the wind aft, the foot of the mainsail crosses her centre line and completes the *gybe* when the mainsail has filled on the other *tack*.

on a tack

A yacht is *on a tack*, except when she is *tacking* or *gybing*. A yacht is on the *tack* (starboard or port) corresponding to her *windward* side.

clear astern and clear ahead; overlap

A yacht is *clear astern* of another when her hull and equipment in normal position are abaft an imaginary line projected abeam from the aftermost point of the other's hull and equipment in normal position.

The other yacht is *clear ahead*. The yachts *overlap* if neither is *clear astern*; or if, although one is *clear astern*, an intervening yacht *overlaps* both of them. The terms *clear astern*, *clear ahead* and *overlap* apply to yachts on opposite *tacks* only when they are subject to rule 42, Rounding or Passing Marks and Obstructions.

leeward and windward

The *leeward* side of a yacht is that on which she is, or, of *luffing* head to wind, was, carrying her mainsail. The opposite side is the *windward* side.

A is to windward of B
B is to leeward of A

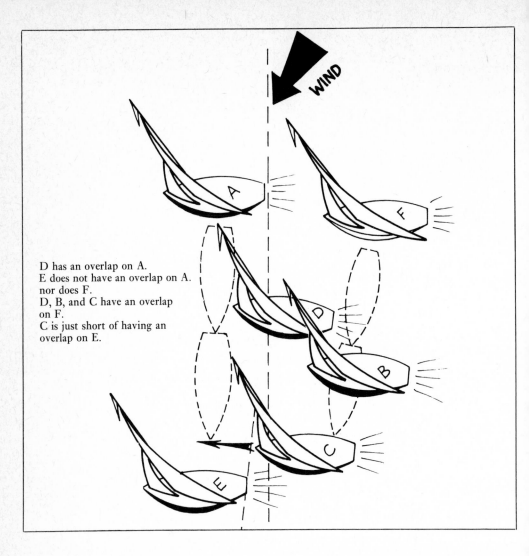

D has an overlap on A.
E does not have an overlap on A.
nor does F.
D, B, and C have an overlap
on F.
C is just short of having an
overlap on E.

*B is clear astern of A but is nevertheless considered to have an overlap on A because an intervening yacht, D,
overlaps both of them.*

The terms *clear astern*, *clear ahead* and *overlap* apply to yachts on opposite *tacks* only when they are subject to rule 42, Rounding or Passing Marks and Obstructions.

proper course

A *proper course* is any course which a yacht might sail after the starting signal, in the absence of the other yacht or yachts affected, to finish as quickly as possible. The course sailed before *luffing* or *bearing away* is presumably, but not necessarily, the yacht's *proper course*. That is to say that if, for example, there is a current flowing, a yacht may sail a course other than the direct course in order to get to the mark sooner, or to make better speed where there is no current (see chapter 2, Sailing in Currents).

There is no proper course before the starting signal.

That is to say that before the starting signal a yacht may sail in any way she thinks is most advantageous, as long as she respects the rights of the other yachts.

racing

A yacht is *racing* from her preparatory signal until she has either *finished* and cleared the finishing line and finishing *marks*, or until the race has been *cancelled*, *postponed* or *abandoned*.

starting

A yacht *starts* when, after fulfilling her penalty obligations, if any, under rule 51.5(c), Sailing the Course, and after her starting signal any part of her hull, crew or equipment first crosses the starting line in the direction of the first *mark*

A's crew is in normal position.

mark

A *mark* is any object specified in the sailing instructions which a yacht must round or pass on a required side.

obstruction

An *obstruction* is any object, including craft under way, large enough to require a yacht, if not less than one overall length away from it, to make a substantial alteration of course to pass on one side or the other, or any object which can be passed on one side only, including a buoy when the yacht in question cannot safely pass between it and the shoal or object which it marks.

finishing

A yacht *finishes* when any part of her hull, or of her crew or equipment in normal position, crosses the finishing line from the direction of the last *mark*, after fulfilling any penalty obligations, if any, under rule 52.2, Touching a Mark.

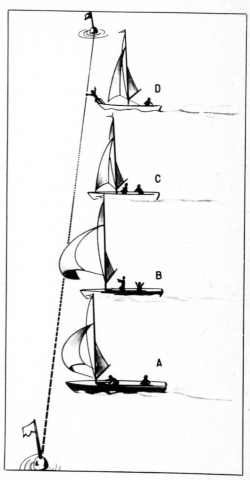

B and D cannot be considered as having finished because D's crew and B's spinnaker are not in normal position.

basic rules

yachts on opposite tacks

Rule 36—Fundamental Rule

A *port-tack* yacht shall keep clear of a *starboard-tack* yacht.

The port-tack yacht must bear away or tack to keep clear of the starboard-tack yacht which has right of way.

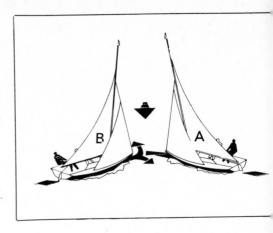

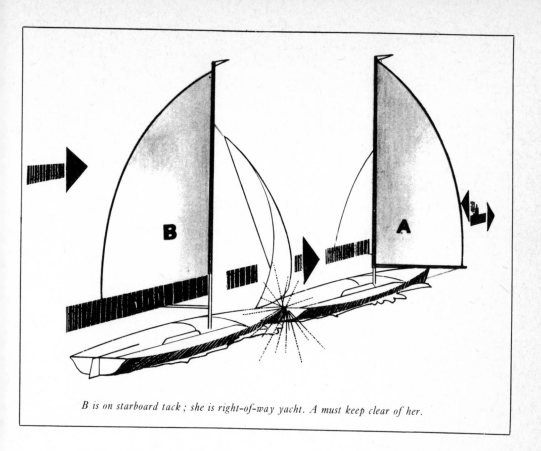

B is on starboard tack; she is right-of-way yacht. A must keep clear of her.

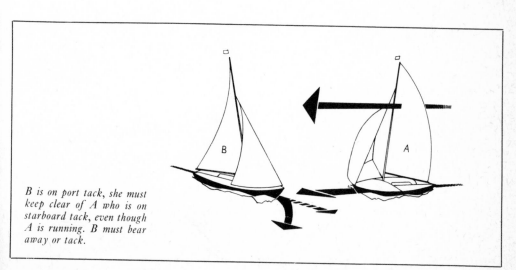

B is on port tack, she must keep clear of A who is on starboard tack, even though A is running. B must bear away or tack.

yachts on the same tack

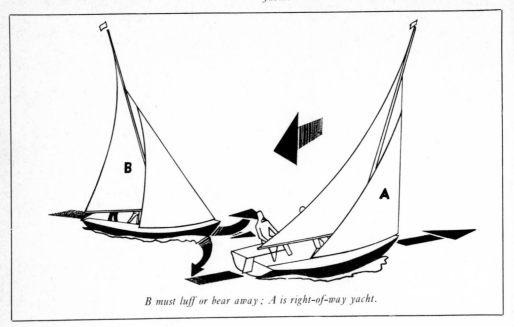

→ *Rule 37—Fundamental Rule*

1. A *windward yacht* shall keep clear of a *leeward yacht.*

B must luff or bear away; A is right-of-way yacht.

2. A yacht *clear astern* shall keep clear of a yacht *clear ahead.*

B is sailing faster than A; she must alter course to pass either to windward or to leeward of A.

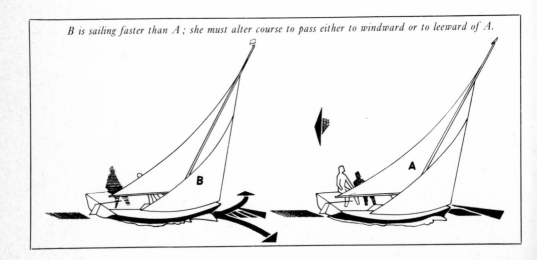

3. A yacht which establishes an *overlap* to *leeward* from *clear astern* shall allow the *windward yacht* ample room and opportunity to keep clear and, during the existence of that *overlap*, the *leeward yacht* shall not sail above her *proper course* (rule 37.3).

B has gone to leeward of A, but she must give A ample room to respond to her new obligation. B is not allowed to luff above her proper course while she is to leeward of A. She must sail her proper course to the next mark while the overlap exists.

changing tack rules
tacking
or gybing (rule 41)

1. A yacht which is either *tacking* or *gybing* shall keep clear of a yacht *on a tack*.

2. A yacht shall neither *tack* nor *gybe* into a position which will give her right of way unless she does so far enough from a yacht *on a tack* to enable this yacht to keep clear without having to begin to alter her course until after the *tack* or *gybe* has been completed.

3. A yacht which *tacks* or *gybes* has the onus of satisfying the race committee that she completed her *tack* or *gybe* in accordance with rule 41.2.

4. When two yachts are both *tacking* or both *gybing* at the same time, the one on the other's *port* side shall keep clear.

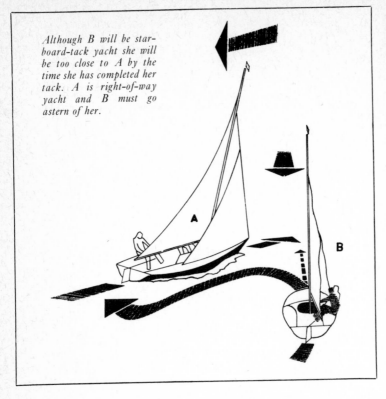

Although B will be star-board-tack yacht she will be too close to A by the time she has completed her tack. A is right-of-way yacht and B must go astern of her.

infringements when meeting other yachts

(Failure to concede right of way, mainly under fundamental rules 36, 37 and 41)

In place of disqualification, which is sometimes harsh on a transgressor, the IYRU has suggested that the latter shall be able to exonerate himself by sailing two complete circles (720°), keeping clear of all other yachts while he does so.

This rule would only be applicable if agreed by the appropriate national anthority. Nevertheless, I recommend its use for instructional races any-way. Some helms-men have a convenient tendency to forget rights of way in order to achieve a brief success; this lowers values all round. The kind of penalty now proposed will quickly restore a good sporting spirit among an instructor's young flock.

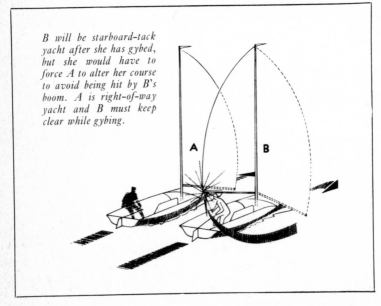

B will be starboard-tack yacht after she has gybed, but she would have to force A to alter her course to avoid being hit by B's boom. A is right-of-way yacht and B must keep clear while gybing.

avoiding collisions (rule 32)

A right-of-way yacht which fails to make a reasonable attempt to avoid a collision resulting in serious damage may be disqualified as well as the other yacht.

touching a mark (rule 52)

1. A yacht which either:
   (a) touches:
   (i) a starting *mark* before *starting*;
   (ii) a *mark* which begins, bounds or ends the leg of the course on which she is sailing; or
   (iii) a finishing *mark* after *finishing*, or

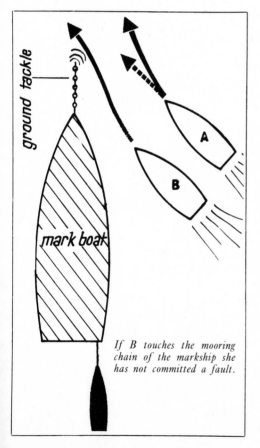

If B touches the mooring chain of the markship she has not committed a fault.

(b) causes a *mark* or *mark* vessel to shift to avoid being touched, shall immediately retire, unless either:
   (i) she alleges that she was wrongfully compelled by another yacht to touch it or cause it to shift, in which case she shall protest; or
   (ii) she exonerates herself in accordance with rule 52.2.
2. (a) Unless otherwise prescribed by the national authority or in the sailing instructions, a yacht which touches a *mark* surrounded by navigable water may exonerate herself by completing one entire rounding of the *mark*, leaving it on the required side, and thereafter she shall re-round or re-pass it, without touching it, as required to sail the course in accordance with rule 51, Sailing the Course, and the sailing instructions.
   (b) When a yacht touches:
   (i) a starting *mark*, she shall carry out the rounding after she has *started*; or
   (ii) a finishing *mark*, she shall carry out the rounding, and she shall not rank as having *finished* until she has completed the rounding and again crosses the finishing line in accordance with the definition of *finishing*.

yachts re-rounding after touching a mark (rule 45)

1. A yacht which has touched a *mark* and is about to correct her error in accordance with rule 52.2, Touching a Mark, shall keep clear of all other yachts which are about to round or pass it or have rounded or passed it correctly, until she has rounded it completely and has cleared it and is on a *proper course* to the next *mark*.
2. A yacht which has touched a mark while continuing to sail the course and until it is obvious that she is returning to round it completely in accordance with rule 52.2, Touching a Mark, shall be accorded rights under the rules of Part IV.

rendering assistance (rule 58)

Every yacht shall render all possible assistance to any vessel or person in peril, when in a position to do so.

rounding or passing marks and obstructions (rule 42)

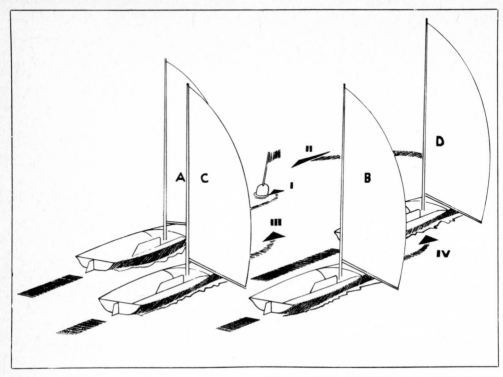

Above: Although D is in the lead, A has right-of-way over her and over all the other yachts.
On the right: B rounds last. C rounds in second position, because C has an overlap on B and D. The order of rounding the mark is A, C, D, B.

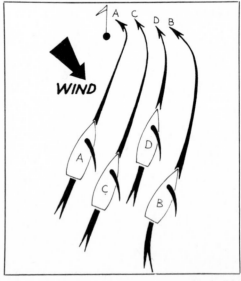

This rule comprises many paragraphs and is very complex. I am not quoting them because they are difficult to assimilate for the beginner. The important thing is that he should avoid incidents.

The essence of the rule is:

When two or more yachts are about to round an obstruction or a mark, the inside yacht has right of way.

A is right-of-way yacht and B must keep clear to give A room to manoeuvre.

Finn No. 75 is going to collide with No. 61; she has gybed too soon, not leaving enough room for No. 61 to gybe. ▶

Experienced helmsmen may wonder at my deliberate attempt to send the beginner on his way with a rather perfunctory knowledge of the rules.

It seems to me preferable that a new helmsman should have an elementary knowledge of his **duties** (not so much his **rights**) rather than be completely ignorant of the code of the sea, before embarking on the purely technical part of racing.

I am convinced that with a perfect knowledge of the definitions and the basic sailing rules a beginner can be sure not to make a fool or a nuisance of himself when he is first called upon to respond to a situation.

the course

The course is defined by marks, which are usually buoys topped by conspicuous flags. Their colour, numbering, position and the side on which they are to be rounded or passed is always set out in the sailing instructions issued by the organizing authority.

The course is generally laid out in relation to the true wind so that all boats have to sail on all points from running to close-hauled. Since windward work requires the largest degree of skill, as well as quick reactions and sound judgement, the wind very rarely being steady in strength or direction, beating to windward accounts for the larger part of the course. It is not enough to sail fast, above all the helmsman must choose the shortest course by making the best use of wind shifts and currents.

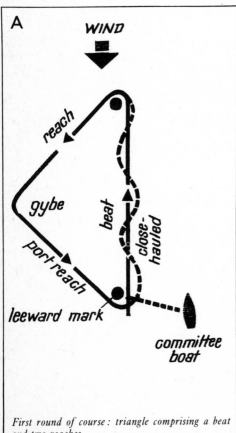

First round of course: triangle comprising a beat and two reaches.

Second round of course: a shuttle comprising a beat and a run.

In a classical Olympic course beating accounts for more than 55% of the course, reaching for about 26% and running for scarcely more than 18%.

the three rounds of an Olympic course, marks to be left to port

(diagrams A, B, C)

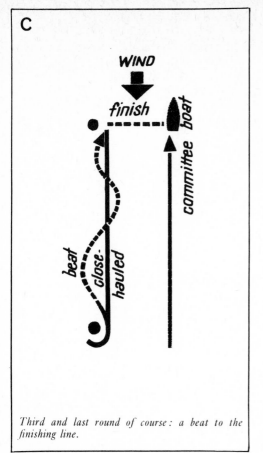

The course is made up of three marks forming a triangle and spaced in such a way as to give the following proportions:

Three windward legs 55%
Two reaching legs 26%
One downwind leg 19%

In the one-man dinghy classes the distance between the leeward and the windward mark is 1·3 miles.

On paper, the entire course measures about 7 miles. In practice, though, the boats cover a much longer distance because on the three beats they have to do nearly twice the theoretical distance. In fact, the distance covered over the entire course is around 11 miles.

In the two-man dinghy classes and the Star class the distance between leeward and windward mark is 2 miles, for the Dragon and the Soling 2·2 miles.

Third and last round of course: a beat to the finishing line.

Many national authorities and class associations stipulate this type of course for their championships, and recommend to the organizers to provide for a distance not less than 1 mile between the leeward and windward marks.

Diagram of a complete Olympic course, marks to be left to port.

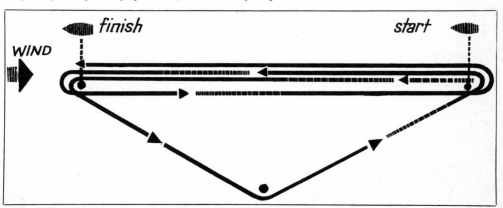

the starting line

In order to give all boats an equal chance at the moment of crossing, the starting line is not laid exactly at right angles to the wind. This will be dealt with later. The most important thing to know is which way round the course is sailed so as not to pass marks on the wrong side and be a menace to other boats.

Often, if the starting mark is to starboard of the committee boat, the course is sailed clockwise, if it is to port of the committee boat, anticlockwise.

starting line (definition, rule 6)

1. The starting and finishing lines shall be either:
   (*a*) a line between a *mark* and a mast or staff on the committee boat or station clearly identified in the sailing instructions;

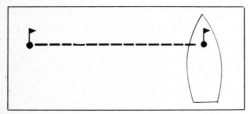

(*b*) a line between two *marks*; or

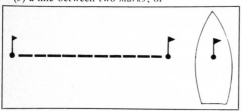

(*c*) the extension of a line through two stationary posts, with or without a *mark* at or near its outer limit, inside which the yachts shall pass.

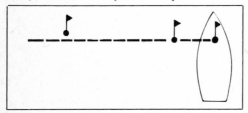

For types (*a*) and (*c*) of starting lines the sailing instructions may also provide that a *mark* will be laid at or near the inner end of the line, in which case yachts shall pass between it and the outer *mark*.

starting area (rule 7.1)

The sailing instructions may define a starting area which may be bounded by buoys. If so, they shall not rank as *marks*.

timing the start (rule 7.2)

The *start* of a yacht shall be timed from her starting signal.

sailing the course (rule 51)

1. (*a*) A yacht shall *start* and *finish* only as prescribed in the starting and finishing definitions.

(*b*) Unless otherwise prescribed in the sailing instructions, a yacht which either crosses prematurely, or is on the course side of the starting line, or its extensions, at the starting signal, shall return and *start* in accordance with the definition.

(*c*) Unless otherwise prescribed in the sailing instructions, when after a general recall, any part of a yacht's hull, crew or equipment is on the course side of the starting line or its extensions during the minute before her starting signal, she shall thereafter return to the pre-start side of the line across one of its extensions and *start*.

(*d*) Failure of a yacht to see or hear her recall notification shall not relieve her of her obligation to *start* correctly.

2. A yacht shall sail the course so as to round or pass each *mark* on the required side in correct sequence, and so that a string representing her wake from the time she *starts* until she *finishes* would, when drawn taut, lie on the required side of each mark (see diagram of Olympic course).

3. A *mark* has a required side for a yacht as long as she is on a leg which it begins, bounds or ends. A starting line *mark* begins to have a required side for a yacht when she *starts*. A starting limit *mark* has a required side for a yacht from the time she is approaching the starting line to *start* until she has left it astern on the first leg. A finishing *line mark* and the finishing *limit mark* cease to have a required side for a yacht as soon as she finishes.

4. A yacht which rounds or passes a *mark* on the wrong side may correct her error by making her course conform to the requirements of rule 51.2.

5. It is not necessary for a yacht to cross the finishing line completely. After *finishing* she may clear it in either direction.

advertisements (rule 26)

1. The hull, crew or equipment of a yacht shall not display any form of advertisement except that:

(*a*) One sailmaker's mark (which may include the name or mark of the manufacturer of the sail cloth) may be displayed on each side of any sail. The whole of such mark shall be placed not more than 15% of the length of the foot of the sail or 300 mm from its tack, whichever is the greater. This latter limitation shall not apply to the position of marks on spinnakers.

(*b*) One builder's mark (which may include the name or mark of the designer) may be placed on the hull, and one maker's mark may be displayed on spars and equipment.

2. Marks (or plates) shall fit within a square not exceeding 150 mm × 150 mm.

3. A yacht shall not be disqualified for infringing the provisions of this rule without prior warning and adequate opportunity to make correction.

note

During the Olympic Games in Rome the courses were sailed leaving the marks to port. The reasons were the following:

If the marks are left to starboard and the yachts get to the windward mark on the starboard tack in order to claim right of way (fundamental rule 36), they must necessarily tack to round the mark and are now on port tack. Since boats are usually very close together when they reach the mark, the leading boat cannot tack until all the following yachts have done so first, making him lose the advantage of his lead. Besides, practice has shown that very few respect rule 36, and this has led to some spectacular collisions.

On the other hand, if the course leaves the marks to port, yachts approaching the mark on starboard tack need only bear away to round it. They must, however, respect rule 42.

I would therefore advise race organizers (race committees) to adopt the Olympic course. They will avoid damage being done and also ease the work of those charged with applying the racing rules and passing sentence.

To be sure of starting at the correct moment in your first race, it is a good idea to be familiar with the ceremony which precedes the start. Ten minutes before the start the race committee breaks out the flag of the class in which you are racing (warning signal). It is important not to miss it and stay close to the committee boat so that there is no risk of mis-interpreting it. Five minutes before the start the race committee breaks out a second flag (preparatory signal, this time the letter P (Blue Peter) of the International Code, which is a blue rectangle with a white square inside. This means that from now on the racing rules apply.

You would be well advised to acquaint yourself with all the International Code Flags to be on the safe side. In fact, the race officers, with regard to unfavourable conditions, may break out flags indicating a postponement or cancellation of the race, or a change in the course.

The following section deals with different international signals, but race committees may use any other signals as long as they are explained in the sailing instructions.

It is essential, therefore, to read the sailing instructions carefully before the start of the race.

signals

(see coloured chart at end of chapter 1, page 40)

1. international code flag signals

Unless otherwise prescribed by the national authority or in the sailing instructions, the following International Code Flags shall be used as indicated:

'AP', Answering pendant—postponement signal.

(*a*) Means:

All races not started are *postponed*.

The warning signal will be made one minute after this signal is lowered. (One sound signal shall be made with the lowering of the AP).

(*b*) When displayed over one ball or shape, means:

'The scheduled starting times of all races not started are *postponed* fifteen minutes.' (This *postponement* can be extended indefinitely by the addition of 1 ball or shape for every 15 minutes.)

(*c*) When displayed over one of the numeral pendants 1–9 over a class signal, means:

'The scheduled time of the start of the designated race is *postponed* 1 hour, 2 hours, etc.'

(*d*) When displayed over the letter 'A', means:

'The races not started are *postponed* to a later date.'

(*e*) When any of the above signals are displayed over a class signal, means:

'The above signals apply to the designated class only.'

'B'—Protest signal.

When displayed by a yacht means: 'I intend to lodge a protest.'

'L'—When displayed means:

'Come within hail', or 'Follow Me.'

'M'—Mark signal.

When displayed on a buoy, vessel or other object, means:

'Round or pass the object displaying this signal instead of the *mark* which it replaces.'

'N'—Abandonment signal.

Means:

'All races are *abandoned*.'

'N over X'—Abandonment and re-sail signal.

Means:

'All races are *abandoned* and will shortly be re-sailed. Watch for fresh starting signals.'

'N over First Substitute'—Cancellation signal.

Means:

'All races are *cancelled*.'

'P'—Preparatory signal.

When displayed, means:

'The class designated by the warning signal will *start* in 5 minutes exactly.'

'R'—Reverse course signal.

When displayed alone, means:

'Sail the course prescribed in the sailing instructions in the reverse direction.'

When displayed over a course signal, means:

'Sail the designated course in the reverse direction.'

'S'—Shorten course signal.

(*a*) at or near the starting line, means:

'Sail the shortened course prescribed in the sailing instructions.'

(*b*) at or near the finishing line, means:

'*Finish* the race either:

(*i*) at the prescribed finishing line at the end of the round still to be completed by the leading yacht' or

(*ii*) 'in any other manner prescribed in the sailing instructions under rule 3.2(a) (vii)'.

(*c*) at or near a rounding *mark*, means:

'Finish between the nearby *mark* and the committee boat'.

'First Substitute'—General recall signal.

When displayed, means:

'The class is recalled for a fresh start as provided in the sailing instructions.'

2. signalling the course

Unless otherwise prescribed by the national authority, the race committee shall either make the appropriate course signal or otherwise designate the course before or with the warning signal.

3. changing the course

The course for a class which has not *started* may be changed:

(*a*) by displaying the appropriate *postponement* signal and indicating the new course before or with the warning signal to be displayed after the lowering of the *postponement* signal, or

(*b*) by displaying a course signal or by removing and substituting a course signal before or with the warning signal.

The race committee should use method (*a*) when a change of course involves either shifting the committee boat or other starting *mark*, or requires a change of sails which cannot reasonably be completed within the 5-minute period before the preparatory signal is made.

4. signals for starting a race

(*a*) Unless otherwise prescribed by the national authority or in the sailing instructions, the signals for starting a race shall be made at 5-minute intervals exactly, and shall be either:

(*i*) Warning signal—Class flag broken out or distinctive signal displayed.

Preparatory signal—Code flag 'P' broken out or distinctive signal displayed.

Starting signal—Both warning and preparatory signals lowered.

In system (1) when classes are started:

(*a*) at 10-minute intervals, the warning signal for each succeeding class shall be broken out or displayed at the starting signal of the preceding class, and

(*b*) at 5-minute intervals, the preparatory signal for the first class to start shall be left flying or displayed until the last class has started. The warning signal for each succeeding class shall be broken out or displayed at the preparatory signal of the preceding class.

(*ii*) Warning signal—White shape.

Preparatory signal—Blue shape.

Starting signal—Red shape, for the first class to start.

In system (*ii*) each signal shall be lowered 30 seconds before the hoisting of the next, and in starting yachts by classes, the starting signal for each class shall be the preparatory signal for the next.

(*b*) Although rule 4.4 (*a*) specifies 5-minute intervals between signals, this shall not interfere with the power of a race committee to start a series of races at any intervals which it considers desirable.

(*c*) A warning signal shall not be given before its scheduled time, except with the consent of all yachts entitled to race.

(*d*) Should a significant error be made in the timing of the interval between any of the signals for starting a race, the recommended procedure is to have a general recall, *abandonment* or *postponement* of the race whose start is directly affected by the error and a corresponding ·*postponement* of succeeding races. Unless otherwise prescribed in the sailing instructions a new warning signal shall be made. When the race is not recalled, *abandoned* or *postponed* after an error in the timing of the interval, each succeeding signal shall be made at the correct interval from the preceding signal.

5. finishing signals

Blue flag or shape. When displayed at the finish, means: "The committee boat is on station at the finishing line."

6. other signals

The sailing instructions shall designate any other special signals and shall explain their meaning.

7. calling attention to signals

Whenever the race committee makes a signal, except 'R' or 'S' before the warning signal, it shall call attention ot its action as follows:
    Three guns or other sound signals when displaying 'N'. 'N over X', or 'N over First Substitute'.
    Two guns or other sound signals when displaying the '1st substitute', 'AP', or 'S'.
    One gun or other sound signal when making any other signal, including the lowering of 'AP' when the length of the postponement is not signalled.

8. visual signal to govern

Times shall be taken from the visual starting signals, and a failure or mistiming of a gun or other sound signal shall be disregarded.

cancelling, postponing or abandoning a race and changing or shortening course (rule 5)

1. The race committee:

(*a*) before the starting signal may shorten the course or *cancel* or *postpone* a race for any reason, and

(*b*) after the starting signal may shorten the course by finishing a race at any rounding *mark* or *cancel* or *abandon* a race because of foul weather endangering the yachts, or because of insufficient wind, or because a *mark* is missing or has shifted or for other reasons directly affecting safety or the fairness of the competition.

(*c*) after the starting signal may change the course at any rounding *mark* subject to proper notice being given to each yacht as prescribed in the sailing instructions.

2. After a *postponement* the ordinary starting signals prescribed in rule 4.4 (*a*) shall be used, and the postponement signal, if a general one, shall be hauled down before the first warning or course signal is made.

3. The race committee shall notify all yachts concerned by signal or otherwise when and where a race *postponed* or *abandoned* will be sailed.

fair sailing (rule 49)

A yacht shall attempt to win a race only by fair sailing, superior speed and skill, and, except in team races, by individual effort. However, a yacht may be disqualified under this rule only in the case of a clear-cut violation of the above principles and only if no other rule applies.

setting and sheeting sails (rule 54)

1. **Changing sails.** While changing headsails and spinnakers a replacing sail may be fully set and trimmed before the sail it replaces is taken in, but only one mainsail and, except when changing, only one spinnaker shall be carried set.

2. **Sheeting sails to spars.** Unless otherwise prescribed by the national authority or by the class rules, any sail may be sheeted to or led above a boom regularly used for a working sail and permanently attached to the mast to which the head of the working sail is set, but no sails shall be sheeted over or through outriggers. An outrigger is any fitting so placed, except as permitted in the first sentence of rule 54.2, that it could exert outward pressure on a sheet at a point from which, with the yacht upright, a vertical line would fall outside the hull or deck planking at that point, or outside such other position as class rules prescribe. For the purpose of this rule: bulwarks, rails and rubbing strakes are not part of the hull or deck planking. A boom of a boomed foresail which requires no adjustment when *tacking* is not an outrigger.

3. **Spinnaker, spinnaker boom.** A spinnaker shall not be set without a boom. The tack of a spinnaker when set and drawing shall be in close proximity to the outboard end of a spinnaker boom. Any headsail may be attached to a spinnaker boom provided that a spinnaker is not set. A sail tacked down abaft the foremost mast is not a headsail. Only one spinnaker boom shall be used at a time and when in use shall be carried only on the side of the foremost mast opposite to the main boom and shall be fixed to the mast. Rule 54.3 shall not apply when shifting a spinnaker boom or sail attached thereto.

forestays and jib tacks (rule 27)

Unless otherwise prescribed in the class rules, forestays and jib tacks (not including spinnaker staysails when not close-hauled) shall be fixed approximately in the centre-line of the yacht.

outside assistance (rule 59)

Except as permitted by rules 56, Boarding, 58, Rendering Assistance, and 64, Aground or Foul of an Obstruction, a yacht shall neither receive outside assistance nor use any gear other than that on board when her preparatory signal was made.

means of propulsion (rule 60)

A yacht shall be propelled only by the natural action of the wind on the sails, spars and hull, and water on the hull, and shall not pump, ooch or rock as described in Appendix 2, nor check way by abnormal means, except for the purpose of rule 58, Rendering Assistance, or for the purpose of recovering a man who has accidentally fallen overboard. An oar, paddle or other object may be used in emergency for steering. An anchor may be sent out in a boat only as permitted by rule 64, Aground or Foul of an Obstruction.

manual power (rule 62)

A yacht shall use manual power only, except that if so prescribed by the national authority or in the sailing instructions, a power winch or windlass may be used in weighing anchor or in getting clear after running aground or fouling any object, and a power pump may be used in an auxiliary yacht.

anchoring and making fast (rule 63)

1. A yacht may anchor. Means of anchoring may include the crew standing on the bottom and any weight lowered to the bottom. A yacht shall recover any anchor or weight used, and any chain or rope attached to it, before continuing in the race, unless after making every effort she finds recovery impossible. In this case she shall report the circumstances to the race committee, which may disqualify her if it considers the loss due either to inadequate gear or to insufficient effort to recover it.

2. A yacht shall be afloat and off moorings before her preparatory signal, but may be anchored, and shall not thereafter make fast or be made fast by means other than anchoring, nor be hauled out, except for the purpose of rule 64, Aground or Foul of an Obstruction, or to effect repairs, reef sails or bail out.

aground or foul of an obstruction (rule 64)

A yacht, after grounding or fouling another vessel or other object, is subject to rule 62, Manual Power, and may, in getting clear, use her own anchors, boats, ropes, spars and other gear; may send out an anchor in a boat; may be refloated by her crew going overboard either to stand on the bottom or to go ashore to push off; but may receive outside assistance only from the crew of the vessel fouled. A yacht shall recover all her own gear used in getting clear before continuing in the race.

skin friction (rule 65)

A yacht shall not eject or release from a container any substance (such as polymer) the purpose of which is, or could be, to reduce the frictional resistance of the hull by altering the character of the flow of water inside the boundary layer.

increasing stability (rule 66)

Unless otherwise prescribed by her class rules or in the sailing instructions, a yacht shall not use any device such as a trapeze or plank to project outboard the weight of any of the crew, nor, when a yacht is equipped with lifelines, shall any member of the crew station any part of his torso outside them, other than temporarily.

limitations on the right-of-way yacht to alter course (rule 34)

When one yacht is required to keep clear of another, the right-of-way yacht shall not so alter course as to prevent the other yacht from keeping clear, so as to increase any alteration of course required of the other yacht in order to keep clear; or so as to obstruct her while she is keeping clear, except;

(*a*) to the extent permitted by rule 38.1, Right-of-Way Yacht Luffing after Starting, and

(*b*) when assuming a *proper course* to *start*, unless subject to the second part of rule 44.1(b), Yachts Returning to Start.

yacht ranking as a starter (rule 50)

A yacht whose entry has been accepted by the race committee and which sails about in the vicinity of the starting line between her preparatory and starting signals shall rank as a starter, even if she does not *start*.

racing for the first time

In order to make a good start, the beginner must know certain rules, ignorance of which, after the preparatory signal, may result in his being disqualified for committing serious offences towards other competitors, or alternatively in being unjustly hindered or forced to give·way by others.

rules at the start

It will be easier to interpret the rules concerning the start if we divide them into three sections:

I. before the starting signal

There is no proper course before the starting signal (definition).

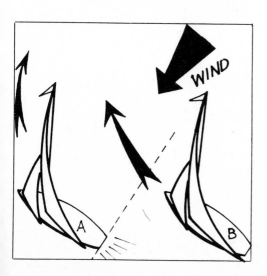

A may luff because she is clear ahead.

right-of-way yacht luffing before starting (rule 40)

Before a yacht has *started* and cleared the starting line, any *luff* on her part which causes another yacht to have to alter course to avoid a collision shall be carried out slowly and in such a way as to give the *windward yacht* room and opportunity to keep clear, but the *leeward yacht* shall not *luff* or sail above a *close-hauled* course, unless the helmsman of the *windward yacht* (sighting abeam from his normal station) is abaft the main-mast of the *leeward yacht*. Rule 38.3, Hailing to Stop or Prevent a Luff; 38.4 Curtailing a Luff; and 38.5, Luffing Two or More Yachts, also apply.

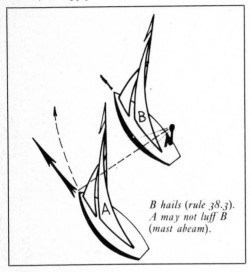

B hails (rule 38.3). A may not luff B (mast abeam).

hailing to stop or prevent a luff (rule 38.3)

When there is doubt, the *leeward yacht* may assume that she has the right to *luff* unless the helmsman of the *windward yacht* has hailed "Mast Abeam" or words to that effect. The *leeward yacht* shall be governed by such hail, and, if she deems it improper, her only remedy is to protest.

hailing (rule 35)

1. Except when *luffing* under rule 38.1 Luffing after Starting, a right-of-way yacht which does not hail before or when making an alteration of course which may not be foreseen by the other yacht may be disqualified as well as the yacht required to keep clear when a collision resulting in serious damage occurs.

2. A yacht which hails in claiming the establishment or termination of an overlap or insufficiency of room at a *mark* or *obstruction* thereby helps to support her claim for the purpose of rule 42, Rounding or Passing Marks and Obstructions.

curtailing a luff (rule 38.4)

The *windward yacht* shall not cause a *luff* to be curtailed because of her proximity to the *leeward yacht* unless an *obstruction*, a third yacht or other object restricts her ability to respond.

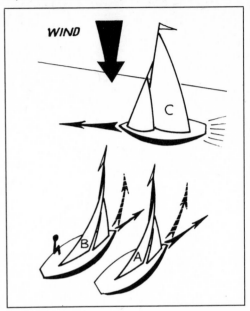

Curtailing a luff (rule 38.4). A cannot force B to alter her course because C, who is on starboard tack, is right-of-way yacht and B must keep clear of her (fundamental rule 36).

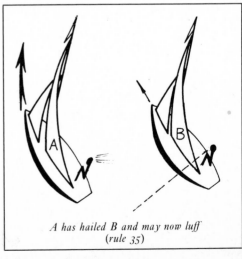

A has hailed B and may now luff (rule 35)

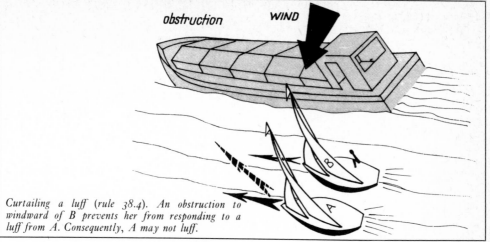

Curtailing a luff (rule 38.4). An obstruction to windward of B prevents her from responding to a luff from A. Consequently, A may not luff.

luffing two or more yachts (rule 38.5)

A yacht shall not *luff* unless she has the right to *luff* all yachts which would be affected by her *luff*, in which case they shall all respond even if an intervening yacht or yachts would not otherwise have the right to *luff*.

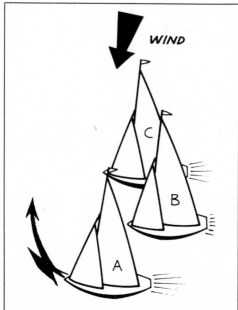

A may luff because her position in relation to B and C gives her the right to. In fact, her mast is forward of C's helmsman. B must respond to A's luff and force C to alter her course, although B's mast is abeam or aft of C's helmsman.

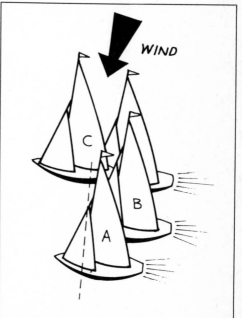

A may not luff B because of her position in relation to C (mast abeam or aft of C's helmsman) does not give her the right to luff C and therefore any of the other yachts either.

However, when approaching the starting line to *start*, a *leeward yacht* shall be under no obligation to give any *windward yacht* room to pass to leeward of a

starting mark

surrounded by navigable water (rule 42.4), but after the starting signal, a *leeward yacht* shall not deprive a *windward yacht* of room at such a *mark* by sailing either above the first *mark* or above . *close-hauled*.

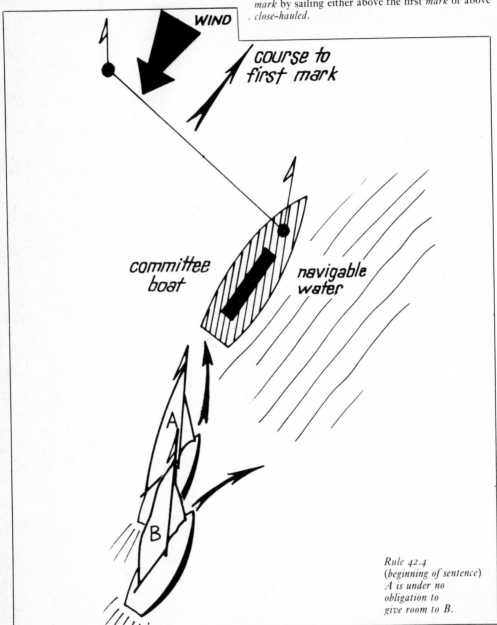

WIND

course to
first mark

committee
boat

navigable
water

A

B

Rule 42.4
(beginning of sentence)
A is under no
obligation to
give room to B.

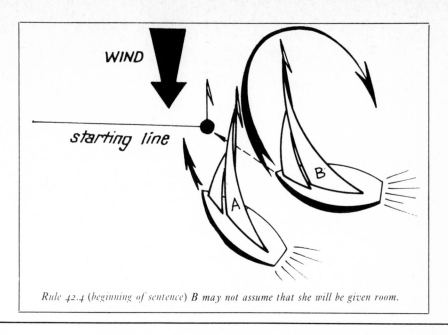

Rule 42.4 (beginning of sentence) B may not assume that she will be given room.

Rule 38.5. Star No. 4705 has definitely no right to luff, her mast being quite obviously abaft the beam of 4704's helmsman.

II. after the starting signal but before having crossed and cleared the line

(rule 42.3, end of sentence)

after the starting signal a leeward yacht shall not deprive a windward yacht of room at a starting mark:

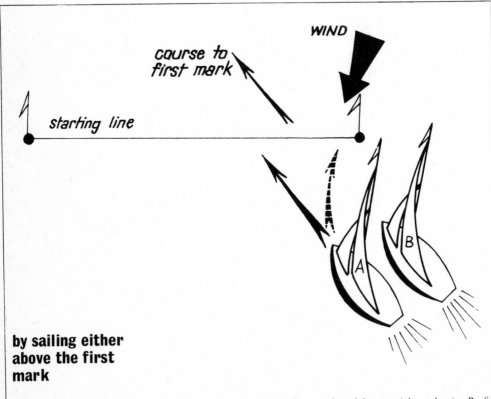

course to first mark

starting line

WIND

by sailing either above the first mark

After the starting signal. A must sail a proper course to the first mark and has no right to deprive B of room (rule 42.3, end of sentence and para i), by heading above the first mark.

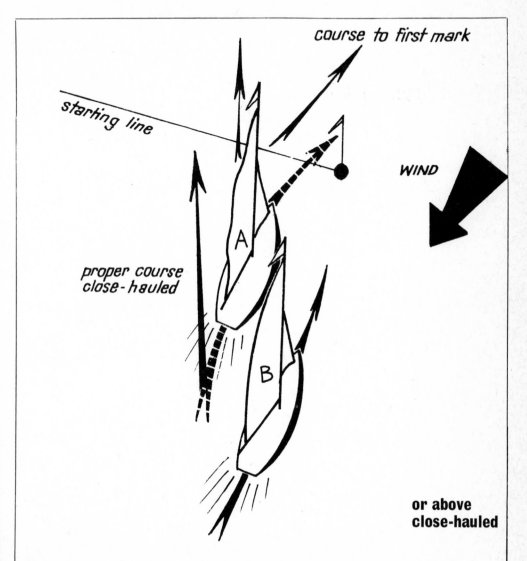

course to first mark

starting line

WIND

proper course
close-hauled

A

B

or above
close-hauled

After the starting signal. A must sail a proper course to the first mark and has no right to deprive B of room (rule 42.3, end of sentence and para ii) by luffing above close-hauled.

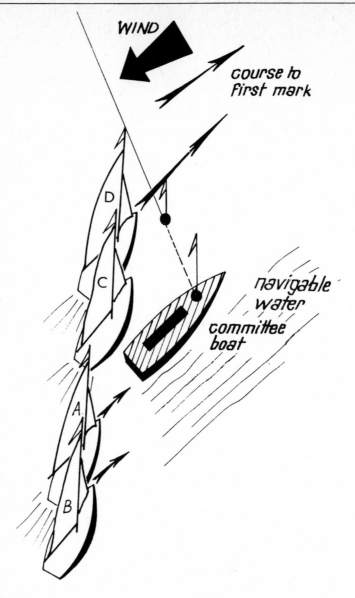

WIND

course to
first mark

navigable
water

committee
boat

D

C

A

B

In this particular case, the starting line being defined by two marks, the committee boat is considered an obstruction. A may not luff B who has an overlap on her. (If the sailing instructions provide that yachts must not pass between the committee boat and the mark, the latter may only be passed on one side and is considered a starting mark.) However, A is not obliged to give B room, since her proper course permits her just to get past the committee boat. As for D, she is on a proper course to the first mark, and since this allows her to clear the starting mark, C cannot claim room to cross the line.

III. after the starting signal and after having crossed the line

It very often happens that several boats are across the line just before the starting signal.

The race committee, rightly considering that these boats have an unfair advantage over the other boats, signals to the culprits to return and re-start.

To do this, the committee uses the following signals:

1. If one boat or a few boats have crossed the line prematurely, the signal for an individual recall is given by displaying the recall numbers of the boats affected accompanied by one sound signal.

2. If a large number of boats have crossed the line too soon, the 1st substitute is broken out, accompanied by two sound signals. This is a general recall.

In the former case, the boats at fault must respect rule 44 in returning to start. In the latter case, all boats are free to return as they like, since the race committee must go through the whole "starting ceremony" all over again, i.e. give the warning signal, then the preparatory signal.

yachts returning to start (rule 44)

1. (*a*) A premature starter when returning to *start* or a yacht working into position from the course side of the starting line or its extensions, when the starting signal is made, shall keep clear of all yachts which are *starting*, or have *started*, correctly, until she is wholly on the pre-start side of the starting line or its extensions.

(*b*) Thereafter, she shall be accorded the rights under the rules of Part IV of a yacht which is *starting* correctly; but if she thereby acquires right of way over another yacht which is *starting* correctly, she shall allow that yacht ample room and opportunity to keep clear.

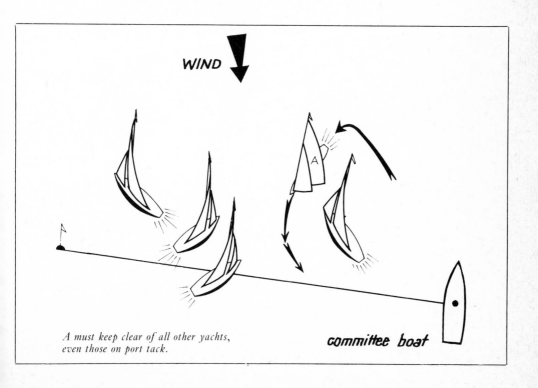

WIND

committee boat

A must keep clear of all other yachts,
even those on port tack.

2. A premature starter while continuing to sail the course and until it is obvious that she is returning to *start*, shall be accorded the rights under the rules of Part IV of a yacht which has *started*.

advice

If, after having crossed the line, you hear a sound signal and are not sure that you have made a correct start, that is if you think you might have crossed the line before the starting signal by however little, you must return to make a new start, otherwise you risk being disqualified at the finish. On the other hand, if you are certain of having made a good start and you think you have heard two sound signals indicating a general recall you must on no account abandon the race until you see the 1st substitute broken out by the race committee, even if all around you everyone is talking of a general recall.

I remember how, in one of my first international championships, I turned back because the boats nearest to me did, claiming there had been a general recall, while others continued the race unperturbed. When I arrived back at the line I found that it had only been an individual recall, and that it did not concern me anyway. My failure to watch the flags on the committee boat had lost me valuable time at the start which I could not make up afterwards.

Talking about recalls, the following is the international rule on recalls:

recalls (rule 8)

1. Unless otherwise prescribed by the national authority or in the sailing instructions, the race committee may allot a recall number or letter to each yacht, in accordance with rule 3.2(*b*)(viii), using yachts' national letters or distinguishing numbers when practicable.

2. When, at her starting signal, any part of a yacht's hull, crew or equipment is on the course side of the starting line or its extensions, or she is subject to rule 51.1(*c*), Sailing the Course, the race committee shall:

(*a*) when each yacht has been allotted a recall number or letter, display her recall number or letter as soon as possible and make a suitable sound signal. As soon as the recalled yacht has wholly returned to the prestart side of the line or its extensions, the race committee shall so inform her by removing her recall number or letter. This is the preferred procedure.

(*b*) When no recall number or letter has been allotted, make a sound signal and leave the class warning signal at "the dip" or display such other signal as may be prescribed in the sailing instruc-

tions, until she has wholly returned to the pre-start side of the line or its extensions, or for such shorter period as the race committee considers reasonable.

The responsibility for returning shall rest with the yacht concerned.

(*c*) Follow such other procedure as may be prescribed by the national authority or in the sailing instructions.

3. (*a*) When there is either a number of unidentified premature starters, or an error in starting procedure, the race committee may make a general recall signal in accordance with rules 4.1, "First Substitute", and 4.7, Calling Attention to Signals. Unless otherwise prescribed by the national authority or in the sailing instructions new warning and preparatory signals shall be made.

(*b*) Except as provided in rule 31.2, Disqualification, rule infringements before the preparatory signal for the new start shall be disregarded for the purpose of *starting* in the race to be started.

mistakes to avoid

All these rules may sound very complicated, but they must be interpreted in a spirit of sportsmanship rather than quibbling.

First of all you must avoid infringing a rule, and that is fairly easy. If you find yourself on port tack after the preparatory signal (letter P) trying to place yourself along the line, you must keep clear of all boats on the other tack. When on port tack you must also avoid stopping the boat head to wind, sails flapping, in order to adjust some gear or other. You will almost certainly, and quite unnecessarily (not to say stupidly) lay yourself open to being disqualified for infringement of rule 36.

Then, as you approach the line, watch carefully the boats to leeward of you and luff slightly to get out of their proximity. This is good starting tactics.

But on no account must you bear away on one or several opponents to stop yourself crossing the line prematurely after you have got there too soon. This is a very serious offence because it does enormous harm to the other boats, and your disqualification cannot restore to them the advantages which they have lost through your fault.

If you find yourself in the unfortunate position of getting to the line too soon, cross it and return to take up your position on the right side of it according to the sailing instructions. You will most certainly have missed your start, but not necessarily lost the race. If you risk any other kind of manoeuvre it is more than likely that a protest will be lodged against you. You will be disqualified and be labelled as a fool for a long time after. When it comes to luffing another boat make sure that your position in relation to your windward opponent really gives you the right to carry out that manoeuvre (rule 35).

Do not be impetuous at your first start, and do not seek trouble just to be able to show that you are not ignorant of these matters; you will only be regarded as a nuisance. Insist on your rights and, above all, honour your obligations towards your opponents, whom you must consider as your friends.

If you have not been recalled do not get carried away by a kind of euphoria, because even if you have successfully negotiated one of the most difficult hurdles in the race you must not relax your attention, because other difficulties, just as severe, lie ahead, as is proved by the racing rules.

right-of-way yacht luffing after starting (rule 38)

1. *Luffing rights and limitations.* After she has *started* and cleared the starting line, a yacht *clear ahead* or a *leeward yacht* may *luff* as she pleases except that:

A *leeward yacht* shall not sail above her *proper course* while an *overlap* exists if, at any time during its existence, the helmsman of the *windward yacht* (when sighting abeam from his normal station and sailing no higher than the *leeward yacht*) has been abreast of forward of the mainmast of the *leeward yacht.*

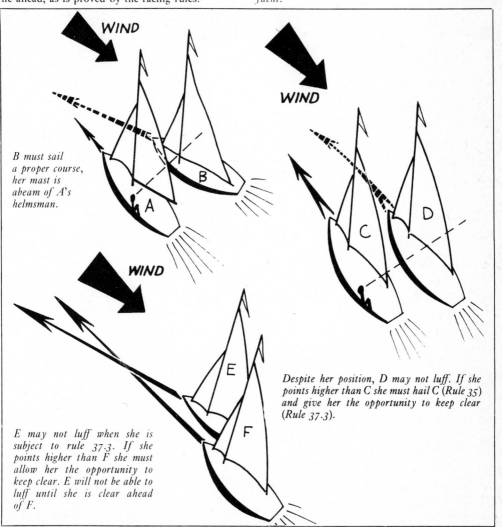

WIND

WIND

WIND

B must sail a proper course, her mast is abeam of A's helmsman.

Despite her position, D may not luff. If she points higher than C she must hail C (Rule 35) and give her the opportunity to keep clear (Rule 37.3).

E may not luff when she is subject to rule 37.3. If she points higher than F she must allow her the opportunity to keep clear. E will not be able to luff until she is clear ahead of F.

2. *Overlap limitations.* For the purpose of this rule: an *overlap* does not exist unless the yachts are clearly within two overall lengths of the longer yacht; an *overlap* which exists between two yachts when the leading yacht *starts*, or when one or both of them completes a *tack* or *gybe*, shall be regarded as a new *overlap* beginning at that time. The following paragraphs of this rule: (3) Hailing to stop or prevent a luff, (4) Curtailing a luff, (5) Luffing two or more yachts have already been explained.

sailing below a proper course after starting (rule 39)

A yacht which is on a free leg of the course shall not sail below her *proper course* when she is clearly within three of her overall lengths of either a *leeward yacht* or a yacht *clear astern* which is steering a course to pass to *leeward*.

advice

For beginners it is above all important not to start behind the rest of the fleet and be last right from the beginning of the race. In spite of all the trouble you have taken before your first race, it is more than likely that your boat is not yet tuned to perfection, nor will you have had much chance to prove to yourself that you can handle it at its best. You must therefore profit from this first contact with the other boats by comparing its speed and weatherliness (ability to go close to the wind) with those of other boats.

Before starting to think in terms of tactics, which includes amongst other things the choice of tacks when beating, you must know how to get the best out of your boat. By watching your opponents carefully, you can first of all improve the boat's trim, then the trim of the sails and finally the adjustment of the centreplate.

If you want to make rapid progress do not try to play "lone wolf" by striking out on a course which makes you lose contact with the others right from the start. Even if you succeed in beating everybody to the first mark you cannot draw any other conclusion from this than that you were extraordinarily lucky. Rather stay close to the other boats and

never cease to study the behaviour of their crews.

Above all you must avoid putting yourself into a position where you get "dirty" wind from a nearby boat. If this happens, alter course immediately, for if you stay close to him you may be led to pass a hasty and inferior judgement on your own boat's performance.

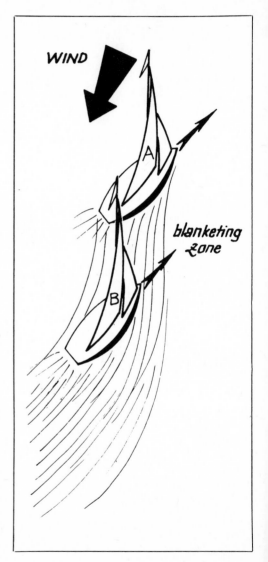

Wind shadow. *B is in the hopeless position.*

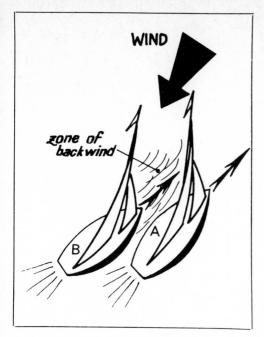

WIND

zone of
backwind

B

A

The wind coming off A's sails violently disturbs the airflow past the lee side of B's sails.

B is in the hopeless position. A is in the safe leeward position.

A good start will put you into a position where you can compete with the best of crews, but you must not, in the heat of the battle, forget the rules. One failure to respond to a starboard-tack yacht, and the best start is ruined. If a wind shift after the start forces you to go onto port tack, make quite sure beforehand that in going about you will not be in another yacht's way. Remember rule 41.

However, on approaching some kind of danger: steep shore, shoal or some other kind of obstruction, you may demand to be allowed to tack, even if another boat is very close to you.

close-hauled, hailing for room to tack at obstructions (rule 43)

1. *Hailing*—When two *close-hauled* yachts are on the same tack and safe pilotage requires the yacht *clear ahead* or the *leeward yacht* to make a substantial alteration of course to clear an *obstruction*, and if she intends to *tack*, but cannot *tack* without

colliding with the other yacht, she shall hail the other yacht for room to *tack*, but she shall not hail and *tack* simultaneously.

2. *Responding*—The hailed yacht at the earliest possible moment after the hail shall either:

(*a*) *tack*, in which case, the hailing yacht shall begin to *tack* either:

(*i*) before the hailed yacht has completed her *tack*, or

(*ii*) if she cannot then *tack* without colliding with the hailed yacht, immediately she is able to *tack* and clear her, or

(*b*) reply "You *tack*", or words to that effect, if in her opinion she can keep clear without *tacking* or after postponing her *tack*. In this case:

(*i*) the hailing yacht shall immediately *tack* and

(*ii*) the hailed yacht shall keep clear.

(*iii*) the onus shall lie on the hailed yacht which replied "You *tack*" to satisfy the race committee that she kept clear.

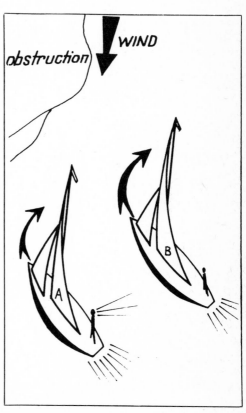

obstruction WIND

B

A

A hails B on approaching an obstruction.

3. Limitations on right to room (rule 43 cont.).

(*a*) When the *obstruction* is a *mark* which the hailed yacht can fetch, the hailing yacht shall not be entitled to room to *tack* and clear the other yacht and the hailed yacht shall immediately so inform the hailing yacht.

(*b*) If, thereafter, the hailing yacht again hails for room to *tack* and clear the other yacht, she shall, after receiving it, retire immediately.

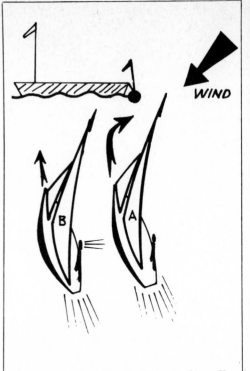

A cannot fetch the mark without tacking. Her helmsman has previously refused to respond to a hail from B asking him to tack. A must retire. Limitation on right to room. Rule 43.3 (c).

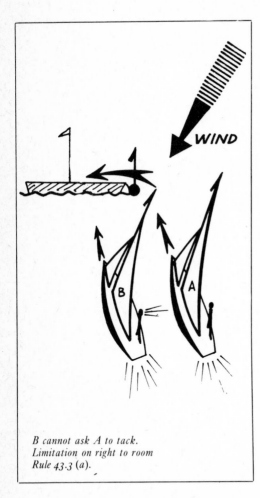

B cannot ask A to tack.
Limitation on right to room
Rule 43.3 (a).

(*c*) If, after having refused to respond to a hail under the rule 43.3 (*a*), the hailed yacht fails to fetch, she shall retire immediately.

But your real difficulties will start on approaching the first mark.

It may be that the wind or the tide or both have shifted the mark. If the race committee know their job they will have provided a "replacement".

mark missing (rule 9.1)

(*a*) When any *mark* either is missing or has shifted, the race committee shall, if possible, replace it in its stated position, or substitute a new one with similar characteristics or a buoy or vessel displaying the letter "M" of the International Code—the *mark* signal.

(*b*) If it is impossible either to replace the *mark* or to substitute a new one in time for the yachts to round or pass it, the race committee may, at its discretion, act in accordance with rule 5.1.

mark unseen (rule 9.2)

When races are sailed in fog or at night, dead reckoning alone should not necessarily be accepted as evidence that a *mark* has been rounded or passed.

Advice on approaching a mark which has to be passed or rounded: Come up to the mark on *starboard tack.* If you are on port tack you are condemned to letting boats on starboard tack pass first, even if you are ahead of them. The longer the string of boats behind you, whose helmsmen have had more foresight than you, the more your chances will dwindle.

At the moment you are about to pass or round a mark, you are bound by the following rules:

rounding or passing marks and obstructions

(rule 42)

When yachts either on the same *tack* or, after *starting* and clearing the starting line on opposite *tacks,* are about to round or pass a *mark* on the same required side with the exception of a starting mark surrounded by navigable water or an *obstruction* on the same side:

when overlapped (rule 42.1 (a))

(i) An outside yacht shall give each yacht *overlapping* her on the inside, room to round or pass the *mark* or *obstruction,* except as provided in rules 42.1 (*a*)(iii) and (iv) and 42.3. Room includes room for an *overlapping* yacht to *tack* or *gybe* when either is an integral part of the rounding or passing manoeuvre.

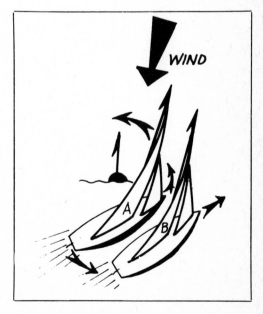

Rule 42.1 (*a*).
B must give A room to tack. If, during the manoeuvre, A's stern comes into contact with B, B has not kept sufficiently clear.

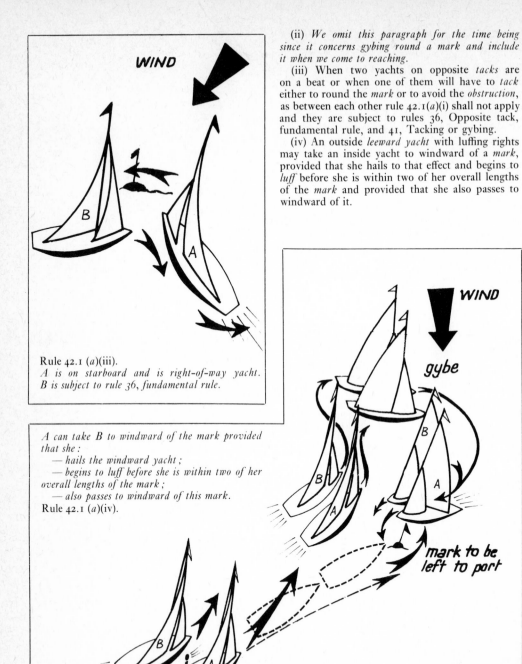

(ii) *We omit this paragraph for the time being since it concerns gybing round a mark and include it when we come to reaching.*

(iii) When two yachts on opposite *tacks* are on a beat or when one of them will have to *tack* either to round the *mark* or to avoid the *obstruction*, as between each other rule 42.1(*a*)(i) shall not apply and they are subject to rules 36, Opposite tack, fundamental rule, and 41, Tacking or gybing.

(iv) An outside *leeward yacht* with luffing rights may take an inside yacht to windward of a *mark*, provided that she hails to that effect and begins to *luff* before she is within two of her overall lengths of the *mark* and provided that she also passes to windward of it.

WIND

Rule 42.1 (*a*)(iii).
*A is on starboard and is right-of-way yacht.
B is subject to rule 36, fundamental rule.*

A can take B to windward of the mark provided that she :
— *hails the windward yacht ;*
— *begins to luff before she is within two of her overall lengths of the mark ;*
— *also passes to windward of this mark.*
Rule 42.1 (*a*)(iv).

WIND

gybe

mark to be left to port

when clear astern and clear ahead (rule 42.1 (*b*))

(i) A yacht *clear astern* shall keep clear in anticipation of and during the rounding or passing manoeuvre when the yacht *clear ahead* remains on the same *tack* or *gybes*.

(ii) A yacht *clear ahead* which *tacks* to round a *mark* is subject to rule 41, Tacking or gybing, but a yacht *clear astern* shall not *luff* above *close-hauled* so as to prevent the yacht *clear ahead* from *tacking*.

Tacking to round a mark. (Rule 42.1 (b)(ii)). A cannot tack to round the mark so close to B that B is forced to alter course to avoid a collision. A is subject to rule 41 in its entirety.

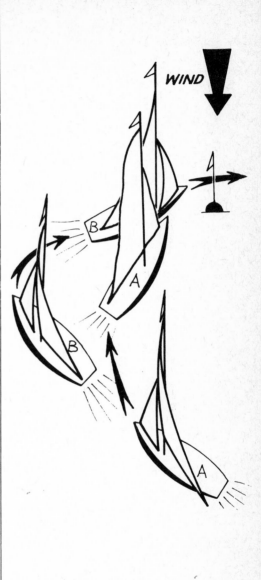

B is clear ahead and can tack to round the mark without interfering with A. A luffs above close-hauled and is going to collide with B. A has infringed the rule.(Rule 42.1(b)(ii), end of phrase.)

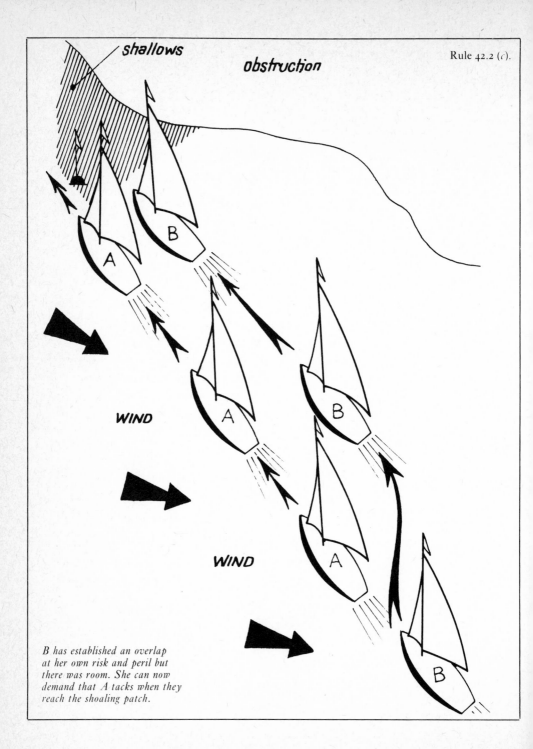

shallows

obstruction

WIND

WIND

B has established an overlap at her own risk and peril but there was room. She can now demand that A tacks when they reach the shoaling patch.

restrictions on establishing and maintaining an overlap (rule 42.2)

(*a*) A yacht *clear astern* shall not establish an inside *overlap* and be entitled to room under rule 42.1 (*a*)(i) when the yacht *clear ahead*:

(*i*) is within two of her overall lengths of the *mark* or *obstruction*, except as provided in rule 42.2 (*b*), and 42.2 (*c*).

(*ii*) is unable to give the required room.

(*b*) The two-lengths determinative above shall not apply to yachts, of which one has completed a *tack* within two overall lengths of a *mark* or an *obstruction*.

(*c*) A yacht *clear astern* may establish an *overlap* between the yacht *clear ahead* and a continuing *obstruction* such as a shoal or the shore, only when

there is room for her to do so in safety (diagram on opposite page).

(*d*) (*i*) A yacht *clear ahead* shall be under no obligation to give room to a yacht *clear astern* before an *overlap* is established.

(*ii*) A yacht which claims an inside *overlap* has the onus of satisfying the race committee that the *overlap* was established in proper time.

(*e*) (*i*) When an outside yacht is *overlapped* at the time she comes within two of her overall lengths of a *mark* or an *obstruction*, she shall continue to be bound by rule 42.1 (*a*)(i) to give room as required even though the *overlap* may thereafter be broken.

(*ii*) An outside yacht which claims to have broken an *overlap* has the onus of satisfying the race committee that she became *clear ahead* when she was more than two of her overall lengths from the *mark* or an *obstruction*.

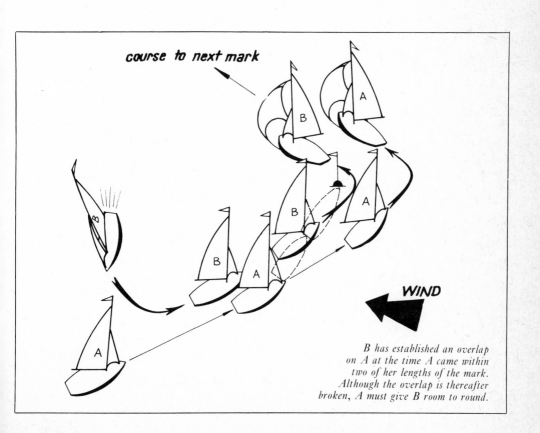

*B has established an overlap
on A at the time A came within
two of her lengths of the mark.
Although the overlap is thereafter
broken, A must give B room to round.*

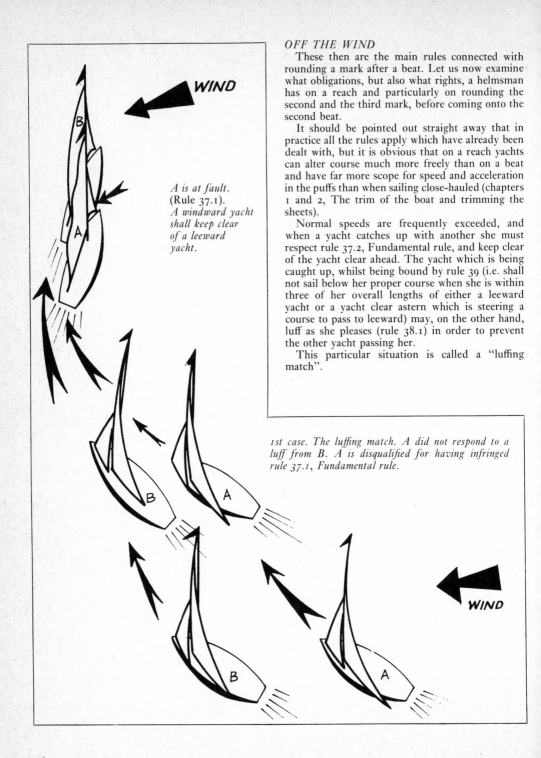

WIND

*A is at fault.
(Rule 37.1).
A windward yacht
shall keep clear
of a leeward
yacht.*

1st case. The luffing match. A did not respond to a luff from B. A is disqualified for having infringed rule 37.1, Fundamental rule.

WIND

OFF THE WIND

These then are the main rules connected with rounding a mark after a beat. Let us now examine what obligations, but also what rights, a helmsman has on a reach and particularly on rounding the second and the third mark, before coming onto the second beat.

It should be pointed out straight away that in practice all the rules apply which have already been dealt with, but it is obvious that on a reach yachts can alter course much more freely than on a beat and have far more scope for speed and acceleration in the puffs than when sailing close-hauled (chapters 1 and 2, The trim of the boat and trimming the sheets).

Normal speeds are frequently exceeded, and when a yacht catches up with another she must respect rule 37.2, Fundamental rule, and keep clear of the yacht clear ahead. The yacht which is being caught up, whilst being bound by rule 39 (i.e. shall not sail below her proper course when she is within three of her overall lengths of either a leeward yacht or a yacht clear astern which is steering a course to pass to leeward) may, on the other hand, luff as she pleases (rule 38.1) in order to prevent the other yacht passing her.

This particular situation is called a "luffing match".

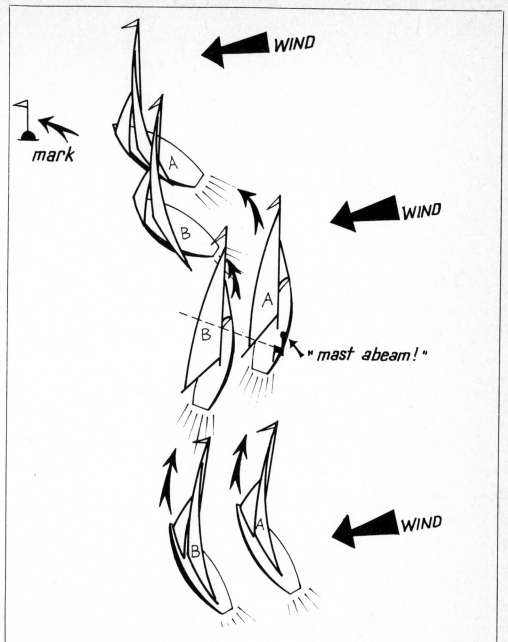

WIND

WIND

mark

"mast abeam!"

WIND

2nd case. The luffing match: A responds to a luff from B, but as soon as A's helmsman comes abeam of B's mast, A must hail "Mast Abeam" and B must immediately resume her proper course to the next mark (rule 38.1, second phrase).

It is thus possible for a yacht to defend herself legally, but once the match is lost (mast abeam) she must accept defeat gracefully. I do not advise beginners to try their skill in an attack of this kind during their first outings, because they risk falling a prey to the "old hands" who will let them come up without batting an eyelid and then suddenly luff, quite unexpectedly. Rule 35 does not apply here. If you are lucky enough to have a faster boat than some of your opponents, pass courteously to leeward of them, but far enough not to be blanketed, or equally far to windward so as not to interfere with them in any way. I know of nothing more odious than to put all one's efforts into pulling the maximum out of a boat and then to see oneself "robbed" of the wind by some bully who passes within several feet to windward. It makes me think of some ruffian who comes along and pushes you away from a good dinner with the sole excuse that he is stronger and he is hungry. This is a case of legitimate defence where one must luff, I nearly said "strike", first.

We now approach the mark round which we will certainly have to gybe. Even if you are well prepared for this manoeuvre, the proximity of others may cause you a moment's anxiety. Stay calm and think about your racing rules. If you have established an inside overlap for some time, hail him to give you room to gybe.

Here paragraph (a)(ii) of rule 42.1 comes in, which I withheld earlier on.

when overlapped : reaching or running on opposite tacks

42.1 (a)(ii). When an inside yacht of two or more *overlapped* yachts either on opposite *tacks*, or on the same *tack* without *luffing* rights, will have to *gybe* in order most directly to assume a *proper course* to the next *mark*, she shall *gybe* at the first reasonable opportunity.

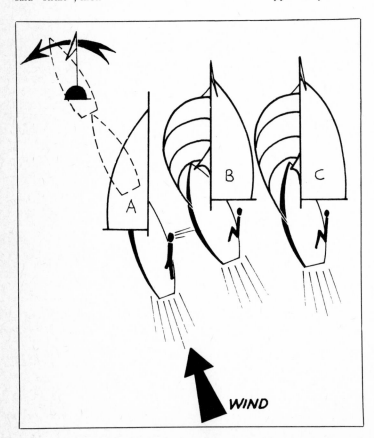

Rule 42.1 (a) (ii). A on the inside is right-of-way yacht. She has to gybe to assume a proper course. The other yachts must keep clear. If there is a collision, they will be at fault.

If you have not established an overlap in time (within two lengths of the mark), keep clear.

You are bound by rule 42.1 (*b*)(i) which we examined earlier on and which is explained, for this particular case, by the illustration below:

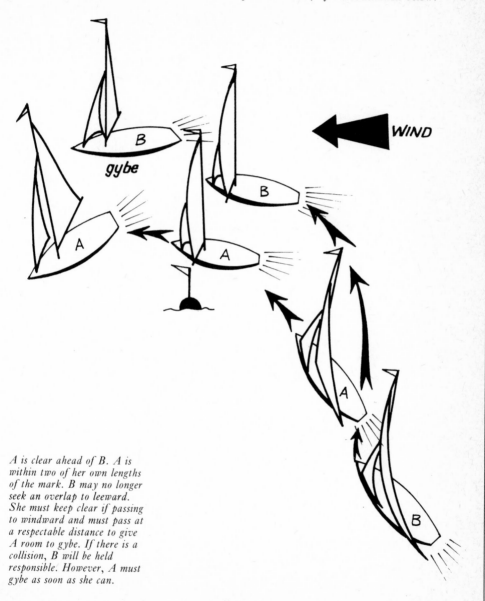

gybe

WIND

A is clear ahead of B. A is within two of her own lengths of the mark. B may no longer seek an overlap to leeward. She must keep clear if passing to windward and must pass at a respectable distance to give A room to gybe. If there is a collision, B will be held responsible. However, A must gybe as soon as she can.

If you are sailing the classic course (marks to port) and have gybed well before reaching the mark and at the same time as some other yacht, watch out if she is overlapping you to leeward, because she may force you to respect rule 42.1 (*a*)(iv), which we have already examined. Her helmsman may only do this strictly according to the rule and, above all, must hail you in good time.

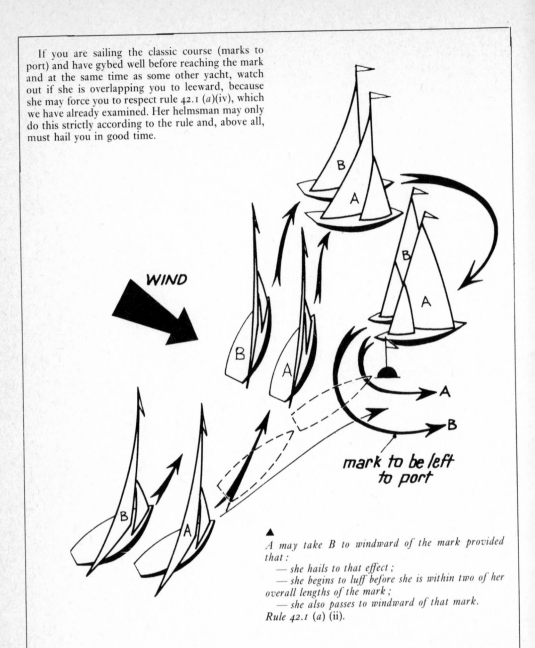

WIND

mark to be left to port

▲

A may take B to windward of the mark provided that :
— she hails to that effect ;
— she begins to luff before she is within two of her overall lengths of the mark ;
— she also passes to windward of that mark.
Rule 42.1 (a) (ii).

Planing towards the mark which 2071 has already rounded.

Finally, if the wind is very fresh and you are not, after all, too happy about gybing, get away from the bunch, go to windward of the mark and gybe there. In this way you may give one or two places away to boats which insist on rounding without losing an inch of ground, but it does by no means follow that they will negotiate such a tricky gybe to perfection, and here is your chance to catch them up on the next leg.

The important thing is always to sail a fair race. You can improve your gybing technique during practice runs. Do not be one of those who do their first (controlled) gybe on the day of their first race.

And if you really feel gybing is beyond you at first, and you think you might capsize and do some damage, do not hesitate to tack round instead. It is better to be modest in the beginning than get a reputation for always having to be rescued.

All you have to do now on the second reaching leg is to get your boat to go well. Think of the hull trim, watch and trim your sails, make use of the puffs, and above all learn by what everybody around you does. Whatever your chances against your opponents, you will discover the joys of racing, probably more so on this point of sailing than in windward work.

Rule 38.

A, faster than B, catches B up and passes to leeward of her. However, A has never been clear abeam of B. She can force B closer to the wind without herself sailing above her proper course for the mark, but she cannot take B to windward of the mark (rule 42.1 (d)). If there is still an overlap between the two within two lengths of the mark, A must give B room to round the mark.

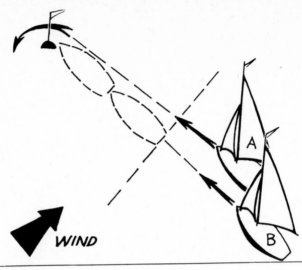

Rule 38.

A, sailing faster than B, has caught B up and is closing in on her from leeward, but at a distance greater than two lengths, i.e. clear abeam. She may luff B and take her to windward of the mark (rule 42.1 (d)).

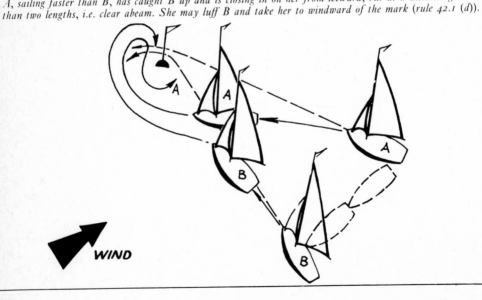

5.5 Metres racing. The leeward yacht is luffing, but the windward yacht seems not to want to respond to the luff. This is an illustration of rule 38 (Right-of-way yacht luffing after starting), particularly of paragraph 3.

Nearly everything has been said now concerning the racing rules. You will still have to round the leeward mark to set off on the second beat, but if you avoid getting yourself into tricky situations, like, for instance, a belated overlap, this rounding should be a mere formality because you can stay on the same tack, coming up from a reach to close-hauled.

Make sure everything is in order as you come onto the beat: lower the centreplate which you have had up on the reach, adjust the kicking strap if necessary and also the position of the mainsheet block on the horse. On the reach you will most certainly have had it set right down to leeward.

As you start off on that beat watch the yachts ahead of you. If they are all going off on port tack, do the same. Do not abandon yourself to the absurd hope that the leading boats are all making a gigantic mistake and that you are going to beat them to the mark on the starboard tack. Of course, if the wind starts heading you, do not hesitate to tack, but never forget rule 41 and keep well clear of following boats.

Be watchful while you are on port tack. Believe me, even "old shellbacks" are caught out like greenhorns in the excitement of tacking on a "header".

As you approach the windward mark you will probably meet the leading boats coming back downwind. Remember that a starboard-tack yacht, whatever her course, has right-of-way over a port-tack yacht. So, if you are on port tack, keep clear. But if you are on starboard tack, you have right-of-way over them (rule 37.1, windward yacht shall keep clear of leeward yacht). In this case you are considered to be sailing closer to the wind. Do not forget to give proper warning by shouting, for example, "close-hauled" if you are on the same tack as the yacht coming towards you, or "starboard" if a port-tack yacht is about to cross your bows.

We have already studied the rounding of the windward mark, so there is no need to go into it again. On the downwind leg, though, follow the advice given earlier. Very often when a spinnaker is used helmsman and crew are so preoccupied while setting it that they forget to keep an eye open for what goes on around them and risk a collision at every instant.

As soon as your spinnaker is trimmed ascertain your position in relation to the other boats going downwind with you.

reaching or running on opposite tacks

A port-tack yacht sailing before the wind is subject to rule 36 in relation to an approaching starboard-tack yacht which is also sailing before the wind. On

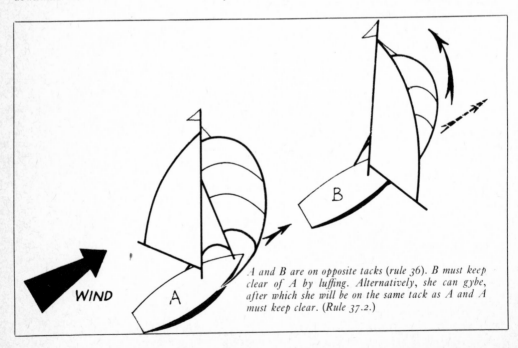

A and B are on opposite tacks (rule 36). B must keep clear of A by luffing. Alternatively, she can gybe, after which she will be on the same tack as A and A must keep clear. (Rule 37.2.)

WIND

F 50, sailing free, attacks to windward.

opposite tacks rule 37.2 does not apply because it is directed at yachts on the same tack.

The only answer for a port-tack yacht is to gybe quickly or to luff in order to keep clear of the right-of-way yacht.

Luffing matches are frequent on that leg. Do not allow yourself to be taken by surprise. Do not yourself luff unless you are sure you are not infringing any part of rule 38. On approaching the leeward mark, watch your overlap. If you have to gybe, and the moment is bound to come sooner or later on this downwind leg, make sure beforehand that in doing so you do not hinder anybody (rule 37.1, 2, 3) and also note whether you are overlapped by other boats (rule 41). Keep your eyes open right to the end of the race. Very often you relax your vigilance through getting tired. It is then that you fail to respond to a right-of-way yacht only a few feet before the finishing line.

Finally, be sure you know where the finishing line is, how it is positioned in relation to the wind and the course you are sailing. Very often a mis-interpretation of the line results in crossing it in a bad place and thereby losing one or even several places.

The finishing line is always defined in the sailing instructions and must conform to rule 6 of the International Racing Rules, which has been explained at the beginning of this chapter.

finishing (rule 10)

Unless otherwise prescribed by the national authority or in the sailing instructions, in races where there is a time limit, one yacht *finishing* within the prescribed limit shall make the race valid for all other yachts in that race.

The finishing signal is described in rule 4.5.

Finishing signals (rule 4.5). Blue flag or shape. When displayed at the finish means: "The committee boat is on station at the finishing line."

Paragraph 5 of rule 51 says: "It is not necessary for a yacht to cross the finishing line completely. After finishing, she may clear it in either direction." However, the sailing instructions usually stipulate that a yacht must clear the finishing line completely and must leave its proximity and the finishing area by rounding either the committee boat or the finishing mark so as not to be in the way of boats crossing the line after her.

If, during the course of a race, you have been put at a disadvantage by an opponent who has infringed some rule or other, you have to lodge a protest with the race committee as soon after the race as possible and then bow to certain formalities which will be dealt with in the following section: protests, disqualifications and appeals.

protests, disqualifications and appeals

contact between yachts racing

1. When there is contact between the hull, spars, standing rigging or crew of two yachts while racing, and neither of them retires in acknowledgement of an infringement or acts in accordance with rule 68.3 Protests, then upon a protest by a third yacht which witnessed the incident, or by action of the race committee, both shall be disqualified.

2. A third yacht which witnesses an apparent collision between two yachts and sees that one or both of the yachts involved is showing a protest flag is relieved by rule 68.3 (*b*) from the requirement of showing a protest flag when she discovers after finishing that no protest has been lodged.

3. The race committee may waive this rule when it is satisfied that minor contact was unavoidable.

protests (rule 68)

1. A yacht can protest against any other yacht, except that a protest for an alleged infringement of the rules of Part IV can be made only by a yacht directly involved in, or witnessing an incident.

2. A protest occurring between yachts competing in separate races sponsored by different clubs shall be heard by a combined committee of both clubs.

3. (*a*) A protest for an infringement of the rules or sailing instructions occurring during a race shall be signified by showing a flag (International Code flag "B" is always acceptable, irrespective of any other provisions in the sailing instructions) conspicuously in the rigging of the protesting yacht at the first reasonable opportunity and keeping it flying until she has *finished* or retired, or if the first reasonable opportunity occurs after *finishing*, until acknowledged by the race committee. In the case of a yacht sailed single-handed, it shall be sufficient if the flag (whether displayed in the rigging or not) is brought to the notice of the yacht protested against as soon as possible after the incident and to the race committee when the protesting yacht *finishes*.

(*b*) A yacht which has no knowledge of the facts justifying a protest until after she has *finished* or retired may nevertheless protest without having shown a protest flag.

(*c*) A protesting yacht shall try to inform the yacht protested against that a protest will be lodged.

(*d*) Such a protest shall be in writing and signed by the owner or his representative, and should state:

(*i*) The date, time and whereabouts of the incident.

(*ii*) The particular rule or rules or sailing instructions alleged to have been infringed.

(*iii*) A statement of the facts.

(*iv*) Unless irrelevant, a diagram of the incident.

(*e*) Unless otherwise prescribed in the sailing instructions, a protesting yacht shall deliver, or if that is not possible, mail her protest to the race committee:

(*i*) within two hours of the time she *finishes* the race, or within such time as may have been prescribed in the sailing instructions under rule 3.2 (*b*) (*xv*), unless the race committee should have reason to extend these time limits, or

(*ii*) when she does not *finish* the race, within such a time as the race committee may consider reasonable in the circumstances of the case.

A protest shall be accompanied by such fee, if any, as may have been prescribed in the sailing instructions under rule 3.2 (*b*) (*xv*).

(*f*) The race committee shall allow the protestor to remedy at a later time:

(*i*) any defects in the details required by rule 68.3 (*d*) provided that the protest includes a summary of the facts, and

(*ii*) a failure to deposit such fee as may be required under 68.3 (*e*) and prescribed in the sailing instructions.

4. (*a*) A protest that a measurement, scantling or flotation rule has been infringed while *racing*, or that a classification or rating certificate is for any reason invalid, shall be lodged with the race committee not later than 18.00 on the day following the race. The race committee shall send a copy of the protest to the yacht protested against and, when there appears to be reasonable grounds for the protest, it shall refer the question to an authority qualified to decide such questions.

(*b*) Deviations in excess of tolerances stated in the class rules caused by normal wear or damage and which do not affect the performance of the yacht shall not invalidate the measurement or rating certificate of the yacht for a particular race, but shall be rectified before she *races* again unless in the opinion of the race committee there has been no practical opportunity to rectify the wear or damage.

(*c*) The race committee, in making its decision, shall be governed by the determination of such authority. Copies of such decision shall be sent to all yachts involved.

5. (a) A yacht which alleges that her chances of winning a prize have been prejudiced by an action or omission of the race committee, may seek redress from the race committee in accordance with the requirements for a protest provided in rules 68.3 (d), (e) and (f). In these circumstances a protest flag need not be shown.

(b) When the race committee decides that such action or omission was prejudicial, and that the result of the race was altered thereby, it shall *cancel* or *abandon* the race, or make such other arrangement as it deems equitable.

6. A protest made in writing shall not be withdrawn, but shall be decided by the race committee, unless prior to the hearing full responsibility is acknowledged by one or more yachts.

7. Alternative Penalties. When so prescribed in the sailing instructions, the procedure and penalty for infringing a rule of Part IV shall be as provided in Appendix 3, Alternative Penalties for Infringement of a Rule of Part iv.

refusal of a protest (rule 69)

1. When the race committee decides that a protest does not conform to the requirements of rule 68, Protests, it shall inform the protesting yacht that her protest will not be heard and of the reasons for such decision.

2. Such a decision shall not be reached without giving the protesting yacht an opportunity of bringing evidence that the requirements of rule 68 were complied with.

hearings (rule 70)

1. When the race committee decides that a protest conforms to all the requirements of rule 68, Protests, it shall call a hearing as soon as possible. The protest, or a copy of it, shall be made available to all yachts involved, and each shall be notified, in writing if practicable, of the time and place set for the hearing. A reasonable time shall be allowed for the preparation of defence. At the hearing, the race committee shall take the evidence presented by the parties to the protest and such other evidence as it may consider necessary. The parties to the protest, or a representative of each, shall have the right to be present, but all others, except one witness at a time while testifying, may be excluded. A yacht other than one named in the protest, which is involved in that protest, shall have all the rights of yachts originally named in it.

2. A yacht shall not be penalised without a hearing, except as provided in rule 73.1 (a), Disqualification without protest.

3. Failure on the part of any of the interested parties or a representative to make an effort to attend the hearing of the protest may justify the race committee in deciding the protest as it thinks fit without a full hearing.

decisions (rule 71)

The race committee shall make its decision promptly after the hearing. Each decision shall be communicated to all parties involved and shall state fully the facts and grounds on which it is based and specify the rule or rules, if any, infringed. If requested by any of the parties such decisions shall be given in writing and shall include the race committee's diagram. The findings of the race committee as to the facts involved shall be final.

disqualification after protest and liability for damages (rule 72)

1. When the race committee, after hearing a protest or acting under rule 73, Disqualification without Protest, or any appeal authority, is satisfied:

(a) that a yacht has infringed any of these rules or the sailing instructions, or

(b) that in consequence of her neglect of any of these rules or the sailing instructions she has compelled other yachts to infringe any of these rules or the sailing instructions, she shall be disqualified unless the sailing instructions applicable to that race provide some other penalty. Such disqualification or other penalty shall be imposed, irrespective of whether the rule or sailing instruction which led to the disqualification or penalty was mentioned in the protest, or the yacht which was at fault was mentioned or protested against, e.g. the protesting yacht or a third yacht might be disqualified and the protested yacht absolved.

2. For the purpose of awarding points in a series, a retirement after an infringement of any of these rules or the sailing instructions shall not rank as a disqualification. This penalty can be imposed only in accordance with rules 72, Disqualification after protest, and 73, Disqualification without protest.

3. When a yacht either is disqualified or has retired, the next in order shall be awarded her place.

4. The question of damages arising from any infringements of these rules or the sailing instructions shall be governed by the prescriptions, if any, of the national authority.

disqualification without protest (rule 73)

1. (*a*) A yacht which fails either to *start* or to *finish* may be disqualified without protest or hearing, after the conclusion of the race, except that she shall be entitled to a hearing, provided she satisfies the race committee that an error may have been made.

(*b*) A yacht so penalised shall be informed of the action taken, either by letter or by notification in the racing results.

2. When the race committee:

(*a*) sees an apparent infringement by a yacht of any of these rules or the sailing instructions (except as provided in rule 73.1), or

(*b*) has reasonable grounds for believing that an infringement resulted in serious damage, or

(*c*) receives a report not later than the same day from a witness who was neither competing in the race, nor otherwise an interested party, alleging an infringement, or

(*d*) has reasonable grounds for supposing from the evidence at the hearing of a valid protest, that any yacht involved in the incident may have committed such an infringement, it may notify such yacht thereof orally, or if that is not possible, in writing, delivered or mailed not later than 18.00 hours on the day after:

(*i*) the finish of the race, or

(*ii*) the receipt of the report, or

(*iii*) the hearing of the protest.

Such notice shall contain a statement of the pertinent facts and of the particular rule or rules or sailing instructions believed to have been infringed, and the race committee shall act thereon in the same manner as if it had been a protest made by a competitor.

penalties for gross breach of rules (rule 74)

1. When a gross infringement of any of these rules, the sailing instructions or class rules is proved against the owner, the owner's representative, the helmsman or sailing master of a yacht, such persons may be disqualified by the national authority, for any period it may think fit, from either steering or sailing in a yacht in any race held under its jurisdiction.

2. Notice of any penalty adjudged under this rule shall be communicated to the I.Y.R.U. which shall inform all national authorities.

3. After a gross breach of good manners or sportsmanship the race committee may exclude a competitor from further participation in a series or take other disciplinary action.

persons interested not to take part in decision (rule 75)

1. No members of either a race committee or of any appeals authority shall take part in the discussion or decision upon any disputed question in which he is an interested party, but this does not preclude him from giving evidence in such a case.

2. The term 'interested party' includes anyone who stands to gain or lose as a result of the decision.

expenses incurred by protest (rule 76)

Unless otherwise prescribed by the race committee, the expenses entailed by a protest on measurement or classification shall be paid by the unsuccessful party.

appeals (rule 77)

1. Unless otherwise prescribed by the national authority which has recognized the sponsoring organization concerned, an appeal against the decision of a race committee shall be governed by rules 77, Appeals, and 78, Particulars to be supplied in appeals.

2. Unless otherwise prescribed by the national authority or in the sailing instructions (subject to rule 2 (*j*) or 3.2 (*b*) (*xvii*)), a protest which has been decided by the race committee shall be referred to the national authority solely on a question of interpretation of these rules, within such period after the receipt of the race committee's decision, as the national authority may decide:

(*a*) when the race committee, at its own instance, thinks proper to do so, or

(*b*) when any of the parties involved in the protest makes application for such reference.

This reference shall be accompanied by such deposit as the national authority may prescribe, payable by the appellant, to be forfeited to the funds of the national authority in the event of the appeal being dismissed.

3. The national authority shall have power to uphold or reverse the decision of the race committee, and if it is of the opinion, from the facts found by the race committee, that a yacht involved in a protest has infringed an applicable rule, it shall

disqualify her, irrespective of whether the rule or sailing instruction which led to such disqualification was mentioned in the protest.

4. The decision of the national authority, which shall be final, shall be communicated in writing to all interested parties.

5. (*a*) In the Olympic Regatta and such international regattas as may be specially approved by the I.Y.R.U., the decisions of the jury or judges shall be final.

(*b*) Other international regattas shall be under the jurisdiction of the national authority of the country in which the regatta is held, and if satisfied that a competent international jury has been appointed, it may give consent for the decisions of the jury to be final.

6. An appeal once lodged with the national authority shall not be withdrawn.

particulars to be supplied in appeals (rule 78)

1. The reference to the national authority shall be in writing and shall contain the following particulars, in order, so far as they are applicable:

(*a*) A copy of the notice of the race and the sailing instructions supplied to the yachts.

(*b*) A copy of the protest, or protests, if any, prepared in accordance with rule 68.3 (*d*), and all other written statements which may have been put in by the parties.

(*c*) The observations of the race committee thereon, a full statement of the facts found, its decision and the grounds thereof.

(*d*) An official diagram prepared by the race committee in accordance with the facts found by it showing:

(*i*) The course to the next *mark*, or, if close by, the *mark* itself with the required side;

(*ii*) The direction and force of the wind;

(*iii*) the set and strength of the current, if any;

(*iv*) the depth of water, if relevant; and

(*v*) the positions and courses of all the yachts involved.

(*vi*) Where possible, yachts should be shown sailing from the bottom of the diagram towards the top.

(*e*) The grounds of appeal, to be supplied by either:

(*i*) the race committee under rule 77.2 (*a*); or

(*ii*) the appellant under rule 77.2 (*b*).

(*f*) Observations, if any, upon the appeal by the race committee or any of the parties.

2. The race committee shall notify all parties that an appeal will be lodged and shall invite them to make any observations upon it. Any such observations shall be forwarded with the appeal.

yacht materially prejudiced (rule 12)

When, upon the request of a yacht made within the time limit provided by rule 68.3 (*e*) or upon her own initiative, the race committee decides that, through no fault of her own, the finishing position of a yacht has been materially prejudiced, by rendering assistance in accordance with rule 58, Rendering assistance, by being disabled by another yacht which was required to keep clear, or by an action or omission of the race committee, it may *cancel* or *abandon* the race or make such other arrangements as it deems equitable.

note

The whole of this rule rests on the word **may**. In fact the race committee has complete authority in this matter. It alone judges the circumstances. However, one would be justified in asking oneself whether, at that moment, rule 58 which I have quoted among the basic rules (that is to say in its fullest sense) can really be given priority by any committee.

Only recently, at a meeting of a racing rules committee, all the persons present, whose competence cannot be doubted, unanimously agreed that there had never been a case of a race being cancelled or abandoned because of a yacht having been or claiming to have been unduly prejudiced.

One could criticize this at length, but in my opinion rendering assistance to a crew in danger comes before the finishing position one may hope to attain. Of course, rescue services are becoming more and more numerous on the water, and there is hardly a club today that can not raise at least one rescue launch for every five to ten boats in a race.

As far as collisions are concerned, I prefer to let you think this problem out for yourself, hoping that you may never be the one who causes a collision.

In your first race or races, always provided that you are not sailing with other beginners and that everything goes well as far as the racing rules are concerned, you will certainly not stand much chance against the best boats in your class. But after all, they draw on the experience which you, too, hope to acquire.

You will most certainly make the annoying discovery that many boats point higher and go faster than yours. This difference will be one of the reasons for your rather mediocre finishing position in your first races. Your handling of the boat is most probably to blame for this, and before starting a lot of clever "experimenting" as so many young racing helmsmen do, have another look at the theory of sailing and the techniques prescribed by it.

I vividly remember how, during my first races, I

never pointed as high nor went as fast as the other boats. I puzzled over the cause of my bad luck for a long time until, one day, I read Ted Well's "Scientific Sailboat Racing" and realized that one has to luff in the puffs. This for me was a veritable revelation, and without knowing the deeper reason behind this rule, because the book did not give it, I improved my performance beyond my wildest dreams.

Only if after many attempts you are absolutely convinced that your boat is inferior to others of the same class should you consider making alterations to the hull, the rigging and the sails.

You will have to start by re-examining the balance of the boat, i.e. the relation between the centre or centres of effort and the centre of lateral resistance, and also whether the rudder blade is straight (chapter 2).

If it is well balanced the boat should be able to keep up with the best of them. But, as I said earlier on, to be able to compare performances, if only for a few minutes, you must be in close contact with the fleet immediately after the starting signal.

In fact, it may only be in those few moments immediately after the start that you will be close to the best crews and boats.

Experienced helmsmen usually know how to place their boats favourably along the starting line, and it is only logical that while you are "learning the ropes" you should try to copy them.

But there would hardly be any need for this book if all I had to do in each chapter was to advise the reader simply to observe what goes on around him. It is only normal for a keen helmsman to want to be more than just a sheep in a flock, even if he is at the head of the herd.

the start

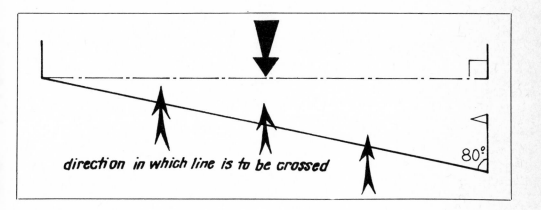

direction in which line is to be crossed

80°

Even in the opinion of experts on yacht racing the start is one of the chief factors essential to success. Some of them go as far as to claim that out of all the racing tactics the start accounts for 40% of the success.

The consequences of a mediocre start in a top class race can be catastrophic. And, other things being equal, the boat that bungles her start suffers a serious handicap by comparison with her opponents.

Before discussing the various manoeuvres which are to help a helmsman to cross the starting line in an excellent or at least in a good position, let me say that we are only dealing here with a windward start, which means a beat to the first mark. Some stretches of water, by their shape, make it impossible in certain wind conditions for the com-

mittee to offer competitors a classical course and its accompanying orthodox start. But for the purpose of this section we will assume the course to be of the kind prescribed for championship races by the national authority.

Theoretically, the starting line, which must have sufficient length for all the contestants to cross easily (allowing 15 to 30 ft. per boat) must be at right angles to the direction of the wind. However, in practice such a line favours the windward-end yachts (starboard tack). The yachts towards the port end usually lose distance by virtue of their position in relation to the windward-end boats and suffer a serious handicap at the start. To avoid this, the starting line is laid in such a way that the port end is slightly further to windward so that the line is at an angle of 75° to 80° to the wind instead of 90°.

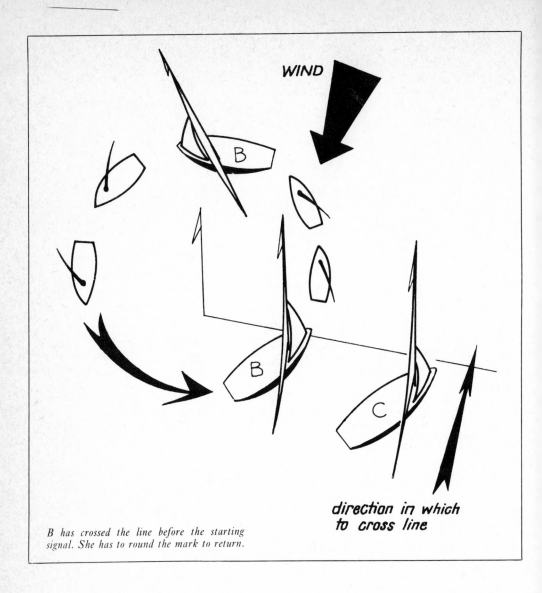

WIND

direction in which
to cross line

*B has crossed the line before the starting
signal. She has to round the mark to return.*

In this way a yacht starting at the leeward (port) end of the line is ahead of a boat starting at the windward end, and all positions along the line can be considered fair.

Beginners must remember that to make a correct start they must know the general and the particular sailing instructions for the race in which they are taking part. They must remember that 10 minutes before the starting signal the race officers display the class flag of the boats which are about to start. This is the signal to be ready. Five minutes later the race officers break out the code flag P of the International Code, known among racing men as the "Blue Peter" (rectangular blue flag with a white rectangle in the centre).

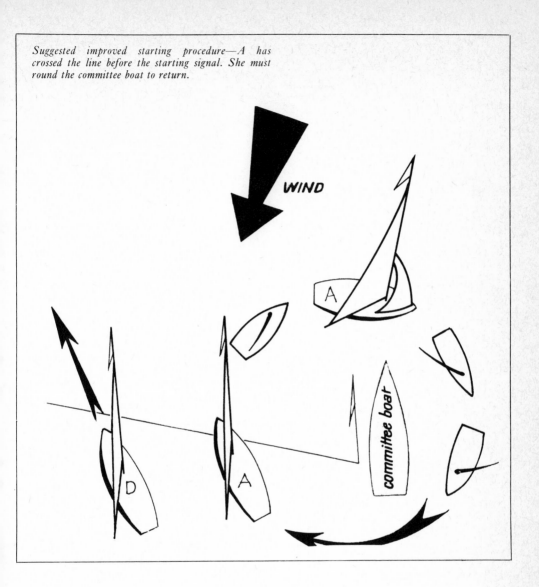

Suggested improved starting procedure—A has crossed the line before the starting signal. She must round the committee boat to return.

WIND

A

D

A

committee boat

This is the preparatory signal. From now on all the contestants engaged in the race of the class indicated at the 10-minute signal have to comply with the racing rules.

Until recently, the national authority imposed the 'five-minute rule' (boats may not cross the line in the wrong direction after code flag 'P' has been broken out but must return round the ends of the line).

The I.Y.R.U. has recognised the benefit of such a rule and now stipulates that any yacht across the starting line less than one minute before the starting signal shall return by rounding either end of the line.

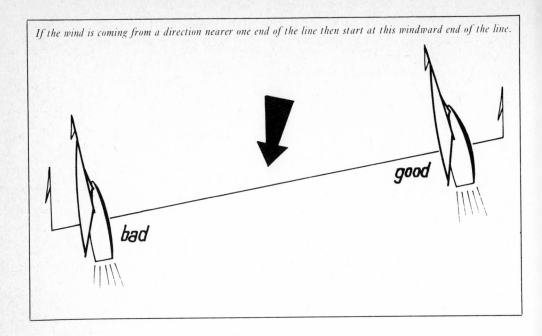

good

bad

After these preliminary explanations we can now come to the start. It is absolutely essential to have a stop watch, by the way. Without this a proper start is impossible.

You should also have a watch synchronized with the clock used by the race committee, so that you know at any moment how much time there is left before the start. This is as useful to old hands as it is to beginners. It happens all too frequently that helmsmen get to the line several seconds before the start, or even several minutes after.

But it is not enough to be at the committee boat in time for the warning signal. Even ten minutes is too short a time to prepare for a good start. Especially if the wind is fresh, you should spend twenty to thirty minutes sailing between the committee boat or the leeward mark and the windward mark. There are several reasons for this. Firstly to warm up your muscles, to make last minute adjustments to the set of the sails, to see that all the gear is functioning properly, and finally—and most important of all—to try and get an idea of the wind shifts to be expected, the state of the sea, the strength of the currents in different parts of the course where you will be sailing during the race. Of course, you must be familiar with the times of change of the tide to know where and when it will turn (chapter 2). Wind shifts, even on an area of water quite distant from the land, frequently

make one tack more favourable than the other. It is a good idea then to determine in plenty of time which is the tack to take after the gun. This will influence where you start on the line. However, the line may have been laid in such a way that the choice of which end to start from is made difficult. How then do you determine the ideal position?

First make a practice start at the windward end of the line on starboard tack and sail close-hauled at maximum speed for two or three minutes. You must time this very precisely. Then estimate the distance travelled along an imaginary line drawn at right angles to the starting line. Go through the same procedure starting at the leeward end of the line on port tack.

Repeat these two tests at least twice to eliminate errors caused by possible wind shifts. You will eventually come to one of three conclusions:

(*a*) The distance made good is virtually the same on either tack. Any point along the line is good to start from and the final choice will depend on which tack you have determined as favourable during your half hour of preparation.

(*b*) The distance made good is greater on starboard tack: start from the starboard end of the line.

(*c*) The distance made good is greater on port tack: start at the port end of the line but nevertheless on starboard tack to have right-of-way.

Example of a perfect port-tack start. No. 2102 crosses the line at the port end (above), cuts across the bows of a large part of the fleet that has started on starboard tack and gets ready to tack (below) to lead the race.

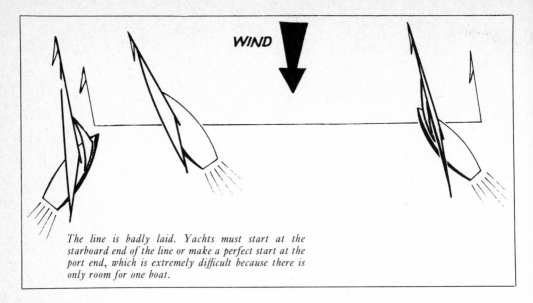

WIND

The line is badly laid. Yachts must start at the starboard end of the line or make a perfect start at the port end, which is extremely difficult because there is only room for one boat.

If the starboard tack is only very slightly more favourable you can consider at least half the line as being good to start from and you need not despair if you fail to get the key position right next to the windward mark. Once you have decided to start from a certain point along the line you must not allow yourself to be put out by anything except of course, by *force majeure*, like for instance a sudden wind shift in the last two minutes before the start. Self-confidence is imperative in these few moments which have such a great influence on the rest of the race.

In high performance classes where one finds many crack helmsmen it is usual to see boats lined up like soldiers on parade in the last thirty seconds before the start.

Lined up before the start.

Above : Flying Dutchmen thirty seconds before the start. Below: after the start ; all boats have started on starboard tack. H.74 is well placed.

You must expect that other helmsmen, too, will have worked out the best point to start from. If you arrive too late you risk being deprived of the best position. But once you have got it you must hang on to it, and that is a most tricky problem.

It is always difficult and even practically impossible to keep a sailing boat stationary for more than a few seconds (5 to 10) as soon as the wind exceeds 5 knots. Even with the sails stalling, i.e. shaking, the boat still moves very slightly.

The stronger the wind, and especially if the sea is rough and there is some current, the more the boat will drift. If it is a case of wind against tide, the latter will take the boat inexorably towards the line.

It follows that you must not arrive at the line too soon, but neither must you get there too late or you may find the place already occupied. Through plenty of practice you will soon acquire this sense of timing. There is yet another piece of advice which you should bear in mind: avoid placing yourself next to someone very much better than yourself, because for sure he will get the better of you immediately after the gun and put you in an impossible position. For example:

1. If you get a helmsman shrewder than you to leeward of you, he will very quickly work himself into a *safe leeward position* and backwind you. It will be impossible for you to break away by going on the other (port) tack, because the other yachts sailing on starboard tack prevent you from doing so. You will then be condemned to wait until all the yachts up to windward have passed before you can get out of this fix.

2. If a champion starts to windward of you he will quickly blanket you because he will have got his boat moving at maximum speed, at the same time sailing very close to the wind. In no time you will find yourself in a tricky situation and be in the same unfortunate position.

Above: F.D. start. Opposite page: 5.0.5 start.

Let us assume then that we have one or two minutes to go before the start. All our attention must now be focussed on the stop watch. It must be frequently consulted, and to make this easier it should not be hung round the neck as some skippers do but fastened to the wrist or placed somewhere *in the cockpit where it can easily be seen.* Single-handers have no other choice. But skippers with a crew can entrust the stop watch to them. The crew must call out every 30 seconds up to the last minute, from then on every 10 seconds to the half minute and finally every 5 seconds until the gun. If preferred the crew can call out the last 10 seconds one at a time, but this "count down" may unnerve the helmsman because at this moment "the die is cast" and all his attention ought to be fixed on handling the sheet and the tiller.

But before this decisive moment there are these 120 seconds, these two little minutes, in which the start is "composed". These are certainly the most important seconds, and one false move would cause the loss of all the advantages gained through careful placement along the line.

what should you aim at ?

1. Make a flying start and cross the line at speed, not on the gun, though, for that is very difficult and there is always the risk of crossing too soon. You must be very careful and try to cross *immediately after the starting signal.*
2. Having no-one to leeward of you, and this is the most important. A leeward yacht will try to

stop you passing by luffing hard—that is her right—and thus prevent you from gathering speed. You will then be passed by the boats to windward. (Rule 38.1, 2, 3, 4, 5.)

Let us wind our "film" back and start again at zero minus 2 minutes. We are going to prepare for a flying start which will be followed by a close-hauled course sailed at maximum speed.

There is one way to make a flying start: as soon as you are very close to the line bear away to fill the sails thus gathering speed, and then luff to come back on the wind again. But the rule is clear: it is forbidden to bear away on another yacht, the leeward yacht always having right-of-way and the windward yacht having to keep clear (rule 37). However, it is not forbidden to bear away 10 to 15 ft. to gather speed if there is no boat to leeward for at least 30 ft. (Definitions: *Proper Course,* last sentence.) At such a distance the leeward yacht will not be inconvenienced and it will be impossible for her to interfere with the windward yacht by luffing since she would be left without speed, sails flapping. The answer is therefore to create a "hole" to leeward, a space some 30 ft. deep.

To do this, we employ the same rule as before, but this time to our advantage, that is to say we luff the boat or boats to windward *slowly* (rule 40) but progressively, thus making room to leeward. There again this manoeuvre must not be started too soon because there is the risk of making a present to another helmsman who has been lying in wait to take advantage of this exceptional amount of room. This final phase of the start can only be started during the last 30 seconds.

A difficult start at the port end of the line very well negotiated by No. 1847.

Flying Dutchman start. The complete sequence will be found in the section on "Racing Tactics" on the fold-out panel.

Having thus crossed the line at full speed at a chosen point and relatively unhindered by opponents the helmsman has nothing further to do than sail as fast as possible and point high. After two or three minutes of this "sprint" he can concentrate on local and general tactics.

Apart from the training courses run for racing helmsmen by some classes and organizations where complete sessions are devoted to the practice of starting techniques, a young racing helmsman can only practice this first and difficult phase of the course in races organized by the clubs. There are usually no more than three regattas in any one class per day, and they are most frequently held on Sundays. This is not really enough to acquire a high degree of skill quickly, and it often takes more than one season to get good results.

The many imponderables that can intervene (wind shifts, daring opponents who steal your place at the last moment, and almost invariably fools who jostle or bear down on you) make even old hands "miss" a start sometimes.

But we do not want to indulge in pessimism. One thing is certain: a correct start which allows you to sail in close contact with the best boats at the beginning of the race will show you whether or not your boat is well tuned.

If you are certain that the balance is right, that the centre of effort and the centre of lateral resistance are correctly placed, and yet the boat lacks speed or will not sail as close as the others, you can only come to the conclusion that the "engine" is to blame, in other words that your sails are defective and do not pull as well as the rest.

the sails

There is a veritable psychosis among racing men over the sail "which pulls". One win in a championship is enough to attract a flood of orders to the maker of the winning sails. Since the performance of a suit of sails cannot be measured with speed indicator and chronometer certain people do not hesitate to indulge in the most painstaking and often puerile experiments while others dare not part with a suit of sails with which they have once won a race.

If often happens that a suit of sails, in particular the mainsail, does not set particularly well. This can be cured by changing the bend of the mast in making adjustments to the crosstrees or where the mast is held at deck level. But let it be said at once that a good sail will always set well on a good mast whatever the strength of the wind and however hard it is sheeted in.

If you are sure that you have a good mast, there is nothing left but to take the sails along to the sailmaker. As with a sculptor, the sailmaker's manual skill and craftsmanship only form the basis of a complex and exacting trade. In order to achieve good results the sailmaker must have considerable experience, accumulated by observations made over years. He must have a certain knack and the kind of affinity with his materials which alone ensures success in this race for performance.

Any kind of sail, as long as it is strongly made, is suitable for the leisurely sailor who is not out to squeeze the highest possible speed out of his yacht. But when it comes to a racing sail, other problems have to be considered.

To start with the sailmaker knows very well that however good his cut he cannot get lasting and unvarying results unless he uses the best quality material.

If a sail sets badly and gets worse as the wind freshens then this is largely due to the choice of a poor quality cloth.

As in all things there is a choice between several qualities of sail cloth. This was already so in the days of cotton, which could be strong and very fine at the same time and made into high performance sails, and it is still so today in the age of synthetic materials. But it must be said that quality always pays.

The conscientious sailmaker, with a trained eye, knows how to choose the material which is capable of taking the strains imposed on it by the strong pull of ropes and winches. That is to say it must possess a perfect resistance to tearing and a relatively low coefficient of stretch.

This latter property is definitely the more important. One rarely sees a sail tear, but quite often, in fact much too often, one can see sails that stretch excessively.

In strong winds a sail of medium fullness can thus quickly take on the scarcely aesthetic appearance of a "sack of potatoes", or the entire luff may stretch and flatten or distort the sail so much that the boat can no longer compete with others in speed or weatherliness.

However, since dinghies are equipped with flexible spars the cloth must have a certain "give" in it, and it would be quite wrong to use a material which is too rigid and refuses to stretch at all.

Synthetic sail cloth is made up of pre-stretched synthetic threads whose tensile strength is determined exactly and its fineness is expressed in "deniers".

It is thus possible to obtain a whole range of threads of different tensile strengths.

The cloth is woven in the classical manner by interweaving at right angles the threads constituting the warp (lengthwise) and the threads constituting the weft (across) in a ratio of two to one. Thus we have two warp threads to every one weft thread, and it follows that the latter will have to have a greater "denier" strength than the warp threads.

For example, 80-denier threads are used for the warp and 130-denier threads for the weft.

After having been woven the cloth undergoes various thermo-chemical processes aimed at fusing the threads together so as to give the cloth its final finish and quality.

The cloth generally comes in bales of several hundred yards 36 in. wide and is of varying thickness, weight and strength according to the strength of the threads used. This is expressed in oz. per sq. yard. The cloth used for dinghy sails is generally between $3\frac{1}{2}$ and $7\frac{1}{2}$ oz. per sq. yard.

In calculating the shape of the sail the sailmaker must take into account two particular properties of the cloth. To start with, despite meticulous precautions taken during manufacture to obtain a stable material, synthetic cloth has an *initial stretch*. This appears when the cloth is put under strain and more particularly in the ready-made sail when it is used for the first time.

After this the cloth becomes stable and the sail will take up its full shape even in the faintest breeze.

Nevertheless the cloth will always possess a certain elasticity. That is to say that under the pressure of the wind or the bending of the spars the cloth "gives", stretching slightly and returning to its former size as soon as the tension is removed.

This property is an advantage since it allows the cloth to adapt itself better to changes in the shape of the spars, but if the elasticity is too great the sail stretches excessively and takes on a disastrous shape.

It is a good idea, before proceeding, to have a look at how the sails work and what rôle they play in the *speed* and *weatherliness* of a yacht.

Whether we are talking about a mainsail, a jib or a spinnaker, the terminology is the same:

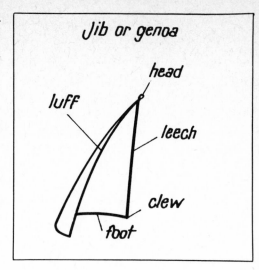

Luff : leading edge of the sail.

Leech : trailing edge by which the larger part of the airflow escapes.

Foot : lower edge of the sail.

The action and the movement of the airflow is more or less the same for the different types of sail, but a mainsail, being usually made fast to a boom, has a pocket along its foot which prevents the air from escaping at the lower edge of the sail. Jibs and spinnakers are loose-footed and allow the air to escape in this way.

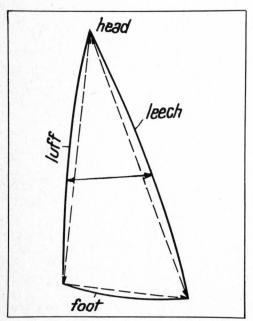

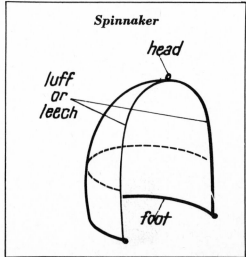

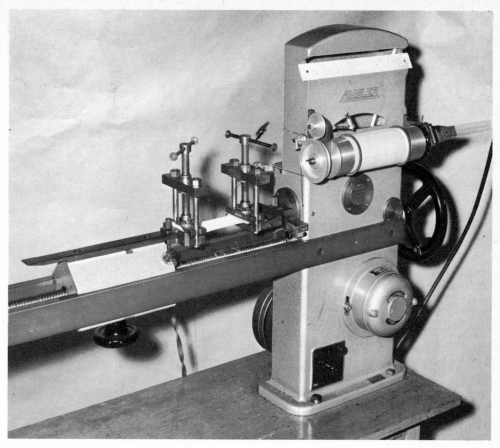

A machine for testing sail cloth.

The sails are influenced by the apparent wind, which gives rise to the aerodynamic force. By means of the mast and the running and standing rigging this is transmitted to the hull where it acts as driving force. The sails in effect are the engine of the sailing boat.

A sail, as was pointed out earlier on, has two sides: a concave or windward side and a convex or leeward side.

This sail is used on the wind (at an angle of incidence of less than 25° to the apparent wind) when the airflow is *laminar* (unstalled), and with the wind aft, when it is *turbulent*.

On the wind, in order to benefit from the optimum aerodynamic force, the angle of incidence between the chord of the sail and the apparent wind must be around 22° and the sail must have a camber of 1/7 (maximum depth of curvature/ratio chord) (chapter 1).

However, when it comes to sailing close-hauled a sail with a camber of this magnitude would demand an angle of incidence in the neighbourhood of 22°, as mentioned before, to make it fill and take up its proper shape.

We know that such an angle is not desirable when close-hauled (chapter 1) and that it is much more profitable to diminish the angle of incidence.

The ideal solution consists in being able to modify the curvature of the different sails according to the point of sailing. Since most jibs are loose-footed, the foot and at the same time the whole sail can be given a more pronounced curvature by easing the sheets. The same solution cannot be applied to mainsails because they are made fast to the boom along the foot.

It is therefore the mainsail for which some means of adjustment has to be found.

For several years experiments have been made in an effort to find a compromise: a sail with a variable curvature, flat on the wind, full off the wind.

Two Olympic classes, first the Star and then the Finn, were used to try out this new technique.

In the case of the Star the complex rig with shrouds, lower shrouds and runners allows *certain changes to be made in the shape of the mast*.

On the Finn the mast can be bent quite simply by putting tension on the sheet.

In both cases, *the mast, by bending, "absorbs" much of the camber of the sail and modifies its shape*.

When the boat is close-hauled in a fresh breeze it is necessary to get the upper part of the sail completely flat, allowing for the helicoidal shape of the sail. High up the sail the angle of incidence is very small, and it must be reduced even more to lessen the strong heeling force. If the mast is very flexible in its upper part it brings about this flattening of the sail by pulling the cloth forward. In this way the camber is taken up completely and, what is more, the leech is opened out to allow a swifter exit of the airflow on the windward side of the sail.

Another system, consisting of a zip fastener along the foot of the sail, has recently been abandoned. In fact, the changes in the camber which could be obtained in this way has but little effect on the efficiency of the sail.

The most recent solution is to have a full sail with the biggest camber very low down so that it has no effect on the performance of the sail close-hauled, even in a fresh wind. Following the example set by the Finn, most dinghies of all types are now equipped with flexible masts.

The airflow escaping by the leech can be compared in its effect with the exhaust of an internal combustion engine.

Everyone knows that the exhaust of an engine influences the input. If the expulsion of the burnt gases does not function smoothly, the motor gets choked. The output of an engine can be improved by accelerating the exhaust (by polishing the ducts or improving their design, for example).

In a strong wind the "exhaust" of a sailing boat can be accelerated by allowing a certain amount of heel. The sails are then no longer normal to the direction of the apparent wind and the exit of the airflow is eased.

The stronger the wind, the more air strikes the sail and the more the leech must be capable of delivering the airflow, taking into account the fact that the suction on the leeward side of the sail increases at the same rate. The leech must be made to open up further and further the more the wind increases in strength.

A flexible mast solves this problem; in bending it stretches out part of the sail, takes up the excess of camber and opens out the leech at the same time as tension is applied to the sheet.

If the theory appears simple enough, the application of these principles is much less so. In fact the sail must be so cut that it adapts itself to the changing shape of the mast without developing folds and creases that would be detrimental to its performance.

Since mainsail, jib and spinnaker have a concave form, the sailmaker must calculate their *area* by projection and make sure that the dimensions conform to the class rules.

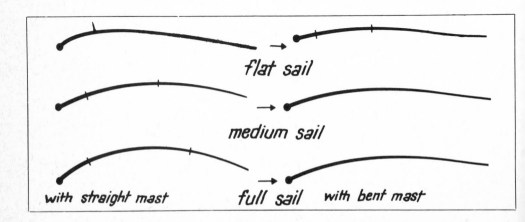

flat sail

medium sail

with straight mast   full sail   with bent mast

mainsails

Lofting—The class rules usually stipulate four measurements for mainsails. While working to them the sailmaker must take into account the residual stretch of the cloth in calculating the camber.

(*a*) the height of the luff;

(*b*) the length of the leech;

(*c*) the length of the foot;

(*d*) distance between point half way up the luff and point half way up the leech. This is intended to limit the amount of roach. For a Finn, for example, the measurements are 5700 mm. for the luff, 3270 mm. for the foot, 6000 mm. for the leech, and 1950 mm. for the mid-width. The amount of excess cloth allowed by the mid-width measurement is not put exclusively on the leech, because in this way the luff would remain straight. Since the sail, once hoisted, is completely one with the mast and the changes in shape which it undergoes, it is essential that a round of some size be put into the luff so that when the sail fills the excess cloth will make its surface concave. It is this operation of lofting the round that demands particular care on the part of the sailmaker. Under the pull of the mainsheet and by the intermediary of the boom and the sail itself the mast bends in a fore-and-aft direction, and in doing so absorbs part or all of the round made by the excess cloth on the luff.

Distributing the excess cloth between the luff and the leech presents a tricky problem to the sailmaker, for, as one might imagine, there are scarcely two masts having the same flexibility or rigidity and bending in exactly the same way.

This brings us again to the property of instant stretch in the cloth. Since this amounts to a few millimetres only it follows that the calculation and lofting of the luff needs to be very precise. An important consideration in this connection is the fact that *the cloth stretches more along the weft than along the warp.*

Some curvature is also given to the sail by a round on the foot, the excess cloth being taken up when the sail fills.

But this is not all that is needed to produce a sail in which the camber is correctly distributed and stays well distributed, even when the mast and boom are acutely bent.

Some of the camber has to be pre-shaped by darts, and tucks either incorporated in the seams of the panels (true seams) or placed between the seams (false darts).

Their number, width and length varies from one sailmaker to another. Presumably this is a trade

Lofting table on which a long, flexible batten is laid out to trace out the rounds.

secret. Along the leech too, the two or three lower panels can be darted for a certain length to get a better set to the leech in the lower part.

When lofting is completed the sailmaker proceeds to lay out the cloth over the top and cut the panels according to the lofting.

Assembling the sail—The panels are assembled and the sail in its rough shape matched up against the lofting in order to mark off the three sides of the sail, taking into account the excess cloth needed for sewing into the bolt ropes along the luff and foot.

The sailmaker uses stabilized and pre-stretched rope, so that whatever the tension applied to the luff and the foot when the sail is in use, these two sides return to their original length.

The following operations are only mentioned as a matter of interest, because they have no influence on the efficiency of the sail:

— putting in the batten pockets;

— sewing the tabling (hem) along the leech;

— reinforcing the clew, tack and head of the sail, the latter with a headboard consisting of two triangular pieces of light alloy or plastic material;

— sewing on insignia and sail number.

The sail is now finished and it is in use that the racing helmsman will assess its quality. However, even a sail made of top quality cloth can become distorted in the long run. If this happens the sailmaker can restore its shape. He can also "correct" a sail which does not give complete satisfaction from the start.

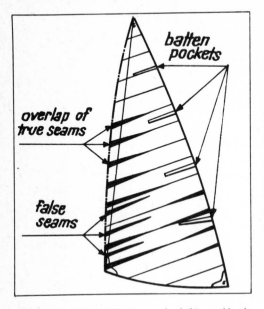

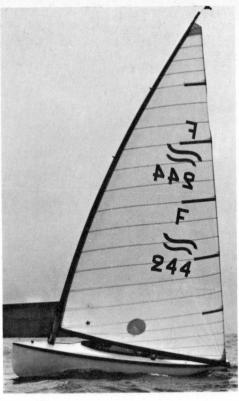

When the cloth is laid out on the lofting table the darts can be arranged with great precision.

Mast and sail on this Finn are perfectly matched. Note the darts along the lower third of the luff.

▼

But it must be said straight away that the fullness obtained by the darts along the luff cannot be reduced and that only the rounds on the luff and foot as well as the darts in the leech can be altered when sailing.

Here are a number of things which can go wrong:

(1) Despite the mast being bent to its maximum, the sail remains too full at the top. Conclusion: the luff has too much round in its upper part.

Alterations to be made: unrope the luff over a good length; to be quite sure unrope the whole of the luff; re-cut the round to make it less pronounced than before, particularly where you have noticed excessive fullness.

(2) When the sail is hardened in, creases run from the luff to the after end of the foot and split the sail into two parts (ill. below).

Conclusion: the round on the luff is not sufficient for the curvature of the mast.

Alterations to be made: unrope the whole luff; sew on a strip of cloth 2 in. to 4 in. wide down the entire length of the luff and re-cut the round to make it more pronounced than it was before. When you have finished check the mid-width measurement. If the sail does not measure up, which it almost certainly will not, the leech will have to be re-cut as well.

(3) The sail, when sheeted in hard, opens up excessively all down the leech, particularly in its lower part.

Conclusion: the round on the after end of the foot is insufficient.

Alterations to be made: unrope the foot for about 3 to 5 ft. starting at the clew and re-cut the round from a point 1½ to 2 in. higher up on the leech. Or better unrope the entire foot, add a strip of cloth 1½ to 2½ in. wide and re-cut the round to make it more pronounced, particularly in the after part.

Finally, if this is not enough, re-shape the panel seams along the leech, starting by initially taking in about ½ in. over 2 to 3 ft. of seam and on one seam only.

(4) The leech of the sail is too "closed", i.e. curves too much to windward in its upper part.

Conclusion: the round on the luff is too great. Proceed as for (1).

(5) The leech sags in its upper half without any creases appearing near the mast.

Conclusion: the cloth has been stretched at this point. The seams of one or two panels will have to be taken in at the leech.

Light creases appear in the sail of No. 204. In No. 75 they are already more pronounced which suggests that the mast of this Finn bends too much for the round allowed on the luff of the sail.

jibs

While in designing a mainsail the eventual changes in shape of the mast and boom must be taken into account, the design of jibs and genoas is governed by entirely different considerations.

The camber of a mainsail can partly be taken up by the bending of the mast and boom. In the case of a jib it is different: as soon as the luff wire or the forestay "bend", i.e. sag under the pressure of the wind and the pull from the sheet, the jib becomes even fuller.

The stronger the wind, the more rigid the standing rigging must be, and in a dinghy this rigidity is obtained by hoisting the jib up hard. However, when the boat is sailed and particularly so when it is sailed close-hauled, the simultaneous action of the kicking strap and the mainsheet cause the mast to bend.

But at the same time the jib itself has an effect on the mast. The very strong pull exerted at the clew of the jib transmits itself to the tack and the head of the sail. A downward pressure comes onto the mast at the hounds, which tends to "squash" it and thereby accentuates the bend brought about by the kicking strap and the sheet pushing the boom forward.

The pull of the jib is at an oblique angle to the centre-line of the boat and although the mast is held in place at deck level it will manage to escape the stress by bending sideways and to windward. This in itself is not harmful since it widens the slot between the mainsail and the jib and increases the suction effect by accelerating the airflow past the leeward side of the mainsail (chapter 1).

But the curvature of the mast must be kept within limits, and it is possible to control it by cross trees and also longitudinal wedges at deck level.

The bend of the mast both forward and sideways lowers the hounds quite noticeably. The tension on the shrouds is relaxed, and this has an immediate effect on the luff of the jib.

It is therefore obvious that jibs and genoas must on no account be as full as mainsails; the leech too is most frequently straight or even concave, or at best very slightly convex in classes where the rules permit the use of short battens (Star, 5.0.5). This is to prevent the leech shaking or being too strongly cambered, both of which would disturb the exit of the airflow.

The foot may be rounded, though, since this adds to the area of the jib and is very profitable off the wind.

A dart 6 to 12 in. high half way along the foot stops the foot from shaking.

On a mainsail the pull of the sheet comes on the whole of the foot through the intermediary of the boom. On a jib or genoa the pull is concentrated in one point: *the clew*. The sail is consequently subjected to considerable strain which results in an excessive stretching of the cloth. The larger the foresail the more work it does and the greater the force needed at the clew to overcome the resistance. This can easily be proved by handling the jib of a 5.0.5 in comparison with the genoa of a F.D., for example. It takes a much greater effort on the part of the crew to sheet in the F.D.'s genoa than it does to sheet in the 5.0.5's jib. The logical conclusion is that the stretch the cloth suffers is proportional to the size of the sail: a genoa goes out of shape more quickly than a jib, a jib more quickly than a mainsail.

There are several ways of cutting jibs and genoas. The most logical way, if one considers that the sheet pull is on a line more or less coinciding with the bisector of the clew angle (or more precisely a line from the clew to a point half way up the luff) is to cut the jib with a diagonal seam coinciding with the sheet pull.

A mitre-cut requires a good deal of manual skill both in lofting and in assembling the sail, but its advantages are well recognized. Another cut is the "sun-ray" cut which distributes the sheet pull evenly over the entire area of the sail.

All the panels come together at the clew and radiate symmetrically towards the luff. The assembly here is simple, but the sailmaker must reckon on using more material because there is considerable wastage.

Another drawback is that since the leech is cut out of a single panel it is almost impossible to take it in if it stretches out of shape. If this happens the material has to be cut and false darts made.

Different cuts in two 5.0.5 jibs: cross-cut on the left, mitre on the right. No. 1271 has a "sun-ray" or "fan-cut" mainsail.

The jib of the boat on the left shows the kind of cut most frequently used. Lofting, assembly and subsequent alterations are relatively simple with this type. However, one can easily see that the cloth, particularly the seams of the panels, "work" badly. This is very obvious on genoas which stretch out of shape more frequently with this cut than with any other.

Lofting:

The class rules usually stipulate three measurements: luff, leech and foot.

In the Flying Dutchman class only the measurement for the foot is laid down in the rules, the luff and leech are free: they are determined by the position of the mast.

For example, if the mast is placed as far aft as possible and given a rake of 50 thousandths, the luff of the genoa will have a maximum length and the leech a minimum height.

If the mast is positioned as far forward as is permissible and kept absolutely vertical, the luff will be at its shortest and the leech at its longest. In this case the sailmaker must obviously be given very precise instructions by the owner, because the dimensions of the foresail will depend on how he wants to trim his mast.

Light-weather jibs and genoas are cut with a convex luff and sometimes several "genuine" darts not exceeding $\frac{1}{8}$ in. in width are put in to pre-shape the camber, as for the mainsail.

There are no "false" darts, though.

A jib or genoa can be given a very pronounced round at the foot, as long as the class rules permit it, and its area increased in this way. But to ensure that this droop-foot will not be prone to shaking it is advisable to put a vertical dart in the middle or one or two short battens, 4 to 6 in. long. If the leech has a slight roach (between $\frac{3}{4}$ in. and $1\frac{3}{4}$ in. deep) it will be necessary to support it with two or three short battens between 6 in. and 10 in. long.

In a "medium" jib, which is the most commonly used type, the luff may still be slightly rounded, but there must be no darts in the panel seams. There can be a round on the foot, but the leech must be straight, unless battens are allowed.

In a "heavy weather" jib the luff is straight and the upper third or quarter may even be slightly concave. When the sail is sheeted in, this concavity provokes a flattening of the sail and the strong pull of the sheet opens up the leech in its upper part to facilitate the exit of the airflow.

Taking into account the "instant" stretch of the cloth, the shape of genoas is somewhat different. The leech in particular calls for a slightly concave profile, but the foot has a very much greater round.

Assembly:

The panels of cloth are laid out at right angles to the leech and sewn together. The three edges are cut according to the lofting and a hem sewn along the luff which takes the luff wire. It is here that an important stipulation must be made:

It is absolutely essential that the luff of jibs and genoas has a stainless steel wire incorporated in it.

Anyone using anything else shows complete ignorance in matters of aerodynamics and tuning a boat. It is quite obvious that a foresail cannot set correctly, and that means efficiently, if its luff can stretch, because the cloth would stretch with it, the more so the stronger the wind and the stronger the pull on the halyard.

It is equally essential for the tension on the luff hem to be adjusted independently of the wire itself.

It can then be relaxed in light weather and tautened in fresh winds. The hem must be permanently fixed to the wire at the head and loose at the tack, where an eyelet is let into it by which the tension can be adjusted with the help of a line.

Let us now have a look at what can go wrong with jibs and genoas and how faults can be remedied.

Note the different cuts of jibs on these Dragons.

the leech of the jib shakes excessively

This can be caused by the mast being raked too far aft, or the fairlead is too far aft.

If this is not the case, the leech may have stretched. Some sailmakers make their sails with an adjustable leech line by which this undesirable and upsetting shaking can be eliminated. Although it may look and sound better afterwards it is undoubtedly bad practice, because it closes the leech and interferes with the smooth exit of the airflow. It is better to try and find another solution, and there are in fact several which might bring good results:

(*a*) shorten the leech by re-cutting the foot to come up to a point on the leech *above* the clew cringle.

(*b*) undo the tabling along the leech and cut it off, then replace it by a strip of new and stronger cloth. It is fairly certain, though, that the after part of the panels has also stretched. In that case;

(*c*) take in the lower panels very slightly at the seams ($\frac{1}{12}$ in. to $\frac{1}{6}$ in. over 1 ft.);

(*d*) cut a crescent-shaped strip of cloth off the leech to give it a concave profile.

the jib is too full along the luff

If it is impossible to get the sail flat in a fresh breeze the round on the luff is too great. Undo the luff hem, then re-cut the luff. Trace the new luff in pencil before cutting.

the jib is too flat

The round on the luff is insufficient.

(*a*) Proceed as before, but increase the round in re-cutting it.

(*b*) Sew a hem onto the luff the after edge of which is convex, so that it adds fullness to the sail.

(*c*) Take some cloth in at the panel seams to pre-shape the camber. The result will be a light-weather jib which can never be completely flattened.

the foot of the jib shakes

There may be too much round on it. This is not serious if the class rules allow the use of battens. If not, try putting one or two vertical darts along

the foot. Do not cut anything off the round unless it is absolutely necessary.

spinnakers

These headsails are unique in being extremely full, deeply cambered and having to set perfectly even in a very light wind (there are spinnakers with an area of over 5000 sq. ft. (ill. on opposite page).

Attached at three points only, head, tack and clew, the spinnaker seems to symbolize geometry in space.

It is made up from a multitude of panels, the particular cut of which gives it its distinctive, semi-spherical shape, and it is without doubt the sail-maker's masterpiece.

The sailmaker, in fact, proceeds by trial and error in finding the ultimate shape of the spinnaker, but first of all he has to "imagine" this shape. Maybe it is not too far-fetched then to speak in terms of art.

In making a mainsail the sailmaker has two spars to go by: the mast and the boom, which immediately provide him with the general shape of the sail.

For a jib or genoa the only fixed line provided is a rigid hoist, namely the luff wire. But when it comes to a spinnaker, which only takes on its proper shape when it is filled, and then only with the wind behind it, the sailmaker has to rely entirely on his imagination in designing it. He then has to draw up its projection in a two-dimensional plan and in putting it into practice allow for the initial and the elastic stretch of the material he uses. The materials used for dinghy spinnakers are very lightweight ($1-1\frac{1}{2}$ oz. per sq. yd.) and are therefore extremely flimsy. To achieve the deep curves of a spinnaker various cuts have been employed in turn from a herringbone pattern to a star shape.

Just lately, since it has become apparent that spinnakers of round or semi-spherical shape give the best performance on all points of sailing, that is from dead before the wind to a reach, horizontal panels have been the most commonly used. It is relatively simple to achieve a good shape by this method and the waste of material is cut to minimum. This means a saving both in time and material. Since there is no middle seam it is more lightly constructed.

At one time spinnakers were chiefly used before the wind and on a broad reach, but since racing techniques were hotted up helmsmen have taken to using them on a reach.

At this point we will take another look at the behaviour of the apparent wind.

If two boats of different type follow the same course, even if the true wind is identical for both we know that they are in fact moved by an apparent wind made up of the true wind and the wind created by the boat as it moves through the air mass.

The faster the boat, the faster the wind created by it, and consequently the stronger the apparent wind and the more acute the angle at which it strikes the sails (chapter 1).

As shapes of dinghy hulls improved and become faster, so it became necessary to change the shape of spinnakers so that they could be used over a larger range of courses. The increasing use of the Olympic course with its two reaching legs has also supported this development.

If a sail is very full, its angle of incidence with the apparent wind must be rather large to allow the sail to fill, but it must not exceed 25° or else there will be turbulence on the leeward side of the sail (sudden drop in aerodynamic force, chapter 1) when the boat is sailing close-hauled—and fast modern dinghies *do* sail close-hauled on a reach.

As a result of such investigation modern spin-

nakers have a medium camber and are rather flat, but large and round in outline so that they can make use of the maximum sail area allowed by the class rules.

The two edges, leech and luff respectively, are pre-stressed and accentuate the generally concave aspect of the whole sail. The foot is cut with a pronounced round which droops. This is assured of a good set by a vertical dart or two as in genoas.

It can happen that a spinnaker sets in an unsatisfactory way when it is put up: the luff and foot may have a tendency to shake or to curve to windward. This is usually caused by improperly tensioned boltropes, but it can also happen as a result of the panels being badly cut. If shortening the boltropes in the first case or stretching them in

the second does not improve matters, it is advisable not to embark on alterations which might end up in chaos. It is better to return the spinnaker to the sailmaker it came from and tell him what is wrong with it.

As far as the foot is concerned it is possible to make certain alterations yourself, for instance taking in the dart if the droop-foot does not set satisfactorily.

Yet the good behaviour of this capricious sail depends above all on the skill of the crew handling it. The first pre-requisite is therefore to make it a permanent and well-used item amongst the boats' equipment, and not to consider it a dangerous and even mysterious sail for occasional use only in favourable conditions.

fittings

With sails that "pull" well, a boat that is perfectly tuned, a good starting technique and a thorough knowledge of the racing rules a helmsman can hope for a certain measure of success in racing.

But in order to win he must also have plenty of fighting morale, which means also complete confidence in his gear. Nothing must be neglected, and even the smallest detail can play an important part in getting all the luck on his side.

Being faster not only means attaining a greater speed through the water but also not losing time in manoeuvres.

Fittings which are neat and practicable and have been well "run-in" during regular training ensure that all manoeuvres are performed smoothly and practically with closed eyes.

When racing, failure to observe a single one of these rules may lead to unpleasant incidents of which there can be dozens.

The following are the most frequent:

— the helmsman lets the tiller slip out of his hand while he is tacking and the boat goes back on the old tack;

— the jib sheet (the leeward one!) pulls out of the fairlead;

— the jib or spinnaker cannot be set because the jib stick or spinnaker boom is hopelessly fouled up in the halyards in the bottom of the boat;

— the centreplate suddenly comes up during a tack, or the rudder on a reach or a run, when a strong wind and a lively sea running make matters tricky anyhow;

— the spinnaker halyard comes undone at the masthead because a shackle has opened;

— the spinnaker boom drops into the water or simply keeps coming off at the mast or the spinnaker tack. . . .

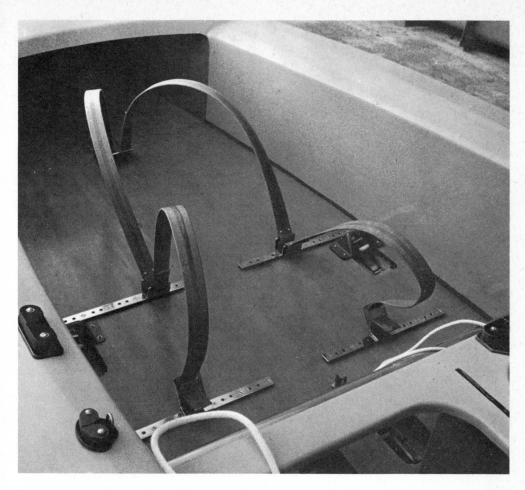

Toestraps which can be adjusted both fore-and-aft and sideways.

We will leave it at that because these things are probably less serious in their consequences than ill-adjusted toestraps or badly hoisted sails.

I want to introduce here an entirely subjective element: the fastest boat cannot do better than its helmsman. The problem has two aspects: firstly it is useless to gain a few lengths on a windward leg if afterwards you throw them away at the mark. Secondly, to keep a boat "fast" from beginning to end of a race, it is essential that certain fittings be capable of adjustment as the wind changes. The height of the toestraps above the cockpit floor is very important, so that the sitting-out position is always efficient and comfortable. Except for the type made of machine belting (Finn), toestraps are prone to frequent expansion and contraction and particularly so during the course of a race under the influence of sun and water. It is therefore important that there should be a means by which they can be re-tensioned quickly. A simple way is drawing them through a buckle. It is equally important that they should be within easy reach of one's feet, that is held up by a piece of shock cord instead of lying limp at the bottom of the boat.

The strap must pass over the instep, not across the toes. By having it pass over your toes you may be able to get out further by an inch or two, but the increased leverage you get in this way is not worth having compared with the extra strain it imposes.

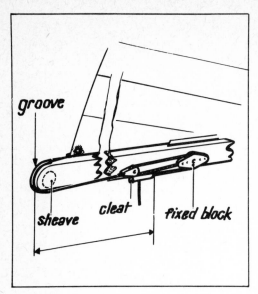

Close-up of clew outhaul tackle.

The sails.

It is not uncommon to meet with considerable changes in the strength of the wind during the course of a race. It is essential, therefore, that the set of the sails should be quickly adjustable to changing weather conditions. Sailing in light weather with the shrouds too taut and the sail stretched out too much along the luff and foot is as disastrous as sailing in heavy weather with the shrouds slack and the sail setting badly (chapter 2).

Adjusting the tension along the luff is always easy because the tack is within reach of the crew, except, of course, on single-handers. But the foot is a different matter. Not only is the clew always securely made fast to prevent the boom track from opening out at this point, but it is also mostly out of reach of the helmsman.

A simple solution is to fit a sheave or a piece of bent tubing to the end of the boom and a simple trumpet-type cleat further forward on the boom. This system can be improved by fitting a purchase between the cleat and the boom end.

With this arrangement the camber of the mainsail can be altered in seconds.

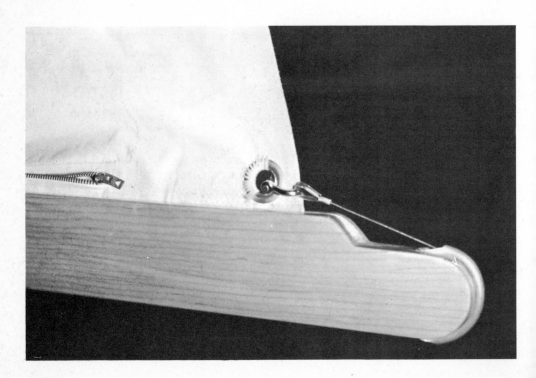

Tack adjustment on a sloop.

On single-handers (Finn and Moth) a particularly well thought-out system compensates for the lack of hands aboard. The problem of adjustments under way is particularly difficult to solve in this case. Off the wind the helmsman must give the sail its fullness by slackening off the luff and foot, and on the wind he must tauten them again without ever letting go of the tiller or leaving his sitting-out position.

Here is one solution:

The tack of the sail is rounded off and fitted with two eyelets, one on the luff about 8 in. above the boom and the other 8 in. from the mast.

A piece of line, one end of which is made fast on deck near the mast, passes through both eyelets, crosses the deck via a fairlead close to the mast and is fixed to the becket of a block.

The block makes a double purchase via a line which can be adjusted equally from a sitting-out position to port or to starboard.

This clever little gadget has immediately attracted the attention of two-man boats, and many crews of 5.0.5's and F.D.'s have adopted it.

The head of the sail is firmly held up by a knot ▶ or a talurit splice on the halyard which locks in the notch of a metal tang fitted to the forward edge of the mast.

The clew is either made fast in the normal way or it can be adjustable. In this way, with the help of two tackles, it is easy to control the tension on both luff and foot (ill. below).

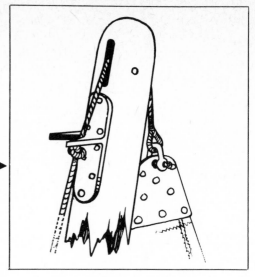

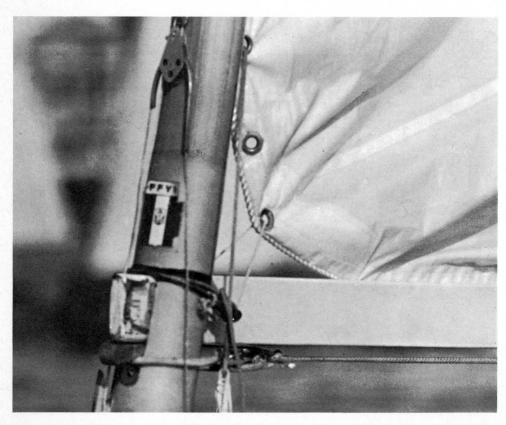

We know that the tension on the jib luff determines the tension on the shrouds. In a fresh breeze it must be very taut, in light winds it must be just enough to prevent the mast from shifting. The forestay is no more than a safeguard and it is unnecessary to attach the jib to it. It is therefore a good idea to leave off the hanks, especially since they tend to be a nuisance to the spinnaker.

But a good tension on the luff wire does not mean that the tension on the jib luff itself has to be the same.

Most boats have their jib set on a stainless steel luff wire which runs freely inside the luff hem. The cloth is fixed to the wire at the head, but at the tack it is left loose and fitted with an eyelet so that the tension on it can be adjusted by means of a simple lashing or better still an adjustable line running through a cleat on deck near the mast.

Advice on tensioning the jib luff: Despite the fact that the luff tension falls entirely on the mast and the forestay plays the rôle of a "preventer" only, it often happens that the luff goes slack and sags, and this is very detrimental to the boat's ability to go close to the wind.

As the mast bends, the jib halyard goes slack: the section of the mast between the jib halyard sheave and the point at which the halyard is attached to the head of the jib now forms an arc, the chord of which is shorter than the arc itself.

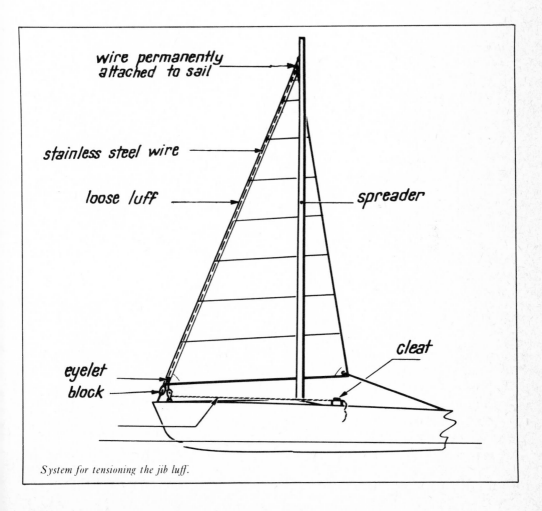

System for tensioning the jib luff.

There are two ways of avoiding this:

— the halyard incorporates a locking device like the one used for the main halyard. During the course of a race tension can then be adjusted from the tack by means of a Highfield lever with a multiple setting. With this method a roller jib cannot be used.

— the halyard, after having been passed through a block, is returned to the tack and made fast with a Highfield lever with multiple setting. With this method the jib can be rolled up.

With either method someone has to go forward to adjust the tension.

On boats carrying a genoa it is essential to be able to open the leech very quickly if the wind freshens otherwise the boat becomes unmanageable.

If the class rules do not allow the sheet leads to be moved aft (e.g. Flying Dutchman) the mast can be raked a little further aft. The shrouds should then incorporate Highfield levers. These are normally released and can be closed to tension the shrouds and at the same time rake the mast aft.

It is sometimes necessary to ease the genoa luff at the same time.

Most sailmakers stick to the traditional custom of making the luff permanently fast to the wire with a medium tension. In that case I would advise you to simply cut the luff loose at the tack and fix a means to make the tension adjustable.

Finally, to stop the foresheets from slipping through their fairleads and to make them easier to get hold of at the moment of tacking it is advisable to tie their ends into a figure-of-eight knot.

▼

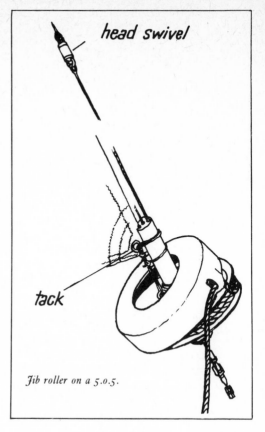

Jib roller on a 5.0.5.

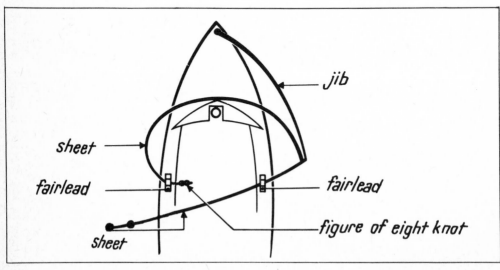

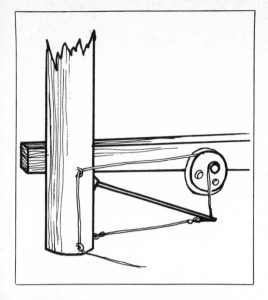

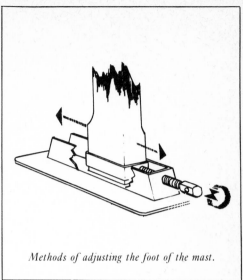

Methods of adjusting the foot of the mast.

More and more these days, pulley-operated kicking straps in racing boats are being replaced by a reel winch; advantages are less space and more power. On dinghies with jibs this reel winch is normally placed at the forward end of the centreboard housing (the photo is of a Flying Dutchman); on una or cat rigged boats, it is normally mounted on the boom itself (see drawing, which shows an OK dinghy).

I do not pretend to have mentioned here all the clever devices that have been thought up to help the helmsman win places . . . and races. There are many more of minor importance which you may have come across yourself, and no doubt you will think of new ones yourself. Thinking them up and fitting them to your boat can keep you busy for many a week-end during the winter, preparing for another successful racing season.

racing tactics

As I said right at the beginning of this chapter tactics are undoubtedly the most interesting part of racing.

There are, however, two entirely different sides to it: tactics in *general* and *local* tactics. The former are intimately linked to a sort of sixth sense, refined by long practice, which allows the helmsman to interpret and put to use the natural elements, wind and current.

We have seen in chapter 2 what it means to sail in tidal waters and near the coasts where the wind is very often modified in strength and direction by the shape of the coastline and also by atmospheric fluctuations (thunderstorms, exposure to sun, etc.).

Local tactics on the other hand are rather more precise since they are bound by the racing rules, applied in a restricted area and directed at opponents in relatively close proximity. If you have a boat which is as fast as the others you can employ local tactics to shake off opponents and outwit them. But local tactics can only be put to successful use if they are backed by a perfect knowledge of the racing rules and a well-tuned and equipped boat, handled with precision and skill by an experienced crew.

Starting technique is part of local tactics and I have gone into this in great detail earlier on in this chapter because I consider it of premier importance in the training of young crews, enabling them to make rapid progress in the accurate trimming of their boat.

Dragon start.

5.0.5 start.

The wind is very rarely steady in strength and above all in direction and often shifts as much as 20 to 40 degrees in either direction. A good position along the line at the moment the gun goes off allows you to set out on the most favourable tack, that is to say the one which leads most directly to the mark.

If, after the gun, you find yourself well clear of the other competitors, do not stay on this tack for too long otherwise you may find that you have to bear away on the other tack to lay the mark.

If several boats have made a better start and are ahead of you and on the better tack, follow them; to split tacks would bring absolutely no advantage, in fact quite the contrary. You have to be patient and wait for a wind shift. It is in this kind of situation that your boat's speed and its ability to point close to the wind are extremely important. You have to concentrate all your attention on getting the boat to go well and react quickly to every wave and every variation in the strength of the wind (chapters 1 and 2).

If you have missed your start and get trapped between several boats, unable to split tacks because you have to respect their right-of-way, try to pass to windward of those ahead of you. However, if it is obvious that they have no intention of letting you pass, do not persist but rather go past to leeward by gathering speed in bearing away. As soon as the opportunity presents itself go onto the other tack to find a clear wind.

If you have managed to make an excellent start

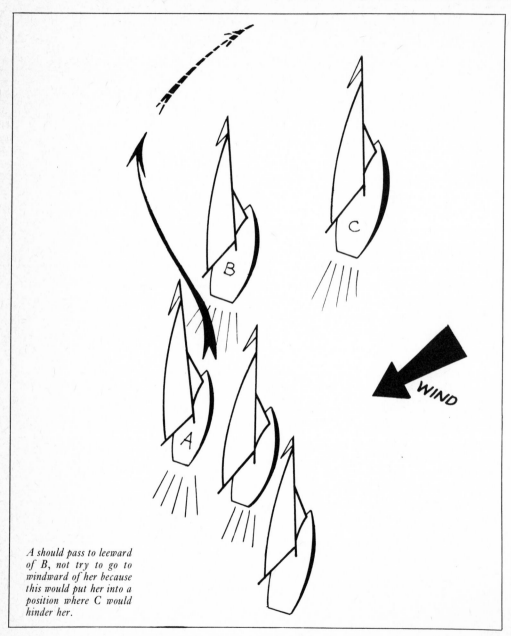

A should pass to leeward of B, not try to go to windward of her because this would put her into a position where C would hinder her.

WIND

and find yourself in the lead after several minutes, watch what your opponents are doing and do not, on any account, let them push you out to windward. As soon as the opportunity presents itself make a short tack across to cover the whole fleet. Do not indulge in the hope, though, that you will "show them a clean pair of heels" and that you will have a considerable lead at the first mark.

It is better to have a lead out in front of the fleet than to windward of it because you must always remember the possibility of a sudden wind shift.

If you are merely out to windward of the others and the wind suddenly goes round and heads you several dozen degrees forcing you to tack, you will immediately find yourself to leeward of the others. If, however, you have managed to get out in front of the fleet and only very slightly to windward, a wind shift need not lose you your lead.

If on the windward leg your nearest opponent persists on the same tack you should on no account abandon covering the others for the sake of this one opponent. Give up covering him and leave him the chance of arriving at the windward mark first. It is better to be second than see a large part of the fleet sail past.

On the first windward leg then local tactics after the start give way to general tactics. Local tactics only come back into their own as you approach the first mark. In fact, local tactics can only be applied when you see your way clear to do so in the race as a whole. It is quite obvious that after the start when all the yachts have crossed the line at the same moment, you cannot afford to concentrate on one or two opponents only.

If, on approaching the mark, a boat is following you closely and you have to tack to round the mark, you must observe rule 41.1. Your opponent will certainly stand a good chance of getting round ahead of you, but if the third boat is still some way away you can defend yourself with the following manoeuvre: Several lengths before the mark, luff as hard as possible to get clear to windward of your opponent. Slow down to force him to overtake you to leeward. Now it is he who must give you room to round the mark (rule 42.2 (b), end of sentence).

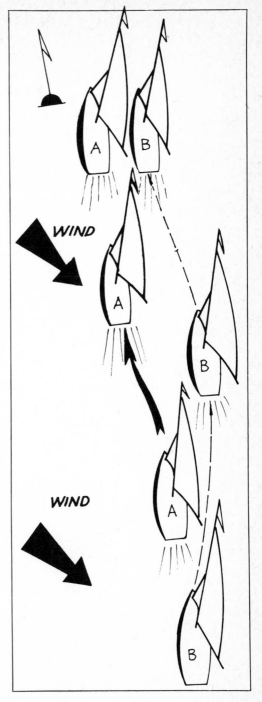

A luffs, forcing B into an overlap to leeward. A can now round the mark first.

Another example:

You are second, down to leeward of your opponent, and the third man is some distance away. Several lengths before the mark slow your boat down by luffing and let yourself be passed by your opponent. After that put yourself in his wake and try to hold this position. Since he has to tack in order to round the mark and you are then very close to him, he will be bound by rule 41.1 and you will go round first.

No. 1332 should bear away slightly to gather speed and catch up with No. 1237 so that she can prevent her tacking first in rounding the mark (imposing rule 41.1).

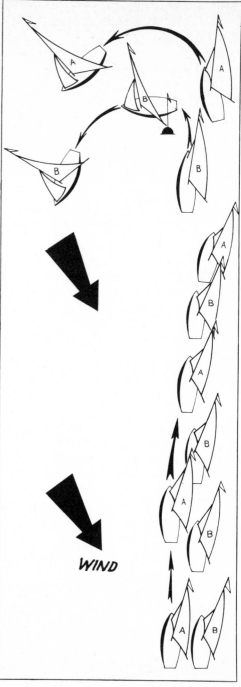

WIND

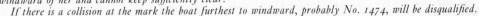
No. 1285 does not seem to have much room to round this mark because No. 839 is hindered by the boat to windward of her and cannot keep sufficiently clear.

If there is a collision at the mark the boat furthest to windward, probably No. 1474, will be disqualified.

1. No. 1441 on starboard tack is right-of-way yacht. Since they are close to the finishing line.

on a reach

The only tactical move used on a reach is the *luffing match*. We have previously seen how it fits in with the racing rules, let us now examine what advantages it holds for the attacking boat.

If the wind is light one cannot really call it a match because all you have to do to stop your opponent luffing you to prevent you from passing is to pass far enough to windward.

But when the breeze is stronger an opponent will not hesitate to luff to stop you passing. Go about your manoeuvre in such a way that you can respond to your obligations at any moment and, if necessary, break the overlap immediately your opponent shows any intention of taking you "off for a ride" without bothering about the rest of the fleet. The others would be the only ones to profit by this piece of good luck and creep through to leeward. Do not indulge in this kind of game yourself, either; it only favours your opponents.

In a fresh wind you must prepare your attack some way ahead, squeezing up in the lulls to windward of your opponent, then bearing away in the puffs to make up ground little by little. When you are sufficiently far up to windward, about three boat lengths, and abreast of your opponent, wait until a strong puff hits you both. If he wants to keep speed on his boat he dare not luff or if he does, he risks heeling over and stopping his boat. Bearing away slightly you will pass him easily.

overlap before rounding a mark

Try to get into the inside position by repeatedly changing course as indicated above.

The tactics will be the same for the second reach as for getting into position for rounding the leeward mark.

However, on that occasion you will be going from a broad reach to close-hauled. Unless the tactical situation forbids it, approach the mark rather wide so that you can round it at the same time as you haul your wind to set off on the beat. In this way you will prevent another boat having hauled her wind perfectly round the mark from getting on your weather.

A hauls her wind and passes astern of B at an increased speed. As she comes up abreast of B she bears away on a run and establishes an overlap. A rounds the mark first.

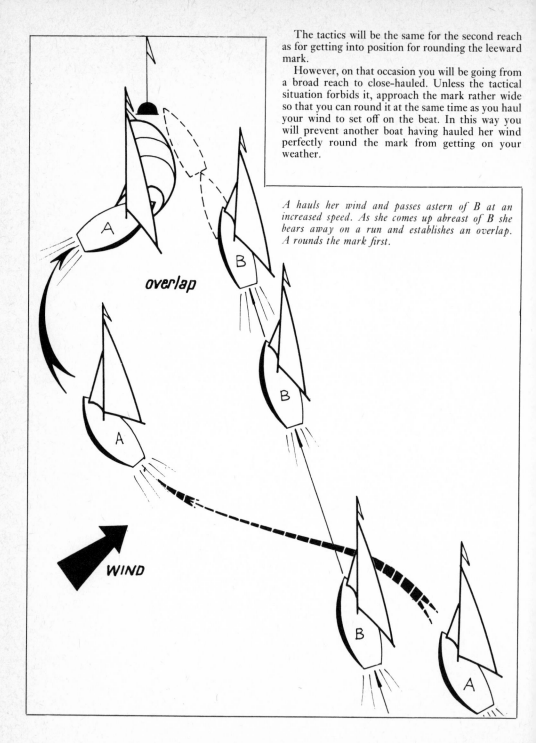

overlap

WIND

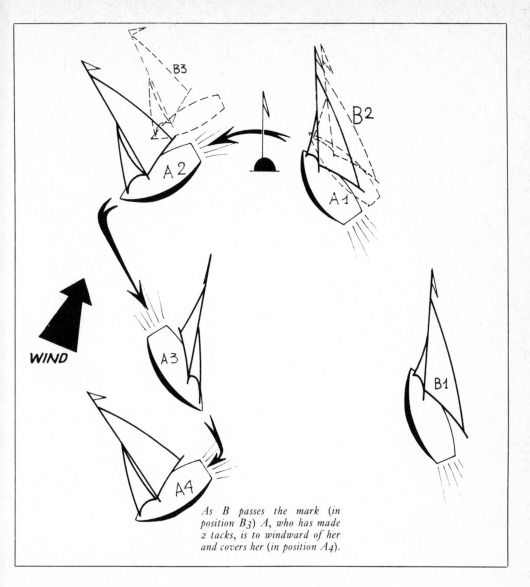

As B passes the mark (in position B3) A, who has made 2 tacks, is to windward of her and covers her (in position A4).

If you are in the lead on the second beat, local tactics will take over from general ones. You will have to cover your nearest opponents, but at the same time you must not hesitate to split tacks if this benefits you.

Generally speaking, follow the advice I have given for the first beat and do not allow yourself to be taken out of your way by blindly covering a single opponent.

If you have gone round the mark with a lead of at least 10 lengths over your nearest opponent, get up speed after the mark and then make a short board of about 3 to 4 lengths. As the second boat comes round the mark you will be on the same tack as her but ahead and to windward.

Once you have got yourself into this position sail to get the maximum speed out of your boat and, above all, never pinch too close, because this would most certainly slow her down. Your opponent would gain by passing you to leeward.

If the wind heads you do not continue to cover your opponent unless you know that the tack both of you are on will later take you to an area of water where the wind will be particularly favourable when you go onto the other tack.

You will have found out about that on your first beat. Alternatively it may be a question of a favourable current or a turning tide (chapter 2). If a third opponent proceeds not to play your game, you can do two things:

— either you are certain you are doing the right thing and it is he who is making a mistake, in which case you take no more notice of what he is doing.

— or you have doubts about the outcome of following the course you are on, in which case you give up covering the second boat for the time being. It is practically impossible to keep an eye on two

Covering: No. 214 tacks across No. 162's bow . . .

opponents shooting off on opposite tacks. The dictum "you cannot chase two hares at once" must be applied here. Above all do not get flustered, concentrate on general tactics, on making your boat go as fast as possible, on profiting from wind shifts. In short: sail your course. You can resume closer contact with your opponents when the opportunity arises. If you have not rounded with the leaders but still look like having a chance of regaining a leading position after having rounded the leeward mark, do not shoot off on an entirely different course to those ahead of you.

There is a big risk that you will do no more than make your position worse. Concentrate on getting the best performance out of your boat and at the same time avoid getting yourself into disadvantageous positions.

. . . and then tacks to windward of him to cover him closely.

There are two exceptions: If you are on "home ground" and know the course better than your opponents you must profit by this knowledge rather than follow them. In this case, you should not have been so badly placed after the first triangle of the course! . . . But I will assume that there are extenuating circumstances in that you made a bad start because of an opponent, or had an accident in the early part of the race.

Finally, if you are a long way back for either of these reasons or even both of them, there remains the solution of this "emergency tack". Sometimes, luck which has turned its back on you at the beginning of the race can come to you in the form of a big wind shift . . . or a dead calm for your opponents who have gone off on the other tack. But you must not count on this. You will learn to your cost that top helmsmen find the best course to victory without having to know your stretch of water intimately.

On the downwind leg there is often an opportunity, particularly in a light breeze, to gain several places by searching out the "cat's paws", planning one's position in relation to the other boats and gaining a favourable overlap before reaching the mark.

Approaching the leeward mark. No. 1271 has started to hand the spinnaker while No. 1332 in the inside position seems to be in no hurry. The two boats in the middle are also getting ready for the manoeuvre.

Having a good look at each other before a luffing match.

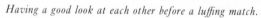

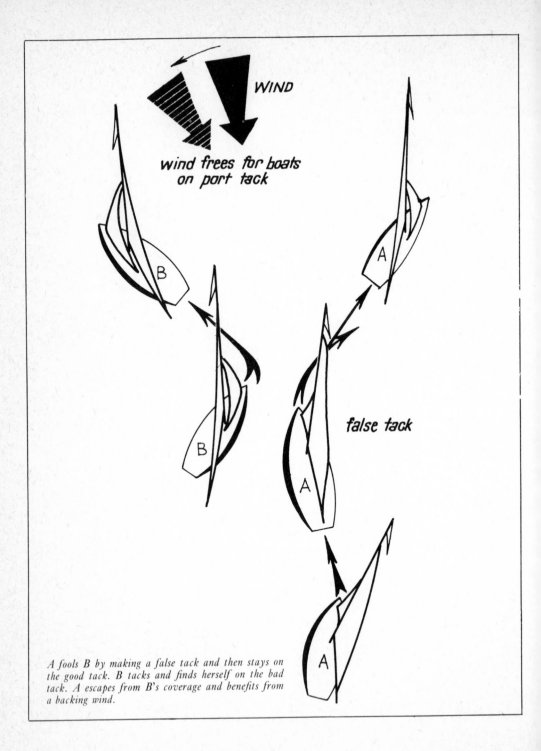

WIND

wind frees for boats
on port tack

false tack

*A fools B by making a false tack and then stays on
the good tack. B tacks and finds herself on the bad
tack. A escapes from B's coverage and benefits from
a backing wind.*

The last beat before the finish will call for local rather than general tactics. The game is by no means over and if you are in the lead at the beginning of this last leg it is essential for you to cover your closest opponents carefully and, if your lead over the others is quite big, even go onto the less favourable tack to keep them "on ice".

Sometimes this "coverage" causes the leading boat serious problems. If covering a single boat leaves the field wide open for the others you must, if necessary, drop the idea. Which means, as I have said at the beginning of this section, that you should face being second rather than be passed on the line by several boats who did not want to get mixed up in this *pas de deux*.

The second boat, as long as the third is not too close, can start a kind of "nautical ballet" in which the two boats tack in quick succession until the leader loses his place or the second boat, who is the ballet-master, abandons the dance.

The attacker in this odd game must never tack nor the defender follow him on the other tack until he is sure that the other has finished his manoeuvre properly. In fact, the second boat can deceive his opponent by making a lot of noise to simulate making a tack while meaning to stay on the same one. If the defender allows himself to be taken in by this ruse, he will immediately lose his coverage and the two boats will go off on opposite tacks.

The second boat starts his attack by tacking as soon as the wind heads. His opponent being ahead and to windward, approximately in the eye of the wind, will be obliged to suffer the first bad effects of a header while he waits for the other to complete the tack. Theoretically, the attacker always has an advantage and can progressively catch up on the other boat.

In a case like this the leading boat will have to deliberately lose ground on his pursuer before reaching the finishing line in order to cover him better and put him in a hopeless position down to leeward.

Once he has managed to do this, and barring accidents or lack of attention, the race "is in the bag" for the leader and the second man has to grin and bear it.

This brings me to the tactics to be followed by the second boat. He will have to beware of the leading boat slowing down, looking for close coverage, and not congratulating himself on having caught up so quickly. If he does, he will have walked straight into a trap from which he cannot escape.

He can resort to a false tack, but it must be done at the very moment the wind frees, so that if the leader falls for it he goes onto the bad tack while the boat simulating the tack, benefits from a freeing wind.

Crossing the finishing line at the nearest possible point would seem a simple matter. Far from it, and many helmsmen allow themselves to be robbed of several places by having misjudged the situation. What you must avoid most of all is being blocked by an opponent astern but slightly to windward (rule 41.1) you then cannot tack.

You must luff to take the wind out of his sails and, at the same time, keep a close watch on him. As soon as he tacks to escape, follow him to keep him covered.

physical fitness in racing

Once helmsman and crew have got their boat perfectly tuned they have by no means done everything to ensure complete success in racing.

Up to a few years ago racing fanatics spent all their time on tuning their boats but neglected their own preparation, their physical training.

Frequently, after one or two days of a championship meeting in a fresh breeze, performances would drop considerably.

Racing tactics, calling for unremitting concentration, demand an excellent physical condition: the ability to sustain prolonged effort and recover quickly. It was the Finn helmsmen who were first to put the accent in racing on physical fitness.

Once the single-hander starts to suffer from fatigue and muscular pain caused by sitting out, he can no longer concentrate on the race. He finishes the course like an automaton, hanging on grimly by his toe straps, incapable of reacting to the attacks of his opponents. He no longer notices any changes in wind direction and he doesn't bother himself about his boat's progress through the water. He has only one thought in his mind: to put an end to this torment.

The crew of a two-man boat in the same situation becomes slow and awkward in movements and often imperils the balance of the boat.

Fatigue in racing slows down your reflexes and dulls your fighting spirit towards the natural elements: wind and water. Helmsman and crew find themselves in a psychological state of abandon. They let themselves be dominated by the elements, they can no longer control their boat with precision and the boat literally runs riot.

On a reach, when the speed is at its highest, when stability becomes precarious, each movement of the helm, each adjustment of the sheets, each change in the position of the helmsman and crew must be done with the greatest precision. If the boat's balance is upset even for a split second the outcome is a capsize. On a keel boat the situation isn't much better.

Let us look at the example of a 5.0.5 or a Flying Dutchman reaching in a wind exceeding Force 5. The crew is on the trapeze and the helmsman, to keep his boat at maximum speed, is concerned with sailing it as upright as possible (chapter 2, the trim of the boat, and trimming the sheets).

In the puffs the sheets are eased and the boat made to bear away. For this manoeuvre to have its maximum effects the mainsheet must be eased very quickly and by a substantial amount. But after the puff has passed and the wind drops abruptly, the boat must be brought back onto the wind and the mainsheet hauled in at great speed. The helmsman is forced to recover several yards of mainsheet in a very short space of time: if he fails to do so the boat will start to heel to windward.

The asymmetrical shape of the hull will make the boat bear away and it will heel even further. No amount of effort on the tiller will make the boat come up into the wind again and it will capsize on top of the crew. It is hardly necessary to add that after such an accident the race is in jeopardy.

This kind of capsize is very common, and while in the case of young helmsmen it can be attributed to their lack of technique it is always caused among old hands by a lack of co-ordination and speed in manoeuvring due to excessive fatigue.

By getting themselves into good physical shape helmsman and crew can delay the onset of this fatigue.

The energy expended in yacht racing can be compared to that expended by mountaineers who must put in constant and prolonged effort, interspersed with energetic, sometimes violent movements and periodic spells of rest. Yacht racing means hard muscular work.

Depending on the type of boat on one hand and the type of racing on the other, the rhythm and nature of the effort can vary a great deal.

In a race which does not exceed three hours a Finn helmsman is forced into sustained effort over the whole of the course, interspersed with violent action, particularly on the reach. For the crew of a two-man dinghy the prolonged effort is less intense (hanging out on the trapeze is less tiring than sitting out by toe straps and the helmsman can allow himself a little rest from time to time) but from time to time he also has to do a bit of quick work in manoeuvres where speed is of primary importance (e.g. tacking). In the keelboat classes the Star crews and helmsmen put in efforts comparable with those demanded of single-handed helmsmen.

In the Dragon or 5·5 Metre class the helmsman's effort is above all one of intense mental concentration, but the crews have spells of concentrated physical activity, particularly when handling the spinnaker. By way of compensation they benefit from very long periods of rest.

In ocean racing the crews are subjected for several days and nights to a very tough life, especially in heavy weather, and often have to do very hard work in changing sails.

In every case, but particularly in ocean racing, the body has to work overtime in combatting the cold and making up to a certain degree the expenditure of muscular energy and the lack of sleep. It is therefore necessary to step up the diet by 300 to 500 calories an hour.

As in all other sports, diet and physical fitness are closely linked.

Before changing your diet or setting out on a course of physical training of whatever sort make a point of finding out whether you are in good health.

In comparison with other sports (such as athletics, swimming, boxing, etc.) the heart and lungs are not called upon excessively in yacht racing, but the spine has to endure long spells of sitting or hanging out. A medical examination should therefore be concentrated on that part of the body. Spinal injuries, quite frequent among inadequately prepared racing men, can put you out of action for a long time (over a year in certain cases).

The doctor should also look for possible functional disorders and metabolic troubles which must be taken into account in preparing a new dietary pattern.

I know of several cases where helmsmen or crews had to suddenly interrupt a course of physical training on account of physiological troubles. A medical examination revealed a disturbance which only had to be treated with an appropriate diet before they could successfully resume their training.

Righting a dinghy after a capsize is hard work.

In yachting, as in other specialized sports, the doctor should be the first to be consulted by the athlete. Not to take his advice would be to expose yourself to serious dangers.

getting fit

We have seen that keeping a dinghy on an even keel requires the crew to take up a position outside the hull. Since this means hanging out by toe straps or on a trapeze it calls essentially for static muscular effort as opposed to the dynamic effort, i.e. the alternate muscular contractions and relaxations required by the manoeuvres during the race.

One can easily see that the muscles intended to produce dynamic effort are ill trained for prolonged contraction.

The muscle first shows fatigue by more and more pronounced trembling and then by violent pain which quickly makes you give up such an uncomfortable position.

However, certain groups of muscles are intended to stand up to prolonged static contraction. They are those which hold the bone structure in position, particularly the muscles of the abdomen that hold the pelvis.

In the classical position of sitting out by using toe straps the abdominal muscles are in constant use, and because of their original function, it is very easy to strengthen them. But they are not the only ones to contribute to maintaining this position. The beginner very quickly realizes by the pain he feels that the muscles at the front of his thighs are equally made to work very hard.

But the problem is more complex than one imagines. Although part of the muscles in the front of the thigh respond quite well to training aimed at making them capable of enduring prolonged static contraction, their original functions having prepared them for this, they do not have to work particularly hard. There is one, though, that shows its disapproval very quickly, and that is the *psoas*, the flexor muscle of the thigh. It is attached to the bones in the following places: at one end to the front of the femur, to the lesser trochanter, at the other end to the front of several lumbar vertebrae.

Although in the thigh its contraction produces no more than a rather unpleasant pain, this is usually accompanied by vertebral displacements and sometimes by spinal lesions.

It is obvious that the most susceptible part or parts suffer first from excessive contractions. The lumbar vertebrae are pulled forward and increase the tendency of the pelvis to move backwards. This shows up in a very marked hollow back, and the consequences can be serious.

Below: static muscular effort is required when sitting out or hanging on the trapeze of a racing dinghy. Here is a Flying Dutchman. Right: on a dinghy like the Finn one is frequently in touch with the elements.

It is very important to take this into account when doing physical exercises, which will initially consist in preventive or compensating gymnastics.

To start with, the body must get accustomed or re-accustomed to physical exercise; I know of nothing better for this than light running interspersed with short sessions of general limbering up (arms, legs, trunk), with particular attention to the spinal column.

Apart from the usual trunk bending forward and sideways, legs straight and apart, support yourself on all fours, again with legs and arms straight, and alternately round and hollow your back.

Still in the same position reach out as far as possible with each arm in turn by stretching your body as far as it will go. Forward and backward rolls are also an excellent exercise.

These exercises make the whole of the spine work, forwards, backwards and sideways. You can do them at home and only a few minutes' practice is necessary every day, morning and evening.

After a few days you can also start on keep-fit exercises to gradually undo the harm done by several years of inactivity.

First of all the pelvis must be got back into its proper position. Scores of people complain of bad backs, and this is usually caused by an excessive forward tilt of the top of the pelvis (hollow back).

The muscles which hold the pelvis in place must be toned up.

Apart from several exercises which I am about to describe you will have to watch yourself constantly for some time: the way you stand, walk and sit. Tilt the base of the pelvis forward by contracting the abdominal muscles and the buttocks. Do not sit with your "seat" stuck out behind you, this aggravates a hollow back.

The exercises aimed at putting the pelvis back into place are done lying on your back.

Start by "testing" your body, and particularly your pelvis with the following exercise: legs half bent, heels firmly on the ground, try to press the hollow of your back flat against the ground by contracting your abdominal muscles and hold this position for some time, then relax. Repeat several times.

When you can do this without too much effort or concentration proceed to raise each leg in turn whilst keeping your back pressed to the ground all the time.

After a certain period of practice which is needed to improve the condition of the muscles involved, do the exercise with both legs raised at the same time.

Gradually increase the time you keep your legs raised and complete the exercise by raising them vertically and moving them in small and large

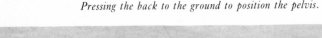

Pressing the back to the ground to position the pelvis.

circles, ten at a time.

It is not until you feel a definite strengthening of the lower abdominal muscles that you should start on the exercises aimed at improving the strength and condition of those abdominal muscles which are affected by the sitting-out position.

One thing is important: the pelvic exercises must be kept up to compensate for possible harm the *psoas* might do.

Above: preventive exercise to strengthen the abdominal muscles. Below: a more strenuous exercise on the horizontal ladder.

233

The exercises for sitting out are quite simple and also belong to the group of abdominal exercises, but this time it is the trunk that is moved while the legs remain stationary, feet held by what represents the toe straps. You can easily make a simple contrivance for yourself to simulate a boat: a small wooden bench for the side deck and a strap screwed to the floor.

You alternately bend and extend the upper part of your body, gradually increasing the length of the exercise. I had this simple set-up at home when I trained for the great international events and the Olympic Games. Every day I spent twenty to thirty minutes "sitting out". To make the exercise less boring I read a book.

Exercise to strengthen the abdominal muscles. The weight in this case is 15 kilos (33 lb.).
Opposite page, top: normal sitting out position on a dinghy, dorsal load of 10 kilos (22 lb.). The abdominal muscles are shown to be doing hard work.

Below : at the beginning of this exercise you lie flat on your back. It looks perfectly simple but is very difficult to do, because it must be done slowly without the soles of your feet coming off the ground. The abdominal muscles have to work very hard.

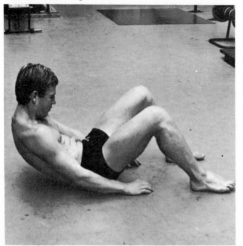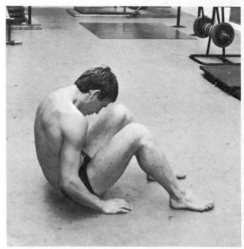

But this is only the first stage of physical training. You also have to strengthen your thigh muscles by a series of leg bending and stretching.

To make a muscle strong you have to increase its size and to increase its size the muscle must be made to work quickly and at full intensity for a very short time. That is to say to make it work against a very powerful resistance. This can be done by using weights. But you "build" a dynamic muscle in this way, whereas for the thighs you want a muscle that is capable of prolonged static effort. This can be achieved by using relatively light weights in a rather slow rhythm and gradually stepping up the duration of the exercise. It is important here that the medical examination has not revealed any heart trouble.

If you have no weights handy you can achieve very good results by doing the leg-bending-and-stretching exercise on one leg. But you can easily make a load with a sack filled with sand or, better still, a piece of car inner tube sealed at both ends.

Top : leg-bend-and-stretching exercise on one leg.

The same exercise with a load, in this case a weight of 80 kilos (175 lb.). In coming up you must be careful not to lean forward. The pelvis must not come up more quickly than the shoulder instead it must help to lift the trunk. At the end of the exercise the pelvis must be well pushed forward. Go down slowly and never take the soles of your feet off the ground.

Opposite page : the three photographs show an apparatus which guides the load and permits greater weights to be used.

236

Every time you go down and even more so when you straighten up you must hold your pelvis correctly. Do not do the exercise with your seat stuck out behind but with your back as straight as possible.

At the beginning the weight should not exceed a third of your body weight for the first two or three series of a dozen movements. You gradually increase the number of movements per series, then the number of series, finally, and still gradually, the load. You get the best results working slowly and lightly. Between each series you should take a rest of about 2 minutes at first, then shorten it until it is only 30 seconds. The load must always be at least 10 to 20% lighter than your own body weight.

The exercises must be done with the heels on the ground. The thighs need not necessarily touch the calves, but the trunk must be kept as near vertical as possible.

237

For "trapeze artists" the limbering-up and preventative exercises are the same, but the special leg-building exercises are different, on account of the fact that they have to make quick use of their legs in pushing themselves outboard. In fact they do the

same leg-bending-and-stretching exercises but take them lower down to the ground by completely bending the legs (buttocks on heels), keeping the heels firmly on the ground.

The training is more dynamic (the exercises are done in a fast rhythm and with heavier weights in ever shorter series). The initial load is one third of the body weight but very quickly (depending on the physical condition of the person in question) rises to two thirds. A man weighing 80 kilos (175 lb.) will start with a series of 10 to 15 movements with a load of 25 to 30 kilos (55 to 65 lb.) gradually reaching 50 to 60 kilos (110 to 130 lb.).

At this point the pattern changes to shorter and shorter series with ever increasing weights.

Example:
3 series of 10 movements with 60 kilos (130 lb.) $1\frac{1}{2}$ minutes apart;
3 series of 6 movements with 70 kilos (150 lb.) 1 minute apart;
3 series of 4 movements with 75 kilos (180 lb.) 30 seconds apart.

I cannot stress too much the importance of being in excellent physical condition before rushing off to do this training. The abdominal muscles must be perfectly fit.

But possibly the arms have to do even heavier work on a boat than the legs and the abdomen.

The best exercise to prepare you for all manoeuvres you might be called upon to perform on a sailing boat is climbing a rope.

I know only too well that there are few people who can install a climbing rope at home, but fortunately a simple table will serve the same purpose.

Lay flat on your back under the table, arms stretched out, hands gripping the edge of the table. Pull yourself up on your arms at rhythmic intervals, each time bringing your chest into contact with the table.

Running and limbering-up exercises continue to form the basis of any successful physical fitness training. Without wishing to discourage future champions I would strongly advise them to get in touch with a specialist, a P.T. instructor, once they have decided to go whole-heartedly into serious racing. He will both guide and supervise their training with complete competence. Only someone who is or has been active in some other kind of sport is in a position to choose wisely and co-ordinate a successful training programme for themselves.

Finally, it is worth knowing that wrestling is an excellent sport to help you build up resistance to fatigue and improve the condition of your muscles quickly.

The Institut National des Sports in Paris is equipped with this rather complicated apparatus which takes up a fair amount of room. It permits a thorough muscular training of the arms and shoulder area in a simulated sitting out or trapeze position. The load can be varied at will.

diet

It was only a short time ago that yachtsmen started seriously to think about the problems of diet. Without the research work done by expert dieticians like Dr. Albert Creff, director of the hospital of Saint-Michel in Paris, and Dr. Hubert Tanguy they would have remained on the verge of a solution and serious mistakes would have been committed.

It is these two doctors in particular who have helped me in working out a special diet for yachtsmen training for Olympic competition or for Olympic trials. It has been found that this diet has a beneficial effect on the physical condition of competitors.

Depending on the means which are put at our disposal, this kind of diet is also applied to national events sponsored by the French National Sailing School at Beg-Rohu. It is regrettable that some other bodies entrusted with preparation and training for yacht racing close their eyes to what is so obvious. Dr. Tanguy is devoted to ocean racing and has particularly studied the problems of nutrition in yachting.

Here are the basic principles of a diet for a

period of training:

Be in good health at the start.
Only athletes in perfect health benefit from normal dieting. It is necessary then at the beginning of the season to have a complete medical examination. If there are any metabolic or functional disorders, the disturbance or illness must be treated first and an appropriate diet prescribed for it.

No sudden changes.
If the daily food ration of an athlete is balanced, it should never be changed suddenly but increased by stages according to the new needs created by the increased muscular work.

The daily food ration should have an average of 3200 to 3500 calories divided into four meals made up of *15% proteins, 30% fats, 55% carbohydrates.*

Four meals per day.
Breakfast should be a substantial meal and include proteins in the form of eggs, meat or fish and sugar in the form of fresh fruit juice.

Do not force yourself.
The likes and dislikes of each individual have to be taken into account: if some prefer fish to meat or eggs, for example, they can still satisfy the same calorific needs, since the biological value of these foods are the same.

No pills.
A balanced diet does not need to be supplemented by vitamins or mineral salts.

This training ration plays an important role in getting an athlete into condition, since they allow him to accumulate reserves of energy and ensure a good functioning of the digestive processes.

actual racing: dinghy racing

Racing corresponds to heavy manual work, that is to say that it has become an athletic sport and needs supplementary food. Taking into account the 3000 to 3500 calories during the training period, it will be necessary during racing to plan for a daily ration of 4000 to 5500 calories (for 3 to 4 hours racing). These calories are apportioned in different ways according to the time of the race.

First case: race in the morning.
It is recommended that you replace breakfast by a complete meal, eaten three hours before the start. This meal should consist of:
— a bowl of cereals with sugar and milk, several rusks or pieces of buttered toast with honey or marmalade;
— a helping of meat, either mince mixed with an

egg yolk and fried in very little fat; or a piece of roast beef or veal eaten hot or cold (no pork or mutton), or chicken;

— a salad dressed with lemon and oil (maize or sunflower oil for preference) or some plain boiled green vegetables;

— one or two very ripe pieces of fruit, peeled;

— weak coffee or tea or an infusion, sweetened with sugar. It is recommended that you should drink very little with your meal. However, between the end of the meal and the start of the race take a "waiting ration" of $\frac{1}{2}$ pint freshly pressed fruit juice with $\frac{1}{2}$ oz. glucose or honey in it about every hour. You should take between $\frac{1}{2}$ and $1\frac{1}{2}$ pints of liquid during the waiting period and stop drinking $\frac{1}{2}$ hour before the start.

Second case: race in the afternoon.
Breakfast should be taken at the usual hour. Lunch should also be taken as near the usual time as possible but in any case to leave 3 to 4 hours between the end of the meal and the start of the race. The meal should be largely the same as the one in the first case; the cereals can be replaced by some raw or cooked vegetables, a salad or an hors d'oeuvre. The same "waiting ration" applies.

Third case: two races a day.
A copious breakfast, the same as in the first case, should be taken 3 to 4 hours before the first race, followed by the same waiting ration. Since two successive races require a considerable expenditure of energy, the interval between the two must be used to "recharge" the body. We recommend taking two plastic containers or preferably Thermos flasks containing easily digested liquid food providing instant energy. In the first container: a mixture of equal parts of weak tea and fresh fruit juice sweetened with 1 oz. of glucose or dextrose or $1\frac{1}{2}$ oz. of honey plus a pinch of salt. In the second container: rice or tapioca or pulped malted cereals with milk, containing 1 gram of bicarbonate of soda and $\frac{1}{2}$ gram of potassium gluconate syrup.

Depending on the outside temperature, these liquid foods will be eaten lukewarm or cold (Thermos flasks). For those who prefer it rice, semolina, tapioca or cereal pulp can be replaced by specially balanced energy foods which come in the form of biscuits, tablets or pastes in tubes. They have been on the market for some time and were used with success at the Olympic Games in Tokyo.

Where there are several escorting boats to follow the competitors round they can take over the task of supply vessels so that the competing yachts need not take the food on board, although it takes up very little room and is easy to stow.

Fourth case: eating during the course of the race itself.
The fact that racing helmsmen have never given a thought to feeding themselves during the course of a race must be put down to their ignorance of the considerable amount of energy used by the body when it is subjected to long, strenuous and repeated efforts in weather conditions which are frequently testing. In our opinion this is a point which must be given some attention, especially if the race looks like being a difficult one. It goes without saying that the food taken must be of a special kind, light and easily assimilable.

The following mixture (to make 2 pints of liquid) should be taken during the race in all weather conditions:

— weak tea made with mineral water (Vittel, Evian, Contrexeville or Volvic);

— fresh fruit juice;

— 2 oz. of glucose;

— 1 gram of potassium gluconate syrup;

— 1.5 grams of bicarbonate of soda.

In addition to liquid nourishment fruit paste, almond paste or nougat are very useful and are easily stowed in a pocket without the risk of them deteriorating in the water. These solid and liquid foods prevent a drop in the output of energy (fall in the blood sugar level), they retard the appearance of signs of fatigue, maintain a good co-ordination of neuro-muscular reflexes, limit the premature accumulation of toxins causing tiredness, prevent acidosis—all of them phenomena which could put the favourable outcome of a race in jeopardy.

ocean racing and passage racing

Although the question of what to eat may seem easy enough to solve, certain environmental factors like the cold and the heat, the wet, heavy weather and a rough sea can complicate matters enormously. The space available on board for stowing provisions must be used in the best possible way. Good quality tinned foods should make up an essential part of the provisions. Modern methods of preservation have made it possible to produce tinned foods with their full vitamin and nutritional value as well as a pleasant taste.

What provisions should be taken aboard before setting out on an off-shore race?
Our list is intentionally selective and only includes foods which, according to modern theories on nutrition, will give a balanced diet.

Vegetables:
Fresh vegetables for consumption during the first 48 hours only (they are liable to deteriorate under the influence of heat and also lose their vitamin value). It is probably better to replace them by tinned vegetables.
Only the following tinned vegetables are recommended: green beans, garden peas, mixed vegetables, selected carrots, leeks, asparagus.

Starchy foods:
Sliced bread packed in cellophane (will keep for 4 to 5 days) or toast wrapped in the same way, which is more pleasant to eat than rusks.
Potatoes in plastic bags.
Various kinds of pasta (spaghetti, noodles, etc.). Rice is tasty and easy to cook and can be prepared at sea in many different ways.
Tapioca for soup.
Breakfast cereals.
Bread, pasta, potatoes and cereals are essentially of the same calorific value and have the same contents of carbohydrates and proteins.
Dry biscuits, gingerbread and chocolate biscuits are always appreciated by those on watch.

Fats:
Tinned butter, lightly salted and pasteurized keeps well.
Vegetable fat, such as margarine, for cooking. Its boiling point is sufficiently high to make it suitable for all culinary uses.
Table oil (maize or sunflower seed) kept in a plastic flask or metal canister.

Meat and protein foods:
Dry sausage (of the Salami type) and smoked bacon are indispensable and always appreciated, easy to eat and easily assimilated, provided they are lean and of the type that keeps well.
Fresh meat for consumption during the first 48 hours. Apart from that cold roast beef and pork will keep for 3 days.
Only the following simple types of tinned meats are recommended: roast chicken, roast pork and boiled beef.
Amongst tinned fish the only two recommended for dietic reasons are plain tuna and hake.

The provisions should include some very fresh eggs and hard-boiled eggs.
Amongst cheeses it is wise to opt for hard or semi-hard types like Gruyere, Edam, Port-Salut and Cantal because they keep well, are rich in fat, are of high nutritional value and easily digested.
For the first few days yoghurt and cream cheeses can also be included in the diet.

Fruit:
Fresh fruit in season can be kept for 48 hours, provided it is not too ripe and stowed where it cannot get damaged. Citrus fruit (oranges, lemons, grapefruit) are much more tolerant. Tomatoes will keep for 4 to 5 days if they are not quite ripe to start with. Besides, fresh fruit, tinned fruit and jam are nice to have on board.

Beverages:
Apart from very long cruises when water is stored in tanks or canisters, it is wise to stock up with mineral water in tins: lightly mineralized waters (Volvic, Evian, Charrier for example) as well as aerated waters (Perrier or Vittelloise) or those containing sodium bicarbonate (like Vichy). The latter two types are particularly recommended for restoring the acid-base balance in cases of fatigue due to acidosis. The daily ration of liquid per head is five to seven pints, and this can include tinned fruit juice. There are also syrups in tubes on the market now which can be added to plain water to make it more pleasant to drink. Easy-to-prepare packet soups containing dehydrated vegetables or bouillon made from stock cubes (e.g. Knorr, Maggi) can form part of the daily intake of liquid. Then there is skimmed milk powder and condensed sweetened milk, both of which can be made into drinks, and not forgetting instant coffee and tea like Nescafe, Decaf and Nestea, as well as tea bags. Nowadays the Express Dairy Longlife Milk can be obtained which keeps virtually indefinitely.

How about wine and alcoholic drinks?
It is worth mentioning that *vin ordinaire* can now be bought in plastic bottles. But that aside, one should always keep in mind that the intake of alcohol must not exceed 10% of the total ration of calories, which means a maximum of $\frac{3}{4}$ pint ($\frac{1}{2}$ litre) of wine per day. It might be as well to point out here that alcohol is not a food: if it is consumed in excess it is poisonous because it prevents the body from taking in the necessary amount of vitamins,

particularly those of the B complex, it interferes with the orderly functioning of the brain, of vision and of the vegetative nerve system (slowing down of reflexes, amongst others). To put it in the best possible way: it is better to drink to a race when it is over than beforehand. . . .

Although many insist that it does, alcohol does *not* combat the cold. It may give a feeling of momentary warmth, but this is rapidly followed by a feeling of even greater cold and depression.

Essential supplementary foods:
Bars of chocolate and powdered drinking chocolate for breakfast; dried fruit (raisins, figs, apricots); nougat, fruit paste, nut and almond paste. All of these are particularly rich in sugar and come in useful in certain situations like night watches, very heavy or very cold weather, when reserves of energy are quickly used up.

Finally, if only to make food more appetizing, one should not forget spices and seasoning, salt, sugar, and certain preparations in tubes such as mayonnaise and tomato sauce, which are very well received by the body.

nutrition in difficult conditions

In cold and wet weather:
It is essential for the body to store more heat and at the same time reduce the dissipation of heat to the outside. To assist this, it must be covered by warm clothing, including the extremities. This is very important because irregularities in the body's heat regulation induce sea-sickness. It is obviously necessary to have a change of clothes handy so that one does not have to keep wet clothes on.

As far as food is concerned it is recommended to step up the fat ration from a daily average of $4\frac{3}{4}$ oz. to 6 oz. The additional $1\frac{1}{4}$ oz. can be made up of an extra helping of butter at meal times or of nut butter or sweet almond paste, both of them vegetable fats which are easily digested and rich in essential fatty acids (containing valuable vitamins). Hot sweetened drinks (tea or coffee) or vegetable or meat stock (made from cubes) should be kept in Thermos flasks and can be taken alternately with fruit juice. Meals should be small but frequent (five per day) and something should be kept ready for when the night watch is relieved: a hot drink and a snack including cold meat, roast chicken, veal or beef.

In heavy weather:
This is a great problem. At the very time when food needs to be particularly substantial and abundant (because of the sustained muscular efforts, nervous tension, lack of sleep and physical exhaustion of the crew) it becomes extremely difficult to prepare and consume it.

Usually there is no time for properly balanced meals, so one eats anything that comes to hand just as long as it can be chewed and swallowed easily: biscuits, chocolate, sugar, chunks of bread are most frequently resorted to in this situation. If the heavy weather does not last very long this make-shift will, though unsatisfactory, at least be tolerable. However, if conditions continue to be bad one has to face up to them. It is then advisable to make use of special emergency rations which in themselves provide a complete and balanced diet of proteins, fats and carbohydrates (15%, 30% and 55% respectively) and are available as biscuits, paste in tubes or tablets, the latter having to be dissolved in cold or preferably warm water though they may, at a pinch, be chewed.

In whatever form they are taken they provide a balanced ration of calories which is enough to make up for the considerable energy expended in sailing in rough weather. It is advisable, for the sake of variety, to alternate between biscuits, paste and tablets.

In heavy weather it is also a good idea to take a tablet of glucose about once an hour. This easily assimilable sugar rapidly replenishes the reserves of glycogen and raises the blood sugar level. Try also a mixture (for 2 pints) of fruit juice, mineral water, weak tea, 2 oz. glucose, $1\frac{1}{2}$ oz. honey, 1 gram potassium gluconate syrup, 1 gram bicarbonate of soda and 1 gram cooking salt which can be kept in a Thermos flask and taken at regular intervals, cold or preferably lukewarm at the rate of 2 pints per day. Its effect is essentially to replenish energy and also to combat the onset of fatigue by helping the body to eliminate quickly the toxines and metabolic residue as well as maintaining the acid–base balance (fatigue gives rise to progressive acidosis which causes cramp and slows down muscular contraction).

Multi-vitamin tablets may be taken, especially if there are night watches to be kept on top of the day's strenuous work and the general lack of sleep. (It is worth mentioning in passing that the vitamin A contained in multi-vitamin tablets helps night vision).

In dry, hot weather:
The body loses considerable quantities of water and minerals, and this process is speeded up by reflection and the lack of shade. To compensate for this it is necessary to provide the body with large amounts of water and minerals, particularly sodium and potassium. Fruit juice and fresh fruit, non-gassy mineral waters containing 4 grams of cooking salt and 2 grams of potassium gluconate per day,

and weak tea, preferably lukewarm, suffice to maintain the hydro-mineral balance.

People's appetites are usually rather small, and it is better to limit food intake almost exclusively to proteins in the form of cold meat and fresh or tinned vegetables. You should eat very little fat because it is not easily assimilated by the body in very hot weather, and only very small quantities of sweetened foods, which only make you thirstier.

Even if the galley is equipped to provide very cold or iced drinks it is never wise to drink them unless you want to run the risk of going down with digestive troubles, painful bouts of gastro-enteritis and diarrhoea.

Seasickness:
This pathological phenomenon, which is the source of great discomfort both for the beginner and the experienced sailor, is caused by over-excitation of the inner ear (the labyrinth, which is the centre of the nervous vegetative system) by the movements of the boat and your position on board. The worse the weather the greater the risk of being seasick. Some people are afflicted very quickly, even in harbour or on the mooring, which suggests that there is also a psychological element in it. The condition is always aggravated by tiredness, cold, lack of sleep and hunger.

How to treat it:
First of all you should be in good physical shape and avoid cold, wet and lack of sleep. Food should be taken frequently and exclude such indigestible dishes as baked beans with sausages, chips and sardines in oil. Lack of appetite and the feeling of nausea are best met with simple foods: fruit, dried fruit, chocolate, cold meat, hard-boiled eggs.

There are various "recipes" whose value is, no doubt, largely psychological: chewing a crust of stale bread or a rusk, chewing gum or drinking a glass of sea water (Slocum).

Various drugs can be taken to combat seasickness, our favourite is Marzine. It comes in two forms: tablets and suppositories (for cases of incessant vomiting) and does not cause drowsiness. Seasickness does not usually last for longer than 48 hours. Two factors which contribute greatly to seasickness are usually overlooked: bad ventilation and a dark cabin. The obvious remedy is to have adequate ventilators and the cabin painted white inside.

Deep-sea asthenia:
This is a condition which occurs parallel to seasickness, a kind of mental "viscosity", an apathy, a slowing-down of motions. If the whole of the crew including the skipper are affected this can be serious. We think that it is due to acute hypoglycaemia (lowering of the blood sugar level) which affects the nerves before it makes itself felt in the functioning of the muscles. To combat this condition take one tablet of glucose until the trouble disappears.

I do not want to close this chapter on nutrition during ocean and passage racing without proposing a daily menu for normal conditions:

Number of meals: 4 proper meals: breakfast, lunch, tea and dinner, plus a night snack. The following are our suggestions on what these meals should consist of:

Breakfast: Tea or black coffee or milk or hot chocolate with water or cooked breakfast cereals or cornflakes. It is most inadvisable to boil a mixture of milk and coffee, milk and tea or milk and chocolate because it is generally indigestible and badly assimilated as has been medically proved. With the drink you can have buttered rusks or toast spread with honey, marmalade or jam and possibly a helping of cold meat, cheese or an egg as well.

Lunch: Raw vegetables or salad dressed with lemon and oil, some kind of meat and potatoes, pasta or rice. For dessert a piece of cheese and fresh or tinned fruit.

To drink: $\frac{1}{4}$ litre ($\frac{1}{2}$ pint) of light red wine.

Tea: Tea or coffee with biscuits and dried fruit.

Dinner: A packet vegetable soup or meat bouillon with noodles in it. Fresh or tinned vegetables (if lunch included a starchy food—or vice versa) cooked in water and dressed with butter. Cold meat or eggs or ham. For dessert tinned or stewed fruit or dried fruit or some biscuits and $\frac{1}{4}$ litre ($\frac{1}{2}$ pint) of light red wine.

recuperation period

On the eve of the race: A hot drink with plenty of sugar, gingerbread, biscuits or buttered rusks. Remember that the daily ration of liquid should preferably be taken between meals in the form of mineral water and fruit juice.

After the race:
In the evening, the first and the second day after a race, whether it is a regatta or a passage race, the body is exhausted by muscular and mental effort and must be helped to get rid of the accumulated toxins quickly and prepare itself for fresh efforts. What in fact happens in the body as it is subjected to the strains of a race?

(*a*) It loses large quantities of water and mineral elements through perspiration, particularly sodium chloride and potassium. Besides, fatigue gives rise to acidosis, which is an acid condition of the blood. Therefore, in the first 24 hours following the race you should drink large quantities of aereated waters with a high mineral content (e.g. Perrier, Vittelloise) or bicarbonated waters (to counteract the acidosis), fruit juice and milk, altogether about $4\frac{1}{2}$ pints of liquid per day. Potassium in the form of 0·5 grams of potassium gluconate syrup should be added to the daily ration of liquid. This helps to accelerate the renal excretion of toxins and metabolic residue contained in the urine.

· (b) The level of glycogen in the liver and muscles is very low, but since glycemic regulation tends to occur spontaneously it is enough to provide the body with vital foods such as fruit, pasta, rice or potatoes in the course of the dinner following the race.

(c) As far as proteins are concerned, their rapid combustion and consumption during physical effort causes the presence of toxic substances in the blood (apart from fatigue toxins) such as urea, uric acid, etc. It is therefore undesirable to increase the level of these substances in the blood even further by replacing the quantity of proteins the body has lost by physical effort by eating large helpings of meat. Instead, you should be content with including some simple and easily assimilated proteins in the dinner immediately following the race, like cereals, grated cheese and milk.

Complex proteins (meat, poultry and fish) should not be reintroduced into menus until dinner on the day following the race.

(d) Among the vitamins contributing essentially to the process of recuperation of the tired body vitamin B-6 (promoting the detoxication and condition of the heart muscle), vitamin B-12 (anti-toxic factor) and vitamin C (influencing above all the elimination of lactic acid and the storage of glycogen in the liver) must be mentioned in particular.

Since these vitamins are contained in sufficient quantity in a simple, balanced diet it is enough to take a weak dose of multi-vitamin tablets with dinner. Large doses of vitamins are useless and even dangerous.

In conclusion we can say then that for the first 24 hours following a race a diet rich in water, sodium chloride and potassium, mineral salts and vitamins, balanced in carbohydrates and fats and poor in proteins should be adopted to ensure the detoxication which a tired and encumbered body needs. As for the rest, you need only follow the natural instinct of any athlete who, on the evening after a competition, is in need of rest and does not require large quantities of food.

You should not revert to a normal diet with meat and fish, until dinner on the day following the race. On the second day after the race and the following days the normal training diet which has been described earlier on takes over again.

etiquette

Apart from flag etiquette this comprises all the rules of courtesy practised by seagoing men which should be observed at all times at sea, in harbour, at home and especially abroad.

Ruling of 19 August 1929: All yachts must wear the Ensign (National Flag) on Sundays, official holidays and feast days, and by order of the Port Authorities; also on entering and leaving harbour and when meeting naval vessels.

saluting

Yachts must salute all naval vessels at sea and in harbour.

The salute is made by lowering the Ensign slowly and then hoisting it three times in succession.

The naval vessel returns the salute by lowering and hoisting her Ensign once. When meeting a fleet of vessels the leader alone returns the salute. Use must never be made of sirens, claxons, whistles and other sound signals which are used in times of distress only.

ensign

The Ensign is worn at the Ensign staff at the stern or the mizzen masthead only, irrespective of the size of the yacht and the type of her rig. The Ensign staff must be three times the height of the Ensign hoist and allow the colours to be flown high and conspicuous and well clear of the deck. The Ensign must always be hoisted at 8 a.m. and lowered at sunset. Yawls and ketches wear the Ensign at the mizzen masthead. To hoist it, the following procedure is followed: With the Ensign held under the left arm, attach the toggle to the eyelet of the mast halyard, then pass the other end of the mast halyard through the eye splice of the Ensign halyard and make fast with a sheet bend.

abroad — courtesy ensign

The foreign Ensign is smaller than the national Ensign of a yacht. Under way, it is hoisted to the masthead attached to a staff. In harbour it is worn to starboard at the height of the cross trees.

mourning

In the case of National mourning the Ensign is half masted. It is also half masted at sea to attract attention or when carrying the corpse of someone who has drowned.

burgee

This is always worn at the masthead. It must be half masted in the event of National mourning or the death of a Club member.

house flag

It is worn from the starboard shrouds if the owner is on board. It is always rectangular in shape and the length is $1\frac{1}{4}$ times the hoist.

It is worn half masted in the event of National mourning, the death of a Club member or the death of the owner.

protest flag

Red flag, minimum length 8 inches.

quarantine flag

Letter Q of the International Code. To be hoisted in foreign ports.

jack

Ensign worn at a jack staff in the bows. Its size is one quarter the size of the Ensign worn by the vessel.

dressing ship

This consists of stretching a line from stem to stern over the masthead and attaching to it the flags of the International Code. This line must always be taut. In addition the House Flag, the Burgee and the Ensign are worn.

It is customary for yachts to be dressed on important national occasions or when the Port Authorities demand it.

When in a foreign port follow the example of the native yachts. "Undress" on weighing anchor and never dress at sea.

life in port

— Do not disturb anyone.

— Use adequate fenders.
— Give others a hand in mooring up and weighing anchor.
— When mooring alongside other yachts face the same way.
— Give a wide berth when passing ahead of other boats.
— Put out mats for people to clean their shoes on.
— Wear plimsolls to avoid ruining decks.
— Always keep your boat clean and tidy, with mooring ropes, sheets and halyards properly made fast and stowed.
— Introduce yourself to the members of the local Yacht Club.
— In all yachting matters try to behave correctly, sensibly and in keeping with good taste.

appendix

part II—management of races
(see also rules on pages 139–141, chapter 3)

RULE 11
ties

When there is a tie at the finish of a race, either actual or on corrected times, the points for the place for which the yachts have tied and for the place immediately below shall be added together and divided equally. When two or more yachts tie for a trophy or prize in either a single race or a series, the yachts so tied shall, if practicable, sail a deciding race; if not, either the tie shall be broken by a method established under rule 3.2 (a) (ix), The Sailing Instructions, or the yachts so tied shall either receive equal prizes or share the prize.

RULE 13
races to be re-sailed

When a race is to be re-sailed:

1. All yachts entered in the original race shall be eligible to start in the race to be re-sailed.

2. Subject to the entry requirements of the original race, and at the discretion of the race committee, new entries may be accepted.

3. Rule infringements in the original race shall be disregarded for the purpose of *starting* in the race to be re-sailed.

4. The race committee shall notify the yachts concerned when and where the race will be re-sailed.

RULE 14
award of prizes, places and points

1. Before awarding the prizes, the race committee shall be satisfied that all yachts whose finishing positions affect the awards have observed the racing rules, the prescriptions of the national authority, the sailing instructions and the class rules.

2. The sailing instructions may prescribe that in a particular instance the race committee may require the member in charge of a yacht to submit within a stated time limit a signed declaration to the effect that "all the racing rules, the prescriptions of the national authority, the sailing instructions and the class rules were observed in the race (or races) on (date or dates of race or races)." A yacht which fails to observe the above requirement may, at the discretion of the race committee, be disqualified, or regarded as having retired.

(Numbers 15, 16 and 17 are spare numbers)

part III—general requirements

owner's responsibilities for qualifying his yacht

A yacht intending to race *shall, to avoid subsequent disqualification, comply with the rules of Part III before her preparatory signal and, when applicable, while* racing.

RULE 18
entries

Unless otherwise prescribed by the national authority or by the race committee in either the notice of the race or the sailing instructions, entries shall be made in the following form:

FORM OF ENTRY

To the Secretary .... Club
    Please enter the yacht .... for
the .... race, on the ....
Her distinguishing flag is..........................
her national letters and distinguishing numbers are...........,
her rig is ....
the colour of her hull is............................
and her rating or class is...........................
    I agree to be bound by the racing rules of the I.Y.R.U., by the prescriptions of the national authority under which this race is sailed, by the sailing instructions and by the class rules.
        Name ....
        Address ....
        Telephone No. ....
        Club ....
    Signed .... Date ....
        (Owner or owner's representative)
Entrance fee enclosed

RULE 19
measurement certificates

1. Every yacht entering a race shall hold such valid measurement or rating certificate as may be required by the national authority or other duly authorised body, by her class rules, by the notice of the race, or by the sailing instructions.

2. It shall be the owner's responsibility to maintain his yacht in the condition upon which her certificate was based.

3. (a) If the owner of a yacht cannot produce such a certificate when required, he may be permitted to sign and lodge with the race committee, before she *starts*, a statement in the following form:

To the Secretary .... Club
UNDERTAKING TO PRODUCE CERTIFICATE
The yacht .... competes in the .... race on condition that a valid certificate previously issued by the authorised administrative body, or a true copy of it, is submitted to the race committee before the end of the series, and that she competes in the race(s) on the measurement or rating of that certificate.
        Signed ....
        (Owner or his representative)
        Date ....

(b) In this event the sailing instructions may require that the owner shall lodge such a deposit as may be required by the national authority, which may be forfeited if such certificate or true copy is not submitted to the race committee within the prescribed period.

RULE 20
ownership of yachts

1. Unless otherwise prescribed in the conditions of entry, a yacht shall be eligible to compete only when she is either owned by or on charter to and has been entered by a yacht or sailing club recognised by a national authority or a member or members thereof.

2. Two or more yachts owned or chartered wholly or in part by the same body or person shall not compete in the same race without the previous consent of the race committee.

RULE 21
member on board

Every yacht shall have on board a member of a yacht or sailing club recognised by a national authority to be in charge of the yacht as owner or owner's representative.

RULE 22
shifting ballast

1. *General Restrictions.* Floorboards shall be kept down; bulkheads and doors left standing; ladders, stairways and water tanks left in place; all cabin, galley and forecastle fixtures and fittings kept on board; all movable ballast shall be properly stowed under the floorboards or in lockers and no dead weight shall be shifted.

2. *Shipping, Unshipping or Shifting Ballast; Water.* No ballast, whether movable or fixed, shall be shipped, unshipped or shifted, nor shall any water be taken in or discharged except for ordinary ship's use, from 21.00 hours on the day before the race until the yacht is no longer *racing*, except that bilge water may be removed at any time.

3. *Clothing and Equipment.*

(*a*) A competitor shall not wear or carry any clothing or equipment for the purpose of increasing his weight.

(*b*) A class which desires to make exception to rule 22.3 (*a*), Clothing and Equipment may so prescribe in its class rules. In so doing, however, the total weight of clothing and equipment worn or carried by a competitor shall not exceed twenty kilograms when wet.

RULE 23
anchor

Unless otherwise prescribed by the national authority or by her class rules, every yacht shall carry on board an anchor and chain or rope of suitable size.

RULE 24
life-saving equipment

Unless otherwise prescribed by the national authority or her class rules, every yacht, except one which has sufficient buoyancy to support the crew in case of accident, shall carry adequate lifesaving equipment for all persons on board, one item of which shall be ready for immediate use.

RULE 25
class emblems, national letters and distinguishing numbers

1. Every yacht of an international class recognised by the I.Y.R.U. shall carry on her mainsail, or as provided in (*d*) (iii) and (iv) on her spinnaker:

(*a*) An emblem, letter or number denoting the class to which she belongs.

(*b*) When *racing* in foreign waters a letter or letters showing her nationality, thus:

A	Argentine	KZ	New Zealand
AL	Algeria	KZA	Zambia
AR	United Arab Republic	L	Finland
B	Belgium	LE	Lebanon
BA	Bahamas	LX	Luxembourg
BL	Brazil	M	Hungary
BU	Bulgaria	MA	Morocco
CA	Cambodia	MG	Madagascar
CB	Colombia	MO	Monaco
CY	Republic of Sri Lanka	MX	Mexico
		MT	Malta
CZ	Czechoslovakia	MY	Malaysia
D	Denmark	N	Norway
DR	Dominican Republic	NK	Democratic People's Republic of Korea
E	Spain	OE	Austria
EC	Ecuador	P	Portugal
F	France	PH	The Philippines
G	Federal Republic of Germany	PK	Pakistan
		PR	Puerto Rico
GO	German Democratic Republic	PU	Peru
		PZ	Poland
GR	Greece	RC	Cuba
GU	Guatemala	RI	Indonesia
H	Holland	RM	Roumania
HA	Netherlands Antilles	S	Sweden
		SA	Republic of South Africa
I	Italy	SE	Senegal
IL	Iceland	SL	El Salvador
IND	India	SR	Union of Soviet Socialist Republics
IR	Republic of Ireland		
IS	Israel	T	Tunisia
J	Japan	TA	Republic of China (Taiwan)
K	United Kingdom		
KA	Australia	TH	Thailand
KB	Bermuda	TK	Turkey
KBA	Barbados	U	Uruguay
KC	Canada	US	United States of America
KG	Guyana		
KGB	Gibraltar	V	Venezuela
KH	Hong Kong	VI	U.S. Virgin I.'s
KJ	Jamaica	X	Chile
KK	Kenya	Y	Yugoslavia
KR	Rhodesia	Z	Switzerland
KS	Singapore		
KT	Trinidad and Tobago		

(*c*) A distinguishing number allotted to her by her national authority. In the case of a self-administered international class, the number may be allotted by the owners' association.

Assuming a Flying Dutchman yacht belonging to the Argentine Republic to be allotted number 3 by the Argentine national authority, her sail shall be marked:

FD

A3

When there is insufficient space to place the letter or letters showing the yacht's nationality in front of her allotted number, it shall be placed above the number.

(*d*) (i) The class emblems, letters or number, national letters and distinguishing numbers shall be grouped so that the centre of the group is above half-height; shall sharply contrast in colour with the sail; and shall be placed at different heights on the two sides of the sail, those on the starboard side being uppermost, to avoid confusion owing to translucency of the sail.

(ii) Where the class emblem, letter or number is of such a design that when placed back to back on the two sides of the sail they coincide, they may be so placed.

(iii) When *racing* in foreign waters, the national letters and distinguishing numbers shall be similarly placed on both sides of the spinnaker, but at approximately half-height.

(iv) When *racing* in home waters, the distinguishing numbers only need be placed on the spinnaker in accordance with rule 25.1 (*d*) (iii).

(*e*) The following minimum sizes for national letters and distinguishing numbers are prescribed:
Height: one-tenth of the measurement of the foot of the mainsail rounded up to the nearest 50 mm.

Width: (excluding number 1 and letter I) 70% of the height.
Thickness: 15% of the height.
Space between adjoining letter and numbers: 20% of the height.
Classes which have a variable sail plan shall specify in their class rules the sizes of letters and numbers, which shall, if practicable, conform to the above requirements.

2. Other yachts shall comply with the rules of their national authority or class in regard to the allotment, carrying and size of emblems, letters and numbers, which rules shall, if practicable, conform to the above requirements.

3. A yacht shall not be disqualified for infringing the provisions of rule 25 without prior warning and adequate opportunity to make correction.

RULE 28

flags

A national authority may prescribe the flag usage which shall be observed by yachts under its jurisdiction.

part IV—sailing rules when yachts meet helmsman's rights and obligations concerning right of way

(see also pages 128–132, 134, 143–171, chapter 3)

The rules of Part IV apply only between yachts which either are intending to race or are racing in the same or different races, and, except when rule 3.2(b)(ii) applies, replace the International Regulations for Preventing Collisions at Sea or Government Right-of-Way Rules applicable to the area concerned, from the time a yacht intending to race begins to sail about in the vicinity of the starting line until she has either finished or retired and has left the vicinity of the course.

SECTION A—RULES WHICH ALWAYS APPLY

RULE 31

disqualification

1. A yacht may be disqualified or otherwise penalized for infringing a rule of Part IV only when the infringement occurs while she is *racing*, whether or not a collision results.

2. A yacht may be disqualified before or after she is *racing* for seriously hindering a yacht which is *racing*, or for infringing the sailing instructions.

RULE 32

avoiding collisions

A right-of-way yacht which fails to make a reasonable attempt to avoid a collision resulting in serious damage may be disqualified as well as the other yacht.

RULE 33

retiring from race

A yacht which realises she has infringed a racing rule or a sailing instruction is under an obligation to retire promptly;

but, when she persists in *racing*, other yachts shall continue to accord her such rights as she may have under the rules of Part IV.

RULE 34

right-of-way yacht altering course

When one yacht is required to keep clear of another, the right-of-way yacht shall not so alter course as to prevent the other yacht from keeping clear; so as to increase any alteration of course required of the other yacht in order to keep clear; or so as to obstruct her while she is keeping clear, except:

(*a*) to the extent permitted by rule 38.1, Right-of-Way Yacht Luffing after Starting, and

(*b*) when assuming a *proper course to start*, unless subject to the second part of rule 44.1 (*b*), Yacht Returning to Start.

RULE 35

hailing

1. Except when *luffing* under rule 38.1, Luffing after Starting, a right-of-way yacht which does not hail before or when making an alteration of course which may not be foreseen by the other yacht may be disqualified as well as the yacht required to keep clear when a collision resulting in serious damage occurs.

2. A yacht which hails when claiming the establishment or termination of an *overlap* or insufficiency of room at a *mark* or *obstruction* thereby helps to support her claim for the purposes of rule 42, Rounding or Passing Marks and Obstructions.

SECTION B—OPPOSITE TACK RULE

RULE 36

fundamental rule

A *port-tack* yacht shall keep clear of a *starboard-tack* yacht.

SECTION C—SAME TACK RULES

fundamental rules

1. A *windward yacht* shall keep clear of a *leeward yacht*.

2. A yacht *clear astern* shall keep clear of a yacht *clear ahead*.

3. A yacht which extablishes an *overlap* to *leeward* from *clear astern* shall allow the *windward yacht* ample room and opportunity to keep clear, and during the existence of that *overlap* the *leeward yacht* shall not sail above her *proper course*.

RULE 38

right-of-way yacht luffing after starting

1. *Luffing Rights and Limitations.* After she has *started* and cleared the starting line, a yacht *clear ahead* or a *leeward yacht* may *luff* as she pleases, except that:

A *leeward yacht* shall not sail above her *proper course* while an *overlap* exists if, at any time during its existence, the helmsman of the *windward yacht* (when sighting abeam from his normal station and sailing no higher than the *leeward yacht*) has been abreast or forward of the mainmast of the *leeward yacht*.

2. *Overlap Limitations.* For the purpose of this rule: An *overlap* does not exist unless the yachts are clearly within two overall lengths of the longer yacht; and an *overlap* which exists between two yachts when the leading yacht *starts*, or when one or both of them completes a *tack* or *gybe*, shall be regarded as a new *overlap* beginning at that time.

3. *Hailing to Stop or Prevent a Luff.* When there is doubt, the *leeward yacht* may assume that she has the right to *luff* unless the helmsman of the *windward yacht* has hailed "Mast Abeam", or words to that effect. The *leeward yacht* shall be governed by such hail, and, if she deems it improper, her only remedy is to protest.

4. *Curtailing a Luff.* The *windward yacht* shall not cause a *luff* to be curtailed because of her proximity to the *leeward yacht* unless an *obstruction*, a third yacht or other object restricts her ability to respond.

5. *Luffing Two or More Yachts.* A yacht shall not *luff* unless she has the right to *luff* all yachts which would be affected by her *luff*, in which case they shall all respond even if an intervening yacht or yachts would not otherwise have the right to *luff*.

RULE 39

sailing below a proper course

A yacht which is on a free leg of the course shall not sail below her *proper course* when she is clearly within three of her overall lengths of either a *leeward yacht* or a yacht *clear astern* which is steering a course to pass to *leeward*.

RULE 40

right-of-way yacht luffing before starting

Before a yacht has *started* and cleared the starting line, any *luff* on her part which causes another yacht to have to alter course to avoid a collision shall be carried out slowly and in such a way so as to give the *windward yacht* room and opportunity to keep clear, but the *leeward yacht* shall not so *luff* above a *close-hauled* course, unless the helmsman of the *windward yacht* (sighting abeam from his normal station) is abaft the mainmast of the *leeward yacht*. Rules 38.3, Hailing to Stop or Prevent a Luff; Curtailing a Luff; and 38.5, Luffing Two or more Yachts, also apply.

SECTION D—CHANGING TACK RULES

RULE 41

tacking or gybing

1. A yacht which is either *tacking* or *gybing* shall keep clear of a yacht *on a tack*.

2. A yacht shall neither *tack* nor *gybe* into a position which will give her right of way unless she does so far enough from a yacht *on a tack* to enable this yacht to keep clear without having to begin to alter her course until after the *tack* or *gybe* has been completed.

3. A yacht which *tacks* or *gybes* has the onus of satisfying the race committee that she completed her *tack* or *gybe* in accordance with rule 41.2.

4. When two yachts are both *tacking* or both *gybing* at the same time, the one on the other's *port* side shall keep clear.

SECTION E— RULES OF EXCEPTION AND SPECIAL APPLICATION

When a rule of this section applies, to the extent to which it explicitly provides rights and obligations, it over-rides any conflicting rule of Part IV which precedes it, except the rules of Section A—Rules Which Always Apply.

RULE 42

rounding or passing marks and obstructions

1. *Fundamental Rules Regarding Room.* When yachts either on the same *tack* or, after *starting* and clearing the starting line, on opposite *tacks*, are about to round or pass a *mark* on the same required side, with the exception of a starting *mark* surrounded by navigable water, or an *obstruction* on the same side:

(a) When *Overlapped*:

(i) An outside yacht shall give each yacht *overlapping* her on the inside, room to round or pass the *mark* or *obstruction*, except as provided in rules 42.1(a)(iii), and (iv) and 42.3. Room includes room for an *overlapping* yacht to *tack* or *gybe* when either is an integral part of the rounding or passing manoeuvre.

(ii) When an inside yacht of two or more *overlapped* yachts either on opposite *tacks*, or on the same *tack* without *luffing* rights, will have to *gybe* in order most directly to assume a *proper course* to the next *mark*, she shall *gybe* at the first reasonable opportunity.

(iii) When two yachts on opposite *tacks* are on a beat or when one of them will have to *tack* either to round the *mark* or to avoid the *obstruction*, as between each other rule 42.1(a) (i), shall not apply. They are subject to rules 36, Opposite Tack Fundamental Rule, and 41, Tacking or Gybing.

(iv) An outside *leeward yacht* with luffing rights may take an inside yacht to windward of a *mark* provided that she hails to that effect and begins to *luff* before she is within two of her overall lengths of the *mark* and provided that she also passes to windward of it.

(b) When *Clear Astern* and *Clear Ahead*.

(i) A yacht *clear astern* shall keep clear in anticipation of and during the rounding or passing manoeuvre when the yacht *clear ahead* remains on the same *tack* or *gybes*.

(ii) A yacht *clear ahead* which *tacks* to round a *mark* is subject to rule 41, Tacking or Gybing, but a yacht *clear astern* shall not *luff* above *close-hauled* so as to prevent the yacht *clear ahead* from *tacking*.

2. Restrictions on Establishing and Maintaining an Overlap

(*a*) A yacht *clear astern* shall not establish an inside *overlap* and be entitled to room under rule 42.1(*a*) (i) when the yacht *clear ahead*

(i) is within two of her overall lengths of the *mark* or *obstruction*, except as provided in rules 42.2(*b*) and 42.2(*c*); or

(ii) is unable to give the required room.

(*b*) The two-lengths determinative above shall not apply to yachts, of which one has completed a *tack* within two overall lengths of a *mark* or an *obstruction*.

(*c*) A yacht *clear astern* may establish an inside *overlap* between the yacht *clear ahead* and a continuing *obstruction* such as a shoal or the shore, only when there is room for her to do so in safety.

(*d*) (i) A yacht *clear ahead* shall be under no obligation to give room to a yacht *clear astern* before an *overlap* is established.

(ii) A yacht which claims an inside *overlap* has the onus of satisfying the race committee that the *overlap* was established in proper time.

(*e*) (i) When an outside yacht is *overlapped* at the time she comes within two of her overall lengths of a *mark* or an *obstruction*, she shall continue to be bound by rule 42.1(*a*) (i) to give room as required even though the *overlap* may thereafter be broken.

(ii) An outside yacht which claims to have broken an *overlap* has the onus of satisfying the race committee that she became *clear ahead* when she was more than two of her overall lengths from the *mark* or an *obstruction*.

3. At a Starting Mark Surrounded by Navigable Water

When approaching the starting line to *start*, a *leeward yacht* shall be under no obligation to give any *windward yacht* room to pass to leeward of a starting *mark* surrounded by navigable water; but, after the starting signal, a *leeward yacht* shall not deprive a *windward yacht* of room at such a *mark* by sailing either above the course to the first *mark* or above *close-hauled*.

RULE 43

close-hauled, hailing for room to tack at obstructions

1. *Hailing*. When two *close-hauled* yachts are on the same *tack* and safe pilotage requires the yacht *clear ahead* or the *leeward yacht* to make a substantial alteration of course to clear an *obstruction*, and if she intends to *tack*, but cannot *tack* without colliding with the other yacht, she shall hail the other yacht for room to *tack* and clear the other yacht, but she shall not hail and *tack* simultaneously.

2. *Responding*. The hailed yacht at the earliest possible moment after the hail shall either:

(*a*) *tack*, in which case, the hailing yacht shall begin to *tack* either:

(i) before the hailed yacht has completed her *tack*, or

(ii) if she cannot then *tack*, without colliding with the hailed yacht, immediately she is able to *tack* and clear her, or

(*b*) reply "You *tack*", or words to that effect, if in her opinion she can keep clear without *tacking* or after postponing her *tack*. In this case:

(i) the hailing yacht shall immediately tack and

(ii) the hailed yacht shall keep clear.

(iii) The onus shall lie on the hailed yacht which replied "You *tack*" to satisfy the race committee that she kept clear.

3. *Limitation on Right to Room when the Obstruction is a Mark*.

(*a*) When the hailed yacht can fetch an *obstruction* which is also a *mark*, the hailing yacht shall not be entitled to room to *tack* and clear the other yacht and the hailed yacht shall immediately so inform the hailing yacht.

(*b*) If, thereafter, the hailing yacht again hails for room to *tack* and clear the other yacht she shall, after receiving it, retire immediately.

(*c*) If, after having refused to respond to a hail under rule 43.3(*a*), the hailed yacht fails to fetch, she shall retire immediately.

part V—other sailing rules
obligations of helmsmen and crew in handling a yacht

(see also rules on pages 133, 138, 141–143, chapter 3)

Except for rule 49, a yacht is subject to the rules of Part V only while she is racing.

RULE 53

fog signals and lights

Every yacht shall observe the International Regulations for Preventing Collisions at Sea or Government Rules for fog signals and as a minimum, the carrying of lights at night.

RULE 55

owner steering another yacht

An owner shall not steer any yacht other than his own in a race wherein his own yacht competes, without the previous consent of the race committee.

RULE 56

boarding

Unless otherwise prescribed by the national authority or in the sailing instructions, no person shall board a yacht except for the purposes of rule 58, Rendering Assistance, or to attend an injured or ill member of the crew or temporarily as one of the crew of a vessel fouled.

RULE 57

leaving, man overboard

Unless otherwise prescribed by the national authority or in the sailing instructions, no person on board a yacht when her preparatory signal was made shall leave, unless injured or ill, or for the purpose of rule 58, Rendering Assistance, except that any member of the crew may fall overboard or leave her to swim, stand on the bottom as a means of anchoring, haul her out ashore to effect repairs, reef sails or bail out, or help her to get clear after grounding or fouling another vessel or object, provided that this person is back on board before the yacht continues in the race.

RULE 59

outside assistance

Except as permitted by rules 56, Boarding, 58, Rendering Assistance, and 64, Aground or Foul of an Obstruction, a yacht shall neither receive outside assistance nor use any gear other than that on board when her preparatory signal was made.

RULE 60

means of propulsion

A yacht shall be propelled only by the natural action of the wind on the sails, spars and hull, and water on the hull, and shall not pump, "ooch" or rock, as described in Appendix 2, nor check way by abnormal means, except for the purposes of rule 58, Rendering Assistance, or of recovering a man who has accidentally fallen overboard. An oar, paddle or other object may be used in emergency for steering. An anchor may be sent out in a boat only as permitted by rule 64, Aground or Foul of an Obstruction.

RULE 61

sounding

Any means of sounding may be used provided that rule 60, Means of Propulsion, is not infringed.

RULE 62

manual power

A yacht shall use manual power only, except that if so prescribed by the national authority or in the sailing instructions, a power winch or windlass may be used in weighing anchor in getting clear after running aground or fouling any object, and a power pump may be used in an auxiliary yacht.

RULE 63

anchoring and making fast

1. A yacht may anchor. Means of anchoring may include the crew standing on the bottom and any weight lowered to the bottom. A yacht shall recover any anchor or weight used, and any chain or rope attached to it, before continuing in the race, unless after making every effort she finds recovery impossible. In this case she shall report the circumstances to the race committee, which may disqualify her if it considers the loss due either to inadequate gear or to insufficient effort to recover it.

2. A yacht shall be afloat and off moorings, before her preparatory signal, but may be anchored, and shall not thereafter make fast or be made fast by means other than anchoring, nor be hauled out, except for the purpose of rule 64, Aground or Foul of an Obstruction, or to effect repairs, reef sails or bail out.

RULE 64

aground or foul of an obstruction

A yacht, after grounding or fouling another vessel or other object, is subject to rule 62, Manual Power, and may, in getting clear, use her own anchors, boats, ropes, spars and other gear; may send out an anchor in a boat; may be refloated by her crew going overboard either to stand on the bottom or to go ashore to push off; but may receive outside assistance only from the crew of the vessel fouled. A yacht shall recover all her own gear used in getting clear before continuing in the race.

RULE 65

skin friction

A yacht shall not eject or release from a container any substance (such as polymer) the purpose of which is, or could be, to reduce the frictional resistance of the hull by altering the character of the flow of water inside the boundary layer.

RULE 66

increasing stability

Unless otherwise prescribed by her class rules or in the sailing instructions, a yacht shall not use any device, such as a trapeze or plank, to project outboard the weight of any of the crew, nor, when a yacht is equipped with lifelines, shall any member of the crew station any part of his torso outside them, other other temporarily.

APPENDIX 1

amateur

1. For the purpose of international yacht races in which yachts entering are required to have one or more amateurs on board, and in other races with similar requirements unless otherwise prescribed by the national authority, an amateur is a yachtsman who engages in yacht racing as a pastime as distinguished from a means of obtaining a livelihood. No yachtsman shall lose amateur status by reason of the fact that his livelihood is derived from designing or constructing any boats or parts of boats, or accessories of boats, or sails or from other professions associated with the sea and ships.

2. Any yachtsman whose amateur status is questioned or is in doubt, may apply to the national authority of the country of his residence for recognition of his amateur status. Any such applicant may be required to provide such particulars and evidence and to pay such fee as the national authority may prescribe. Recognition may be suspended or cancelled by the national authority by which it was granted.

3. The Permanent Committee of the International Yacht Racing Union, or any tribunal nominated by the chairman of that committee, may review the decision of any authority as to the amateur status of a yachtsman for the purpose of competing in international races.

4. For the purposes of participation in the Olympic Regatta an amateur is required to conform to the eligibility rules of the International Olympic Committee. Information on these eligibility requirements is available from all national authorities.

APPENDIX 2

"pumping" sails, "ooching" and "rocking"

"Pumping" consists of frequent rapid trimming of sails with no particular reference to a change in true or apparent wind direction. To promote planing or surfing, rapid trimming of sails need not be considered "pumping".

The purpose of this interpretation of rule 60, Means of Propulsion, is to prevent "fanning" one's boat around the course by flapping the sail similar to a bird's wing in flight. "Pumping"

253

or *frequent*, quickly-repeated trimming and releasing of the mainsail to increase propulsion is not allowed and is not "the natural action of the wind on the sails".

Similarly, frequent, quick-repeated gybing or roll-tacking in calm and near calm conditions fall into the same category as "pumping".

Where surfing or planing conditions exist, however, rule 60 allows taking advantage of "the natural action of water on the hull" through the *rapid* trimming of sails and adjustment of helm to *promote* (initiate) surfing or planing.

The test is whether or not the conditions are such that by *rapid* trimming of sails a boat could be *started* surfing or planing. A skipper challenged for "pumping" will have to prove, through the performance either of his own boat or of other boats, that surfing or planing conditions existed, and that the *frequency* of his *rapid* trimming was geared to the *irregular* or *cyclical* wave forms rather than to a *regular* rhythmic pattern.

Note that the interpretation refers to "promoting" and not to "maintaining" surfing or planing. Once a boat has started surfing or planing on a particular set of wave forms, from then on she must let the natural action of wind and water propel her without further *rapid* trimming and releasing of the sails.

Rapid trimming when approaching marks or the finishing line or other critical points should be consistent with that which was practised throughout the leg.

"Ooching", which consists of lunging forward and stopping abruptly, falls into the same category as "pumping".

"Rocking" consists of persistently rolling a yacht from side to side.

APPENDIX 3

alternative penalties for infringement of a rule of part IV

Experience indicates that the 720° turns penalty is most satisfactory for small boats in relatively short races but that it can be dangerous for large yachts and in restricted waters and not sufficiently severe in long races. The 20% penalty is relatively mild and is designed to encourage acknowledgement of infringements and willingness to protest when not acknowledged. Both systems keep yachts racing.

Either of the following alternatives to disqualification may be used by including in the sailing instructions a provision such as the following (or if preferred the selected penalty may be quoted in full):

"The 720° turns penalty (or the percentage penalty) as provided in rule 68.7, Alternative Penalties, and Appendix 3 of the yacht racing rules shall apply, instead of disqualification, for infringement of a rule of Part IV".

720° turns

A yacht which acknowledges infringing a rule of Part IV may exonerate herself by making two full 360° turns (720°) subject to the following provisions:

1. The yacht infringed against shall notify the infringing yacht at the first reasonable opportunity by hail and by showing a protest flag. (The first reasonable opportunity for a hail is usually immediately.)

2. Upon such notification, the yacht acknowledging fault shall immediately start to get well clear of other yachts and while on the same leg of the course she shall hail adjacent yachts of her intention and then make her turns. While so doing, she shall keep clear of all other yachts until she has completed her turns and is on a *proper course* to the next *mark*.

3. For the purpose of applying this penalty, "a leg of the course" shall be deemed terminated when two boat lengths from the *mark* ending that leg, and the next leg shall be deemed to commence at this point except for the final leg which is terminated when a yacht is no longer *racing*.

4. The turns may be made in either direction but both in the same direction.

5. When the infringement occurs before the starting signal, the infringing yacht shall make her turns after the starting signal and before *starting*

6. When an infringement occurs at the finishing line, the infringing yacht shall make her turns on the last leg of the course before being officially finished.

7. If neither yacht acknowledges fault, a protest may be lodged in accordance with rule 68, Protests, and the sailing instructions.

8. An infringing yacht shall report her infringement and the resulting action taken by her to the race committee, together with such other information as may be required by the sailing instructions.

9. Failure to observe the above requirements will render a yacht which has infringed a rule of Part IV liable to disqualification or other penalty.

10. An infringing yacht involved in a collision which results in serious damage to either yacht shall be liable to disqualification.

percentage

1. A yacht which acknowledges infringing a rule of Part IV shall be penalized by receiving the score for the place worse than her actual finishing position by 20% to the nearest whole number of the number of starters in that race, except that the penalty shall be at least three places and except further that in no case will she receive a score for a position worse than one more than the number of starters. (Examples: An infringing yacht which finishes eighth in a start of nineteen yachts will receive the score for twelfth place (19 × 0.2 = 3.8 or 4); an infringing yacht which finishes thirteenth in a start of fourteen yachts will receive the score for fifteenth place.)

(*a*) A yacht infringing a rule in more than one incident shall receive a 20% penalty for each incident.

(*b*) The imposition of a 20% penalty on a yacht shall not affect the score of other yachts. (Thus two yachts may receive the same score.)

2. The yacht infringed against shall notify the infringing yacht at the first reasonable opportunity by hail and by showing a protest flag. (The first reasonable opportunity for a hail is usually immediately.)

3. A yacht which acknowledges infringing a rule of Part IV shall at the first reasonable opportunity show International Code flag "I", or such other signal as the sailing instructions may specify, keep it flying until she has finished and report the infringement to the race committee.

4. A yacht which fails to acknowledge an infringement as provided in paragraph 3 and which, after a protest and hearing, is found to have infringed a rule of Part IV, shall be penalized 30% or at least five places instead of 20%.

5. A yacht which has shown I.C. Code flag "I" during a race and has not reported the infringement to the race committee shall be liable to the 30% penalty of paragraph 4 without a hearing, except on the two points of having shown the flag and having reported the infringement to the race committee.

6. An infringing yacht involved in a collision which results in serious damage to either yacht shall be liable to disqualification.